SUCCEED
ON YOUR
OWN TERMS

SUCCEED
ON YOUR
OWN TERMS

LESSONS FROM
TOP ACHIEVERS
AROUND THE WORLD
ON DEVELOPING
YOUR UNIQUE POTENTIAL

HERB GREENBERG
PATRICK SWEENEY

McGraw-Hill

New York   Chicago   San Francisco   Lisbon   London
Madrid   Mexico City   Milan   New Delhi   San Juan
Seoul   Singapore   Sydney   Toronto

The inspiration for this book comes directly from our children, who we occasionally try to share lessons with but who, more often than not, continue to teach us.

We also dedicate this book to our parents, whose profound insights and infinite love we carry with us.

And we particularly want to thank our wives, Sunny and Donna, whose unwavering love, abiding understanding, and enduring partnership continually amaze us.

Contents

Introduction

This book is an interior travel guide into the hearts and minds of individuals who have succeeded on their own terms.

THE INDIVIDUALS WE ARE about to introduce you to have succeeded by knowing who they are, understanding the qualities that drive them, playing to their strengths, overcoming their limitations, taking advantage of their defining moments, and having their own definitions of success.

During the last two years we have traveled to over a dozen countries and explored with hundreds of successful individuals questions such as: What are the qualities that distinguish them? Do they simply have more energy, drive, focus, vision, and luck than the rest of us? Or do they also have something above and beyond that, something truly exceptional? Is there one particular quality shared by all successful individuals? And how can we recognize our own defining qualities and tap into our own inner strengths?

Along the way, we learned much about the qualities that distinguish and drive people who are succeeding on their own terms—and how we can recognize those qualities in ourselves.

Through in-depth interviews and insights gleaned from analyzing the comprehensive personality assessments they took, we will provide a one-of-a-kind look into people who are at the top of their game, succeeding beyond their wildest dreams.

From entrepreneurs to star athletes, from inventors of products to impassioned social workers, from mountain climbers to uncompromising politicians, we will take you behind the scenes and give you a real understanding of what motivates people who have a clear sense of purpose, meaning, and personal fulfillment in what they are doing.

We will share the inspiration and insights we've gained along the way about how winners see themselves, how we can identify and develop our own unique qualities, and how we can prepare for our own defining moments.

We wanted to find out: How does a star athlete get ready for a shot at breaking a world record? How does a parent defy the Ku Klux Klan when they are threatening her children? How does a student still in high school develop a company that Michael Ovitz wants to purchase?

Do such individuals even know what makes them tick and what keeps them going? Do they recognize winning qualities in others? Did they always know they were meant to take on their signature challenges? Do opportunities for success keep presenting themselves or come around only once? How do they overcome adversity? What keeps them awake at nights? And ultimately: How do people at the top of their game define their own success?

As we explore these questions, we'll introduce you to some of the incredible people we met, including Roger Staubach, the former quarterback who led the Dallas Cowboys to two Super Bowl victories and now heads his own international realty company; Rebecca Stephens, on how climbing Mount Everest became her all-consuming goal; Paul Schulte, a Paralympic wheelchair basketball player; Samuel Pisar, a Holocaust survivor who went on to become a prominent international lawyer; João Carlos Martins, who lost the use of one of his hands, but still went on to perform a Bach recital at Carnegie Hall; Ben Vereen, the actor, who tells us how he overcame the defining moment of losing his daughter; Senator Barbara Boxer, who talks about the importance of standing up for what you believe in, even when you know you can't win; Marc Koska, who invented a new type of disposable syringe after he could not stop thinking about an article he read which focused on the need to prevent AIDS; Muggsy Bogues, the shortest NBA player of all time, who shares how he overcame the odds; Francis Samuel, who reinvented his currency exchange company when France converted to the euro; Michael Graves, the architect and designer who constantly keeps creative; Emilio Butragueño, the former World Cup soccer player who is now the Vice President for Real Madrid; and Congressman John Lewis, the legendary civil rights advocate who spoke at the historic March on Washington just before Dr. Martin Luther King, Jr. made his "I Have a Dream" speech.

While this is certainly an eclectic group of individuals from various countries and diverse walks of life, they all share one common denominator, which was clear upon meeting them. What became immediately recognizable was the undeniable sense that these individuals are all doing exactly what they should be doing. They are in tune with themselves.

Now, allow us to step back for a moment and share some quick background on who we are and what motivated us to write this book. Caliper was founded by Herb Greenberg over four decades ago to advise companies on hiring and developing employees, building teams, coaching executives, managing performance and on virtually every aspect of ensuring that organizations have the people and systems in place to succeed. Our basic premise has always been that, when it comes to succeeding, an individual's potential is far more important than his or her experience. Don't look to the past. Look to what is inside of someone. The assessment instrument Herb developed and has refined through the past four decades is the Caliper Profile, which is one of the most accurate tools currently available for reading an individual's motivations, strengths and potential. This assessment is the foundation for our consulting approach, which has helped over 25,000 companies around the world, including FedEx, Caterpillar, Johnson & Johnson, and some of the fastest-growing smaller companies to assess and develop the talents of more than two million applicants and employees—from individuals being considered for their first jobs to presidents of companies, and everyone in between. It is our hope in writing this book to share what we've learned about people who find success on their own terms. These significant lessons have important meanings for individuals and corporations alike.

As a unique starting point, this book will begin with one of the authors, Herb, sharing what it was like to lose his sight at the age of 10. He'll also tell you how he accepted certain things about his life—but not others.

xvi SUCCEED ON YOUR OWN TERMS

**What became immediately recognizable
was the undeniable sense that these
individuals are all doing exactly
what they should be doing.
They are in tune with themselves.**

We will go on to pinpoint the defining moments of dozens of inspiring people who have succeeded on their own terms and share with you answers to some of the questions we posed to them, such as: How do you react when your back is against the wall? Did you recognize your defining moment when it was occurring? Did you have a hero? What quality distinguishes you? What was your biggest mistake, and what did you learn from it? What drives you in the face of defeat? Where do you get inspiration? Did you learn anything from your first job? What lessons would you like young people to learn from your life?

Among the key findings we discovered is that inside of all successful individuals are three things: a defining quality that sets them apart, a moment that they each called their own, and a clear definition of their own success.

As a bonus, we are offering you the opportunity to take an online personality assessment which can serve as a starting point to help you discover your own defining qualities. The results may confirm and clarify what you already know about yourself or perhaps uncover a strength of which you were only vaguely aware. It is our hope that the insights you gain from this personality profile can provide a deeper understanding of how you can play to your own strengths.

By the end of the book we will also show you ways to clarify your own definition of success and identify your defining moments before they vanish in the rearview mirror.

By encouraging you to think about success in an entirely different way and showing you how winners see themselves and their world, we want to provide a road map to help you find your own success. We hope some of the stories and insights from this book will help you broaden your understanding of what success really means—whether you are an executive looking to hire employees who can grow with your company or an individual looking to change your life's direction.

PART
1

Knowing Where You're Going and Defining Success

CHAPTER

You've Got to Know Where You Are to Know Where You're Going

*This book has been a truly collaborative process—from the concep-
tion to the interviews to the assessments to uncovering the patterns of
success to the writing. In this chapter, however, since we are focusing
on Herb's own journey of success, it seemed appropriate, for modesty's
sake, to have it written by Patrick.*

I FIRST MET HERB OVER two decades ago at a forum that
Brendan Byrne, then the governor of New Jersey, hosted on the subject
of creating jobs in a tough economy. At that time I was the governor's
speechwriter, and I came to know Herb as a bright, engaging, committed entrepreneur, brimming with ideas and energy. While he was blind,
he didn't let that hold him back at all. I wasn't exactly sure what his firm
did, but I understood it had something to do with helping companies
identify and develop their professional talent.

When I left the governor's office, Herb offered me a position heading up marketing and corporate communications for his consulting
company. That, as Humphrey Bogart says at the end of *Casablanca*, was
the start of a beautiful friendship.

One of the first things I learned was that when it came to being
interviewed by the media, Herb had only one request: he didn't want to
talk about being blind. His concern was that such articles almost always

3

l guy does well," and that was not how he wanted
ad, he was much more interested in talking about
ects and possibilities.

cted his wish. And as I got to know him better, I
If you asked me to come up with a dozen words to
would not be one of them." And that was that.

Then, about a year ago, he and I were racing through an airport.
Time, you learn with Herb, is not to be wasted. Every minute is to be
squeezed for all its worth. We placed our carry-on bags on the con-
veyor belt, and as soon as I started guiding Herb through the doorway
that detects metal objects, alarms went off. The guard asked Herb to
sit down so he could scan him with a metal detector. As I moved forward to escort Herb toward a chair, the guard motioned for me to stay
back. Then, realizing that Herb was blind and not wanting to offend
him, the guard stammered, "I'm sorry. Do you have . . . trouble seeing?" Herb replied, "Well, I can't see very well." And I just cracked up,
saying, "Herb, that is the most upbeat explanation of being blind I've
ever heard."

When I told his wife, Sunny, the story later, she shook her head,
started laughing, and said, "That's Herb."

In all the years we'd known each other, Herb had provided very few
details about how he lost his sight. So, on that plane ride I decided to
ask him to tell me what it was like when he went blind. As we eased back
for a long flight, Herb shared with me how he learned to accept certain
things about his life—but not others.

"When I was nine years old," he began, "I suddenly became very ill
from an infected mastoid, a cranial bone right behind the ear. I was
burning up with fever, so my parents had to get me to the hospital for
an operation right away. My condition was quite serious. They were
told there was a very strong possibility I could lose my hearing and
that there was even a chance that I might die. Now, you also have to
understand that my parents were already in excruciating emotional
pain at that time. About a week before I was rushed to the hospital, my
13-month-old baby sister, Rosalind, had died from strep throat. I can't
imagine what they were going through. And the thing of it is that
penicillin was introduced about a year later—which could have cured
both my sister's strep throat and my mastoid infection. But what can
you do?"

While Herb's operation was successful, he left the hospital weighing only 35 pounds. "I just felt too weak to do anything," he said. "I was also extremely susceptible to infection, and some sort of virus hit my eyes." Slowly over the course of that year, as he got stronger, his vision faded.

"I can remember waking some mornings and seeing little spots in front of my eyes. Little black dots. But they would go away when I rubbed my eyes, so I wasn't especially concerned.

"Then one day, and I'll never forget this," Herb recalled, "I was reading a book to my dad from the Don Sturdy series of adventure stories. You probably don't even know him. He was like Jack Armstrong or Tom Swift, a hero kind of thing. Anyway, as I was trying to read, my father noticed that I was holding the book upside down."

He learned to accept certain things about his life—but not others.

What was going through his mind at that time?

"It was very confusing. It just wasn't making sense anymore. There were all of these black marks and dots on the white paper, but I didn't know what they meant. I could only remember what we read out loud in class. I was just repeating what I had memorized."

So his father rushed Herb and his upside-down book to a doctor, who removed any doubt about what was happening. "I can remember him saying, 'Your son is going blind.'"

Herb paused as he remembered. "It was a slow process, very gradual. There wasn't any one crashing moment when I thought, 'Oh, my God, I'm blind.' And I don't remember crying or asking, 'Why me?' or 'What am I going to do?' I just kept adjusting. I kept trying to look closer and closer at things. And, honest to God, I didn't realize, except for the black dots, that anything was wrong. It didn't really hit me until one of the follow-up doctor visits when I heard him say, 'Your son is now blind.'"

Over the course of the next year, Herb and his parents alternately challenged and accepted what had happened. They got him Braille lessons right away. "But I found memorizing to be a lot easier," Herb recalled. In fact, he claims to have never taken a note in all his school days—from the elementary grades to getting his Ph.D.

His intensity, impatience, and anger merged to defy a well-meaning but inept educational system that wanted to send him away to a special school for the blind. There were three distant schools he could attend, but his parents would have nothing to do with that. They were not about to let their young son be sent away to school. He had just lost his sight, and they didn't want him to lose touch with his family. They were determined to make sure he would live at home. But more important, they wanted Herb to attend a regular school with regular kids. They didn't want him to be segregated because of his blindness. And they clearly understood that their young son felt the same, since he told them, in no uncertain terms, "If you let them send me away, I'll break every window in the building."

So, Herb basically was home-schooled while his parents sorted out the situation with the authorities, resisting enormous pressure to do "the right thing" and send him away to a facility for the blind. Finally, at the end of that year, a representative from the board of education came to their house with news that a school in Brooklyn, P.S. 93, had a Braille class and Herb could attend there the next year.

Looking back on that year, Herb views his parents' strong stance as a turning point. "If they had caved in and sent me away to a school for the blind, I have no doubt, particularly back then, that my options would have been very limited and my life would have been completely different," he said.

One of his fondest adolescent memories was being a Boy Scout. Lionel Goldman, then the scout master of Troop 271 in Brooklyn, created an environment where Herb felt accepted, challenged and just one of the kids. "By allowing a newly-blind boy into his troop, Lionel gave me the chance to make new friends and do things I never would have otherwise, including spending four summers at the camp at Ten Mile River. Lionel was one of the first people outside my family who was comfortable with my being blind. He didn't view it as something that should hold me back. I'm eternally grateful to him for that."

For Herb, what is it like being blind? Can he see anything at all?

"Right now I can make out just a bit of light. Today is a very sunny day. It is very bright, and I can sense some light. I know the sun is over there," he said, pointing upward and somewhat to the west.

Light and shadows, however, are about it.

"I don't see any color," he continued, "just bright and dark areas. I can't see shapes. Not really. I can sense there is something there. But if I was walking along and not expecting to see it, I would bump into it. When I really try to focus, though, I can see something, in effect, blocking the light."

There is a painting in the Philadelphia Museum of Art by the Impressionist Edgar Degas. It is his last known work. At the time, he was then almost totally blind from the paint pigments he had rubbed unwittingly into his eyes. This painting is done entirely in shades of red because, as the curator explained, red was the last color he saw.

I asked Herb if that made sense to him, and he said, "That's interesting. I'm not sure if it was that for me. But I do remember some colors quite well. Red is one of them. I can also envision blue, but it's harder. I can sort of imagine green, and I have vague notions of purple. But I can't tell you what they would go with, so don't ask me to match your clothes for you. Now that you mention it, though, of all the colors, red remains the strongest in my mind."

Often when I am with Herb, I hear people marvel at his accomplishments, not the least of which is founding a global consulting company with over a dozen offices worldwide and an enviable list of clients, including Fortune 500 companies, fast-growing smaller firms, and even professional sports teams. But their admiration usually culminates with something like, "And what's even more incredible is that the guy is blind."

How does Herb feel about that?

"I don't like it," he said definitively. "It makes me very uncomfortable. You know that. The truth is that everyone has some kind of disability, and it does frustrate me that I can't do certain things I know I'd enjoy, like playing basketball. I love sports, and I would have loved to play on a team. But my disability ruled that out. The reality is that being blind can be limiting and very annoying. When I was younger, I was denied certain jobs because I was blind, and there were certain girls who wouldn't go out with me because I was blind. There was one girl I cared a great deal for and who liked me too. We'd gone out on a few dates. But then her parents put a stop to it. They wouldn't let her go out with me anymore. All of that hurt. It really hurt."

As he reflected on how, as a teenager, he was rejected by some girls—and even by some of their parents—simply because he was blind, the psychologist in him considered how rejection can paralyze some people, while causing others to carry on with even more determination.

That triggered a memory of how he'd experienced prejudice in the job market because of his disability. As a 25-year old who had just received his Ph.D. with highest honors from New York University, Herb was excited about making his mark on the world. He'd already consulted for over three years with the New York City Department of Welfare. So he was primed for a new challenge. He'd sent out over 600 applications for positions around the country, ranging from teaching to social work to consulting. Within a week, he received 85 encouraging letters inviting him for an interview. When contacting his potential employers, Herb made them aware that he was blind. And, in short order, the 85 potential interviews were reduced to three actual interviews, resulting in no job offers. "Now *that* was rejection," he said.

How did he come to terms with that kind of rejection?

"I certainly didn't dwell on it," he said, then added, "I honestly believe that I've been able to succeed in my career—not exactly in spite of my blindness but because I was blessed with a creative mind. My parents gave me a solid sense of self-esteem, and I had some incredible mentors along the way. I have also experienced my share of failures. Quite a few of them. I tried many things that did not work out before succeeding with Caliper. So it's not so much about overcoming being blind; it's more a matter of overcoming the hurt that comes from being rejected because I was blind. Somehow I was always able to use that hurt as a motivator to try even harder."

Eventually, Herb was offered an assistant professorship at Texas Tech. After his second year, he remembers one incredibly hot night in July of 1957 when a reporter called and informed him that the Texas Tech Board of Directors had voted not to renew his contract. Herb was stunned, since he had just been offered a sizeable salary increase by the chairman of the department. It turned out Herb was being let go because he had been giving speeches around the state on his Ph.D. dissertation, which was that segregation in education could not create equal opportunities for those who were segregated. His outspoken liberal views apparently offended most of the university's board members.

When Herb was offered his next teaching position at Rutgers, the head of the psychology department said the reason Herb was fired from

Texas Tech made him an even more appealing candidate for this new teaching position.

"When you're in the wrong place," Herb said, "you can't turn yourself inside out to try to fit in. You've got to be true to yourself. You can't let them get to you. You've got to believe things will work out for the best." Ironically, years later, Herb received a settlement from Texas Tech, which was enough for him to put a down payment on a summer home.

While teaching at Rutgers, an insurance company approached him with a consulting project. They wanted a thorough review of all of the psychological tests available at the time to determine if any of them could predict if an individual could sell. Three months later, he wrote them a memorandum which basically said that there was nothing like that in the marketplace.

That's when the entrepreneur in him kicked in. He sensed an opportunity and, with a colleague, spent every spare moment developing a personality assessment that could determine whether an individual was motivated to sell or manage others or provide customer service or lead a company.

In August of 1961, Herb resigned from his teaching position, confident that he and his partner were on to something. Together they borrowed $15,000 from a small stock brokerage firm and started Caliper. "Even back then," Herb said, "$15,000 could not support a start-up business and two young families for very long." Just as they were about to run out of funds, an executive from General Motors decided to take a chance on Caliper's approach to assessing potential and predicting job success.

That gave them the breathing room they needed.

Herb's premise, and Caliper's as well, has always been to look for that which is not so easily seen.

When Herb was interviewed most recently in the *Harvard Business Review*, he was asked: Do managers overemphasize or misread visual clues when evaluating people for jobs or promotions? He responded, "Most people depend too much on their sight. How does someone look? Do they fit the part? Some of those visual cues can be as superficial and inaccurate as 'She seems to carry herself like a leader' or 'He looks like he would fit in with the rest of the department.' That first impression then becomes the context for the rest of the information they gather about an individual. They may hear the person's responses differently because they like what they see or because that person is smiling convincingly at them. That's one of the reasons why, during Freudian therapy, an individual is on the couch, facing away from the therapist, who just listens."

Then he added, "A hiring interview is a very unnatural way to meet someone. Applicants can impress you with the homework they've done on you and your company, and it's not hard to convey an enormous amount of enthusiasm for just an hour. So you have to delve below the surface. Try to get a sense of their character as well as what they've learned from their accomplishments *and* their failures. Try to get at what is genuine. The key to hiring and managing people is to find out what drives them. One of the most important questions to ask is 'why?' This is not something you can see visually. You need to ask the right questions and then really listen."

When Herb was asked, "What sorts of nonvisual cues do you notice?" he responded, "The proverb says that 'the eyes are the windows to the soul,' but I think it's the voice. People can work on their smile. They can convey a certain look. There's so much plastic surgery these days that someone can actually buy a certain look. But voices are genuine. You can tell if a person is comfortable with you, not putting up barriers. Or you can tell if there's no reaching out in a person's voice. When someone's voice is flat or quiet, you don't have any idea what he or she is feeling or thinking. That can be a warning flag."

Herb makes an extra effort to pay close attention to the voices of those around him. Is there warmth there? Genuine enthusiasm? Sincerity? Or do people sound uncomfortable with themselves or with others? He said, "You can hear cues in their voices. Are they really interested? Are they thinking about something else? Or are they trying too hard?"

Here's an interesting experiment to try. Concentrate mainly on people's voices. Do it for a full day. Then see if you can describe the voice of someone you really care about and the voice of someone you don't.

I was with Herb once at a Super Bowl party where the television was playing, but he also had a radio on. I asked him why he had them both on, and he said, "Close your eyes and just listen to the television. Now describe for me what's going on."

I couldn't.

"Television announcers take for granted that you can see what's happening," he explained. "So it would be redundant for them to repeat it." As I closed my eyes and listened, I heard commentators talk about the players and give statistics, but they never described in any detail exactly what was taking place.

"Television," Herb said, "tends to comment on what's going on from somewhat of a distance. But since radio can't give you anything to look at, broadcasters have to paint as complete a picture as possible with sound alone. That's why their voices are so important and, at its best, their work often rises to the level of great art. I guarantee you, you'll learn more about what's happening in this game from listening to it on the radio than you will from watching it on television. There is a big difference in the way each medium tells the same story. For me, the media people who grew up with radio are the best; those who grew up in the age of television fall short when it comes to giving those salient details. Something's been lost in the name of progress."

I can't help thinking that Herb may be hearing the same things I'm hearing but is paying a different kind of attention.

Does the loss of one of your senses improve your others?

"I can't tell you for sure. I don't really have anything to compare it to," Herb said.

This is probably an issue that is impossible to prove one way or the other. But how else can one explain Herb's uncanny awareness of time, distance, and direction? He has a memory for phone numbers like a Rolodex file and can get you from here to there better than MapQuest.

Whether or not it's because he can't see, he seems to have a compass and a clock built in. Here's just one example: we were driving from the airport into downtown Miami to speak at a convention, and we were on in less than an hour. Herb had stayed at our hotel before, but I hadn't. "Head south on A1A," he said. "How far?" I asked. He smiled and said, "Don't worry, I'll tell you." Oh, great, I thought. I'm driving with a wise guy who can't see, and I don't know where in the world I'm going. So I said, "Just give me a hint. Is it 20 minutes away?" He responded, "I'm the navigator. I know where we're going." Knowing how to take a hint, I stopped asking, and we continued planning the last-minute details of our presentation. (With Herb, there is no time like the last minute.) I was in mid-sentence when he interrupted me with "Where are we now?" I looked around and said, "At a light, across the street from a

Texaco station." He said, "No, I meant, what street are we crossing?" I told him, and he said, "Fine. We're only about half a mile away."

How did he do that? On one level he seemed engaged in our conversation. On another level he had an accurate grasp of the geography. And at the same time he had to have been calculating the speed at which we were traveling.

I asked him, "How the hell did you know exactly where we were?" He replied, "It's not that I was thinking about it all that intensely. It's all just peripheral. I'm aware of the same things you are, but in a different way. While both of us were involved in the conversation, you were probably also looking around at the scenery for landmarks or whatever. Right? You're not concentrating on it. It's just part of the background. I'm more aware of the road, the turns, and our speed because my energy and attention are not wasted taking in the scenery." It makes sense. I've seen him do the same sort of thing in the subway systems of Chicago, New York and London.

Directions are more than just getting from point A to point B for Herb. "I've got to know where I am," he says. "Definitely. I want to know if we're on the right track. Are we getting lost? Are we okay? I need to know because most people don't have a clear sense of where they are or where they're going. Maybe it's a control thing. But somebody's got to know where we're going and what's happening. And I feel better if it's me."

I pointed out to Herb that this sounded a lot like his management style.

"I hadn't thought of it that way, but I think you're right," he said. "I don't want to have to tell people what to do all the time. I just want to know what's going on and that we're moving in the right direction. Tell me what's happening. If it's good, that's great. I always love to hear positive things. If it's bad, let me know, and we'll fix it. But I can't know whether we're on track or have a problem until I know where we're headed and what the plan is for getting there."

He paused, then added, "But it's all about knowing directions. It's about knowing where you've been. And where you're going. I like to know the design. What's the layout? Then I can contribute something. But a lot of people just figure they'll kind of meander along and find their way—and they never get anywhere. I need to know the plan. Then I can play along."

"The real winners in this world are those individuals who know their strengths and are able to create situations that play to their unique abilities."

Herb's strong sense of place may come from having grown up in Brooklyn. Several people we interviewed for this book had grown up in Brooklyn. And beyond having moxie, they all shared a strong sense of belonging.

For instance, when we met Senator Barbara Boxer (D-CA), she and Herb immediately launched into reminiscences of Brooklyn. I had been in this position before and knew that if they got around to the subject of the Dodgers leaving, I wouldn't be leaving any time soon. When two people from Brooklyn first meet, they typically play a game of naming streets and places. It's like a test, as if someone might actually fake being from Brooklyn. They ask about Junior's, then Ebbets Field, and then Borough Park. In the senator's case, she went to Wingate High School; Herb went to Bushwick. Whatever Brooklynites go on to become, and no matter where that journey takes them, they know where they're from. Their shared pride wells up when they meet, and you can tell they're okay with one another.

Being okay with one another brings to mind a key point about Herb and trust. Establishing trust is a challenge for everyone; it's at the heart of any meaningful relationship.

But you realize just how important trust is when you walk with someone who is blind. When a blind person is on your arm, they must trust you to look out for them. You are their guide. Where's the wall? A door? The steps? Is there a curb? Are you sure you're paying close enough attention, watching out for both of you?

Even when trust is established, Herb says he still feels a strong sense of self-preservation. Whenever I walk with him, he always wants to link his left arm inside my right arm. It's just a pattern, and I never gave it much thought until one time when we were rushing through an airport and I went to tuck his other arm inside of mine. He went out of his way to switch positions. When I asked him why, he explained that even though the last fistfight he was in was as a kid, he still likes to walk with someone on his left so that his right hand is free to swing. "I can't remember the last time I had to slug anyone. It's just a deep-seated preservation thing," he explained.

He grew up in a neighborhood where someone would attack a blind kid?

"Between the ages of 10 and 13, I attended a school in the heart of Bedford-Stuyvesant, which was in one of Brooklyn's toughest areas. There were quite a few times when I was attacked, punched, and in some cases, really beaten up. That's why I needed my right hand free. So that when the attacks came, I was ready."

Two of Herb's close friends, the venture capitalist Gordon Gund and New York State Senate Minority Leader (and current candidate for Lieutenant Governor) David Patterson, also happen to be blind. Over the years Herb has spent hour upon hour talking with David about politics and Gordon about sports and business. However, they never spoke about being blind. That is, not until we arranged to interview them for this book. This project—discovering what drives successful people—opened the door to Herb's talking with both of them about one of their most obvious similarities, a subject which they had somehow avoided before.

When Herb and Gordon were talking about trust, they both admitted that it took a long time for each of them to allow other people to help them. But as they learned to let down their guard, they realized that acceptance, and the subsequent trust, helped them develop deeper relationships.

After my initial conversation on the plane with Herb about his blindness, we had several more discussions on the topic. But it is not an easy place for him to go. So, I usually came away with more questions than answers about how his being blind has helped define him. That in many ways is what led us to write this book.

Herb, I believe, considers his blindness to be something that simply happened to him as a child. It is just a part of him. Why concentrate on it? By his nature, he is not one to dwell on the past. He is much more interested in talking about what is happening now than about what already took place. Herb prefers the present. Or what might happen five minutes from now. "Some people like to have a five-year plan," he once told me. "But I don't see the point of planning too far ahead." Now that's something you could knit on a pillow.

I remember being in his office one day, and he was outlining three new projects he wanted me to work on. As I got up to leave a few minutes later, he asked me if the first project was done yet. "Now, that's a classic Herb Greenberg moment," I said. He just laughed, adding, "I'm going to hear about this one, aren't I?" "Absolutely," I replied. "Some day I'm even going to write about it." Sometimes you just have to laugh. And Herb does that a lot.

Although Herb may have had doubts along the way, he never doubted he would succeed.

One of the key concepts Herb shares, one that has found its way into his *Harvard Business Review* articles, is that for a person to succeed at anything, it must be fun. As he said, "Everyone has key strengths and key limitations. That is the human condition. The real winners in this world are those individuals who know their strengths and are able to create situations that play to their unique abilities—where their limitations are of little consequence. These are people who are not just succeeding, they are succeeding on their own terms."

In the coming pages you'll get to know many remarkable people, from all walks of life, who have figured out how to make this happen.

But first we need to agree on a definition of success.

CHAPTER

First You Have to Define Success

S*everal individuals share their personal definitions of success, including Fariborz Ghadar, who had to leave Iran during the revolution, and Rebecca Stephens, who climbed Mount Everest.*

INVARIABLY, AS SOON AS WE'D sit down to interview someone for this book, after the pleasantries were out of the way and the coffee or tea had been poured, the person would ask us, "Before we get into this, I need to know, what do you mean by success?"

We would shrug our shoulders and say, "We'd really like to tell you, but you'll have to wait until the book comes out."

The truth is that they were beating us to one of our own most important questions. "What is *your* definition of success?" was one of the first things we wanted to ask everyone we interviewed.

We assumed we'd get some incredible answers.

And we did.

In our eyes, the individuals we selected to assess and interview for this book were all highly successful. But it wasn't because of any empirical formula we had developed. It wasn't because of their wealth or job titles. Most were already at the top of their game. The rest were on their way. They came from all walks of life: business, sports, politics, entertainment—you name it. But their common ground was that the moment you met them, you knew they were doing exactly what they were meant to do. Some of them had even succeeded beyond their wildest dreams. They were at the right place at the right time because they knew what they were about and were playing to their strengths.

Granted, that might sound more than slightly subjective. No doubt it's hard to measure. But the people we encountered tipped the scales when it came to enjoying what they were doing, knowing that they were contributing in a meaningful way—and sharing their enthusiasm. In some cases they even apologized for liking what they were doing so much. They felt lucky, blessed, engaged, challenged, and always peeking around future's corner.

We'll share with you what we've learned.

You must realize, however, that some of the definitions of success, just like some of the qualities it takes to succeed, may seem to contradict one another. And, in fact, they sometimes do. But that's all right. There is no single success formula for all of us. If that's what you're looking for, we are definitely the wrong people to ask. But, we can assure you of one thing: there absolutely is a path that's right for you. And if you can learn from others and recognize parts of yourself in their stories, we believe you'll be able to open the door to your own success.

Which brings us back to the question at hand: What is success?

One of the more classic definitions of success came from Rebecca Stephens, the first British woman to climb Mount Everest. She realized that reaching the highest point on earth was her goal after being assigned to report on a group of climbers who were going to scale the northeast ridge of the world's tallest mountain. At that point she didn't know the first thing about mountain climbing, but it seemed like a plum assignment, so she grabbed it. That was in 1989, and all she was expected to do was file a few stories about what it was like to prepare for the climb. What struck her most was the level of passion every climber felt for getting to the top of Mount Everest. "At first I wondered why they were willing to risk their lives just to climb these rocks," she said. But she soon realized there was a bigger story here and wired her editors, saying, "I'd like to try to answer the question: Why do climbers climb?" At that point, she had gone beyond her assignment and was asking her own questions. She proposed that she climb to the first camp so she could describe firsthand the effects of reaching that altitude. She said, "I knew this was the only way to really understand the desire that was driving these climbers."

We'll tell you later about her defining moment and the qualities that drove her to defy the elements and face the very real possibility of death, first with Mount Everest and then when going on to scale the highest peak on each continent. Most important, in her decision to make the climb, she realized something about herself she hadn't known before.

And it was invigorating.

And clarifying.

Part of that realization had to do with Rebecca finding her own definition of success. For Rebecca, "Success is the achievement of whatever it is you set out to do. And it's up to you to decide what that is. It can't be determined by anyone else. Success is not, absolutely not, what is commonly defined by mercantile societies as the accumulation of wealth. If riches come along with your success, that's great. But money alone is not a measure of true success. You might have done everything in your power to achieve your goal, yet obstacles that are beyond your control prevented you from reaching it. The weather might keep you from reaching the top of the mountain, or the economic climate might hold you back from reaching another goal. But you can still consider yourself successful if you put everything you had into it, and if you learned a thing or two along the way. It's not an easy definition of success, but it's not impossible either. It's all about setting a goal and totally connecting yourself to achieving it."

After four years of intense training Rebecca stood on top of the world for 10 minutes. The summit, as she describes, is a tiny area. It's the point where the three tapered faces of the mountain rise and meet. It's only about 15 feet by 10 feet. That's it. So you don't step back when you're taking a picture. There's also no doubt about it when you reached the very top. From there she could look all the way down the mountain, and see everything—her past, present and her possibilities. "And for those 10 minutes," she said, "that mountain was completely ours. It was just a magical feeling of solitude up there where everywhere you looked there was wilderness. It was exquisitely beautiful." Then they had to descend. Quickly. There was no time to waste. It was all a matter of timing. They had just six hours of daylight, which they had to use with maximum efficiency, in order to get back down the mountain. So they took several quick photographs and made tracks.

Climbing Mount Everest is success on anyone's terms. "It was an incredible challenge. Certainly difficult. And it required boring diligence," Rebecca explained. "It also took enormous respect for the mountain. I had never pursued anything with such conviction as I did my quest to climb Everest. To me that was half the battle won, if not more. To succeed, you first need a very keen awareness of yourself. It requires really listening to your inner voice, so you have the courage to pursue a path which aligns with your desires. When you find that, then you have the impetus to achieve. That's the secret, I believe."

Success has less to do with what you have than with knowing who you are.

Ben Vereen has a somewhat different take on success. This galvanizing Broadway, movie and television singer, dancer, and actor with an electric smile, elastic movements, and exuberant energy said, "What is the top of your game? You know it when you are in it. When you are true to it, when you are honest, and when you have integrity, the top is not a place. The top is eternal.

"There is no final peak," he added, "because you are constantly striving for the highest good. If you feel you've peaked at something, you've placed a ceiling on it, put an end to it."

He paused, then added, "The peak can be very confusing. You can think you're there when you're not. It's like a guy who is driving down the highway and sees a place called The Peak. So he pulls over and rents a room for the night. Then he wakes up and drives off thinking he's been to The Peak. But it was only a rest stop. That's all. Some people never go any farther than that because they think they've been to The Peak. But you've got to keep going. You can't be fooled by the rest stops or the places where you're just fueling your car. Sometimes those stops are diversions or just distractions. Or the filling stations of adversity. You've got to listen to that voice inside that says, 'Keep going. It's farther up the road.' Because there is never going to be a point where you've totally made it. The peak of my game is eternal."

This from a man who became part of America's consciousness when he portrayed Chicken George, the grandson of Kunta Kinte who won his freedom in Alex Haley's landmark miniseries *Roots*, won a Tony Award as best actor in a musical for his role in *Pippin*, and co-starred in *All That Jazz*, Bob Fosse's semi-autobiographical film.

"I'm on that journey," Ben said, his eyes lighting up and his smile igniting. "I'm on that journey," he repeated, as if to himself.

Paul Schulte, the youngest U.S. wheelchair basketball player at the 2000 Paralympic Games in Sydney, reflected on what success was like at the Olympic level. "We were in front of 18,000 people, playing the Australians in their own house. The sound was deafening. It was the only time in my life that I've been as close to someone as you and I are right now, and I was screaming at the top of my lungs to the guy next to me, and he didn't even turn his head. The energy was amazing. The floor shook. I'd never felt a floor shake from the excitement of a crowd. I'd never experienced anything like it. Everybody was over the top. Our team had to resort to hand signals because we couldn't hear each other. Right before the tip-off, I froze the moment in my mind. And I said to myself, 'This is success.'"

Paul's team went on to win. "But the experience itself," he said, "that was the real success. At the tip-off we wanted to win more than anything. But just by being there, we knew we had already succeeded."

Paul said, "Success is focusing on what you have rather than what you don't have. In my life, there were 10,000 things I could have done before my disability. Now there may be only 9,000. You've got to focus on your present opportunities and let the rest go."

Paul often meets people who have just been in an accident and lost the use of one or more of their limbs. It's a fragile time. Their lives have been turned upside down and inside out. "I try to let them know that they are still the same person they were before. Their bodies may have changed, but they are the same person—maybe even better. They just need to accept what's happened and discover their own amazingness."

He recalled a time when he was talking with a young woman who had barely survived an accident and had come out as a paraplegic. He was listening to her and knew exactly where she was coming from: the disbelief, the anger, all of it. Then Paul told her that he felt very lucky, and she said she thought he was off his rocker. He explained, "Let me tell you how you actually have an advantage over most people walking on this planet. First and foremost, you won't be afraid of dying anymore. When you get real close to death, you lose the fear of it. You know what it's like to be that close. And it helps you live your life a little bit differently, more fully. Not that everybody should have a tragic experience; I wouldn't wish that on anyone. But for those of us who have been through it, there is much to be gained. You could look at what happened and say, 'I'm a victim. This happened to me, and everybody should feel sorry for me.' Or you can say, 'This is an opportunity.' If you can view adversity as an opportunity, things will be completely different. That's when you're ready to succeed."

He paused, then said, "Succeeding is not just about the results you produce. It's about what you're actually doing. It's really about aiming for a dream. You're aiming. And it's exciting. You don't worry about failing or succeeding. You're just *in it*. That's all that matters. Success is a by-product."

For a guy who led his team to a gold medal by averaging 17 points a game at the 2002 Gold Cup, it's interesting that he sees such a clear distinction between winning and succeeding.

Paul concluded, "If you lose, that doesn't mean you're not successful. It's a loss only if you don't learn something from it."

Senator Barbara Boxer said that, for her, success is having her own clear sense of what is important, what is right, and what she needs to do. "I don't always *succeed*, if that only means accomplishing what I want. But I can feel successful from just moving my agenda forward. I have an inner strength that helps me see the right thing to do. We all go through this world in such a short amount of time. So if you're not going to do what's right, if you're not going to be brave, then you really don't deserve anyone else's trust. For me, succeeding is being true to myself. I might not always win, and these days I often don't. But I'm still succeeding on my own terms. All I can do is be true to myself."

She was the only senator to formally challenge President Bush's second election victory, the second such challenge in a presidential race since 1877. Senator Boxer joined Representative Stephanie Tubbs Jones (D-OH) in objecting to the certification of Ohio's 20 electoral votes, citing serious voting irregularities in that state.

In President Bush's bitter contest with Al Gore in 2000, black members of the House stood up to protest the results, pleading for a senator to join their objections, but none did.

She said that, in retrospect, "it was a mistake not to object four years ago." She had gone along with Gore's request for a smooth transition, but this time it was different for her. "I think this was the first time in my life I ever voted alone in the U.S. Senate, and I have to tell you, I still think it was the right thing to do." The senator believes that at least she forced the Republican leadership to listen more to concerns about voting rights.

"You don't have to win to be successful," she continued. "And sometimes you can even win by losing if you're standing up for what you know is right. Sometimes you win just by taking up the fight. There are so many different measures of success," she concluded, "but one thing I can say for sure is that success becomes clear when you hear your own inner applause."

For anyone who thinks success can be measured solely by how much money you have, Fariborz Ghadar, Ph.D., an international consultant who was named one of the top 10 Stars of Finance by *Business Week*, can clear up that misconception.

He was the vice minister of finance for Iran, a member of the shah's cabinet who was responsible for identifying global investment opportunities for a country that had more money than it knew what to do with. He was traveling to virtually every nation in the world, recommending that Iran's oil money be invested in everything from pistachios to Persian rugs.

Then the revolution came.

And he didn't have the slightest idea that it was about to break open.

"You can be right in the middle of such events yet not really see them," he said. "Buildings were being burned, there were riots in the streets, people were being killed, and I was saying, 'This will pass. It's just one of those temporary things.' Then my wife called me from London and said, 'Quick, turn on CNN. It's time to get out.' As she was trying to convince me that I wasn't seeing the whole picture, bullets came streaking into our office. We were on the top floor, the seventh, and bullets were flying all over the place. So I agreed that, well, maybe I should get out of there. And I left. It was one of the turning points of my life.

"When I got to the airport, I tried to exchange the Iranian money I had, which was quite a bit. But they would give me only one-fifth of its face value. 'Forget it,' I said. 'I'll be back in a few weeks. I'll keep my money.'"

But his money wasn't the only issue. It was extremely difficult to get a plane out of the country. Fortunately, his father, who was then the ambassador to Jordan, was able to get him on a Jordanian airline. From there he was able to book a flight to London.

He tried to exchange his money in Jordan and this time was offered only one-tenth of its value. Again he said, "Forget it. I'll just hold on to it until this thing blows over." When he arrived in London just a few hours later, his money was completely worthless. Nobody wanted it at any price. "I still have several fistfuls of that money. I keep it in a drawer. It reminds me of how little money is really worth and how transient such values are."

Fariborz learned that success has less to do with what you have than with knowing who you are. "I've always taken pride in being able to see what is going on around me," he explained. "But I've learned that when you are right in the middle of it, you sometimes can't see it, no matter how brilliant you are. You often have to step outside a situation to know what's really happening. That was a valuable lesson for me—even more valuable than the money I lost, which was basically everything I had."

Whose definition of success resonates most with you? Did any of them prompt you to start thinking about your own definition?

From executives to athletes, and from politicians to artists, we've heard some incredible stories about their successes. And each of them has come up with his or her own personal definition of success, a definition that helps define and drive who he or she is.

Perhaps you connect most with Rebecca Stephens, who had a goal that became part of her. Or you may identify more with Ben Vereen, who believes that success starts with believing in yourself as you continue your search on this planet. Or Paul Schulte's definition might speak to you: Success is focusing on what you have rather than what you don't have. Or Senator Barbara Boxer's belief that you need to listen to your inner applause and stand up for what you believe might resonate with you. Or you might get more from Fariborz Ghadar's understanding that success has less to do with what you have than with knowing who you are.

Whose definition of success resonates most with you? Did any of them prompt you to start thinking about your own definition? If that's the case, you're well on your way to being successful on your own terms. Perhaps, just because you are taking the time to read this book, you are thinking, "Maybe there's something else, something more, that I can do." When you arrive at your own personal definition of success, it will help clarify what you have to do next to achieve your dreams, whatever they are.

We'll leave you with one last definition of success, one of our favorites. It comes from an amazing Brazilian author and inspirational speaker, José Luiz Tejon Megido, whom you'll hear more about later. For now, we just want to share with you his particular definition of success, one that seems to transcend all the others and, at the same time, tie them all together: "Success starts with keeping a sense of youth about you. Keep inside of you an image of the child you were. And make sure that child is always part of who you are and what you're doing."

Tapping Into Your Defining Qualities

We all have different strengths. Learn to discover yours and make them your focus.

WE'D LIKE TO START our journey by sharing with you some of what we've learned about the qualities that help people succeed in different walks of life.

Caliper has been working with leaders at companies such as Avis, Caterpillar, FedEx, GMAC, Johnson & Johnson, and some of the fastest-growing smaller firms, helping them select the right people, manage individuals most effectively, develop productive teams, and improve overall corporate performance. Over the past four decades we've grown to include offices in Australia, Brazil, Canada, China, France, Germany, Japan, Mexico, Singapore, Spain, Taiwan, the United Kingdom, and the United States.

Our premise has always been that an individual's potential and motivation make all the difference.

People succeed when they are tapping into their strengths. And are making sure that their limitations don't trip them up.

This is particularly true when it comes to succeeding in leadership, management, sales, or customer service positions, as well as in working on a team.

If we were assessing you for a position, among the questions we would consider are the following:

Do you have the ability to inspire people and the intuition to sense change that are required to lead others?

Do you have the decision-making skills, ability to command respect, and communication talent needed to manage people and projects?

Do you have the persuasive skills, ability to read others, and strength to bounce back from rejection needed to succeed in sales?

Do you have the desire to come through for others, the detail orientation, and the organizational skills required to succeed in a customer service and/or administrative position?

While some people can succeed because of their talents as crafts-people, questions still arise: Do you have the persistence, the attention to detail, and the ability to work with others to be a carpenter, electrician, or any other job requiring a specific craft?

These are the qualities that drive us. We all have different strengths. The idea is to discover them and make them our focus.

Of course there are dozens of other qualities that we measure to help identify an individual's strengths and potential. Then, of course, we also have to take into account the organization's culture, the personality attributes of a person's manager, and the dynamics of the team. When all is said and done, there are myriad combinations of those qualities; that is what makes us who we are and helps explain why we might be successful at one thing and absolutely wrong for another.

Perhaps this concept is demonstrated most dramatically in our work with professional sports teams. The Chicago White Sox and the Detroit Pistons are among the two dozen teams we advise on their draft choices.

Now, these teams don't need us to consider an athlete's speed or agility. They have scouts who can recognize that kind of talent a mile away.

But the coaches and managers of professional teams know that what really matters—after the talent has been established—is whether players have the will, the drive, the motivation to ratchet their talent up to the highest level. Can they handle the pressure? Are they really competitive? Are they team players? These are the qualities that distinguish the best players.

It's what Yogi Berra recognized when he said, "Winning is 90 percent mental; the other half is physical."

Ultimately, we've learned that we all succeed when we tap into our strongest qualities.

Then our *potential* can be realized.

Over the years we've found that when talent is essentially equal, such as in first-round draft picks in professional sports, the difference between the superstars and journeymen is the hunger, the desire, the drive to succeed on their own terms.

Just consider what an edge you'll have if you understand the qualities that drive *you*.

We assume you are a unique blend of several distinct qualities. But, if you start out by identifying the one that is your dominant, driving, defining quality, imagine how far ahead of the game you'll be.

With that in mind, we want to share with you 19 of the qualities we have found that distinguish people who succeed.

There are some of us who are naturally reflective. And some of us just race from point A to point B, rarely looking back unless we've knocked something over.

Of course, all of us possess various levels of several of the qualities we are about to explore with you. But some of the people we came across seemed to own a certain quality, as if it were their middle name.

In this section of the book we're going to tell you about quite a few distinct qualities. These qualities won't be new to you. But hopefully, in the telling of the stories of people who exemplify these qualities, you will see part of yourself: the part we call your defining quality.

Knowing your defining quality, calling it your own, and breathing life into it can go a long way toward making you successful.

Again, please keep in mind that the underlying message of these stories is that there is more than one way to succeed. Each of the people we've selected to exemplify one of these qualities also possesses several other driving motivations.

Here is a quick overview of the 19 qualities we will be telling you about through the stories of some of the incredible people we met:

Perseverance. There are people who, in the face of uncertainty or possible defeat, defy the odds and refuse to accept the idea that there is no way out. Through sheer perseverance, by refusing to cave in, they are able to alter what appears to be the inevitable.

Through the Holocaust, Samuel Pisar lost his father, his mother, and his sister and narrowly escaped death several times. In this vision of hell that eclipsed Dante's Inferno, Samuel would sometimes think he could not make it one step farther. He believes he "survived by drawing strength from the energy of despair," as he said. "Despair can either devastate you immediately or fill you with energy and determination to resist and overcome. When you touch bottom, as I have, and give a hefty kick with everything you've got, you can sometimes return to the surface, and even beyond it. Pain and suffering do not necessarily degrade or embitter you, they can also energize and empower you."

Goal-Oriented. If two people are climbing a mountain together, what is the most important thing they need to get to the summit? Teamwork? Cooperation? The right equipment? Training? Those are all needed, but the most important thing they need is the mountain. You need a clear goal.

From a psychological perspective, we've found that individuals who are goal-oriented have a combination of self-discipline, a strong sense of responsibility, assertiveness, and drive.

Rebecca Stephens, the first British woman to climb Mount Everest, can tell you that when a goal becomes your own, it can change your life. Once she decided to climb the highest mountain in the world, everything else in her life became crystal clear. "It was the first time in my life," she said, "that I actually knew what I wanted to do. Before that I was drifting somewhat aimlessly. Not unhappily, mind you. But I was aware that I was a jack-of-all-trades and master of none. I hadn't really found my direction in life." With climbing to the summit of Mount Everest as her goal, her life came into focus. "I had never sought out anything with such conviction as I did to climb Everest," she said. "For me the battle was already half won, if not more. Because once you have a clearly defined objective, everything else becomes a lot easier."

Self-Awareness. There are some of us who are naturally reflective. And some of us just race from point A to point B, rarely looking back unless we've knocked something over. When we're not clear about what is motivating us, we can trip over ourselves and land in places we never intended. On the other hand, when we know what drives us, we can tap into our strengths and focus them in a clear direction.

The unfortunate truth is that most of us hide from a true examination of ourselves. We avoid asking the tough questions: Do I like this job? Why don't I pursue something that is more fun? Those are tough questions. But only through asking them and finding the answers can we hope to succeed on our own terms.

Ben Vereen has figured this out. He is an extremely talented actor, singer, and dancer who has received the highest recognition for the parts he's played on Broadway, on television, and in movies. But he is also very deep and reflective, as he shares with enormous candor how, after the loss of his child, he slowly, painfully figured out how to pick up the pieces of his life, which had been torn asunder.

Resilience. The way we handle rejection, defeat, or just the discouragement that life has a tendency to send our way has a lot to do with how we succeed. Individuals with a healthy self-esteem are able to brush themselves off after getting knocked down, and carry on with even more determination. This is a quality that psychologists call ego-strength, and it is exemplified by Muggsy Bogues who, at five feet, three inches, was the shortest professional basketball player of all time. In the section on resilience, Muggsy will tell you all about this quality when he describes the feeling he had when he was picked in the first round of the draft. He said, "All the folks saying, 'He's too small.' They said it when I was in grammar school, then junior high, then high school, then college, then the pros. And in one sense it was in and out. You know, in one ear and out the other. But it hurt. So in another sense it was just another measuring stick as far as proving them wrong. And then it gets to the point where it's even more important than just proving them wrong." There's a guy who knows where rejection belongs.

Willingness to Take a Risk. Without taking a risk, or a leap of faith, very little happens. Being willing to take a risk doesn't mean throwing caution to the wind, but it does require assessing a situation, weighing the alternatives, believing something is worth doing, and then stepping out where you may have never been before. That doesn't mean all of us have to go skydiving. Some of us are naturally more prone to taking risks. Part of it has to do with being comfortable exploring the unknown. People who are more cautious prefer things to stay as they know them. But nothing stays the same forever. There's no way to avoid risk, so you might as well take your risks on purpose. In all of our studies of successful people, the willingness to take risks is universal. The reason is that if people were not willing to take risks, going out into the unknown, they would never succeed on their own terms.

Senator Barbara Boxer risked a sure seat in the House of Representatives for a long shot at the Senate. She ended up in a fight for her political life. In winning, she learned much about herself and about how putting it all on the line can get you focused on what you need to do to succeed.

Thriving on Pressure. Most of us wish we could be cool under pressure. But thriving on pressure? That's quite another thing, a whole different psychology. It's not just being able to do well under the worst situations but knowing that for some reason the best in you comes out when everyone else is running for cover.

Roger Staubach, the Hall of Fame quarterback for the Dallas Cowboys from 1969 through 1979 who led his team to two Super Bowls victories, can tell you about thriving on pressure. During his career Roger developed a reputation for finding a way to win when defeat was staring him in the face. He led his team to 14 comebacks in the final two minutes of the game.

When he made those unbelievable last-minute passes with the clock ticking and the fans on edge, it may have looked like luck was with him. But luck doesn't come out of thin air. The harder Roger worked, the luckier he became. He always demanded of himself just a little more. That inner taskmaster, getting to practice early, staying later, working on his game in the off-season, prepared him to recognize and take advantage of the pressure, mistakes, and opportunities that can come out of nowhere and change the results of an important game.

Optimism. Being a fighter with a positive attitude is often central to succeeding on your own terms. It's not that your attitude alone can change things. But it can take you a long way. Optimism starts with the belief that there will always be another opportunity.

When Janet Lasley was diagnosed with terminal cancer, this mother of two young children and owner of a construction company said, "This is not *freaking* going to happen to me. I'm not going down this way!" In the years since, she has undergone six surgeries and six rounds of chemotherapy and is scanned regularly to monitor two tumors that refuse to disappear completely. Sometimes, several times a day, she thinks, "If this were my last day on earth, how would I want to spend it?" And she comes up with some creative ways to spend those days. Ultimately, it's her incredible optimism that gets her through as she fights valiantly, knowing that in the blink of an eye everything could change.

Empathy. The ability to understand others is a quality that is sorely undervalued. Empathy, as we described in *How to Hire & Develop Your Next Top Performer* (McGraw-Hill, 2001), is the ability to sense the reactions of another person, to place oneself in the other person's shoes. Then you can understand where that person is coming from. When we are able to do that, we can make real connections that lead to important relationships. This is vital to succeeding in leadership, management, sales, and virtually any professional or personal relationship.

Someone who gets it is Claude Grunitzky, who, as the son of an ambassador, grew up shuttling between the small African country of Togo, Washington, DC, Paris, and London. He speaks six languages, carries two passports, and is never on one continent for more than a week or two. Those foreign experiences shaped his transcultural philosophy and formed the creative energy behind *Trace* magazine and his advertising company, True. Claude's entire approach is to break down barriers between cultures, languages, editorial, advertising, and all forms of communication, so that we are dealing with each other in a voice that transcends all the babble. "The most important thing I learned was to question everything I was being taught," he said, particularly when the history lessons in the United States, France, England, and Togo contradicted one another.

There's no way to avoid risk, so you might as well take your risks on purpose.

Competitiveness. That burning inner need to beat an opponent with every move—that's competitiveness. Whether it is stealing a basketball from an opponent in the final seconds of a game or hitting a home run with the bases loaded or winning an impossible business deal, competitiveness is that inner burning need to win.

Geoffrey Bodine, honored as one of NASCAR's 50 greatest drivers, narrowly escaped a fiery nine-vehicle wreck in Daytona when his truck hit the wall at about 185 miles per hour and cartwheeled down the track in flames. The top of his vehicle was sheared off, the engine rolled down the straightaway, pieces flew into the stands, and the truck's metal disintegrated until almost all that was left was a roll cage before it was hit again. On a video replay of the accident, even in slow motion, you can't count how many times the vehicle flipped over. The announcer assumed that Geoffrey was no longer with us. Two months after the accident Geoffrey was back behind the wheel. Why? His first explanation was, "I'm competitive." When pushed for a more definitive explanation, he added, "I didn't want to be replaced."

Patience. It takes enormous internal strength to wait for something that is worthwhile. There are always reasons to change the dial, do something else, to go on to the next adventure. But some things are worth holding out for. That, however, takes incredible fortitude, particularly when those around you are losing their heads.

Just ask Daisy Myers, whose family made history in 1957 by being the first people of color to move into Levittown, Pennsylvania. The Ku Klux Klan burned crosses, blasted racist music, picketed her house, threw rocks through her windows, and threatened her children for months even though the state police were sent in to protect them. She says the major quality that kept her and her family going through that ordeal was patience. "I'd wait for the night to become daylight, because they were only brave when it was dark. Then we'd wait to see if they'd be there again the next night. Throughout it, we just had to be patient. Just believe that everything would work out, sit tight, believe and have a little patience," she explained.

Persuasiveness. There are some people who just need to bring others around to their point of view. The world is out of kilter if people are not agreeing with them, nodding their heads in agreement or approval. Ego-drive, as Herb describes it, is a specific need some people have that makes them feel good about themselves when they are persuading others. They want to hear the word "yes." It could be "Yes, I'll buy your product" or "Yes, I'll go out with you" or "Yes, I'll vote for your candidate." Hearing the "yes," seeing the heads nod in agreement—that's what drives someone who is persuasive. It's a need that cannot go unfulfilled.

One person who exemplifies persuasiveness is David Oreck. The guy's all over late-night television in his infomercials, carrying his light-as-a-feather vacuum cleaner under his arm. David is the founder and instantly recognizable spokesperson for the New Orleans-based vacuum manufacturing company that bears his name. "Having the best product is crucial," he said, "but what will distinguish you in today's marketplace is marketing and sales. We've all heard that if you build a better mousetrap, the world will beat a path to your door. But that isn't true. The world first has to get the message. You have to be willing to sell your ideas—usually to people who haven't the faintest idea that they need them. Never underestimate the power of ideas," he added. "Ideas have started religions and nations."

Confidence. If there were a psychological recipe for confidence, it would read something like this: Take one part self-assurance. Mix with an equal part of trust in those you surround yourself with. Shake. Do not stir.

Jeffrey Lurie, Chairman and Chief Executive Officer of the Philadelphia Eagles, read a front-page article in *The Wall Street Journal* saying that he was making the mistake of his life by purchasing the team. The fans were upset. (That's a nice way of describing how Philadelphia fans can get. At one point the Eagles' stadium even had its own judge, courtroom, and overnight jail.) They were upset because they were sure he had bought the team just to move it to Los Angeles. Then, when he and his coach, Andy Reid, chose Donovan McNabb to be the quarterback, the mayor of Philadelphia even introduced a resolution in City Council to have the Eagles draft another player instead of Donovan McNabb. Fans called radio stations and the Eagles' switchboard to express similar feelings. Undaunted, Jeffrey carried on and in a few short years replaced the beleaguered stadium the team used to play in with a world-class facility and got the team to the Super Bowl. Jeffrey exudes a confidence that comes from believing in himself *and* in the people with whom he surrounds himself.

Passion. It is impossible to succeed without loving what you do. Really succeeding means pouring your heart and soul into what you're doing. When you start with passion, all the people around you know they're in the presence of someone who is not just talented but has the potential for greatness. The last time João Carlos Martins played a Bach concert at Carnegie Hall, *The New York Times* said there were fireworks in all directions. His passion for interpreting Bach was rushing through his entire body, his head shooting back, his hands flying off the keyboard, his audience in rapture. They even put 500 seats on the stage.

"I played as I never played in my life," he said. "Any time I go to the stage, I have to perform as if it were the last concert of my life. I have to play with all my passion. It's the only way I know how." At that time João Carlos was just regaining the use of his right hand which had been seriously injured in an accident. He has since recorded a CD called *For the Left Hand Only*.

Integrity. One of the qualities that has to do with our very essence is being honest and true to ourselves. Interestingly, the word *integrity* also means "the state of being complete." We often find out about our integrity when it is tested.

When Connie Jackson was heading up a health-care clinic in Chicago, she became disillusioned with politicians who were unwilling to fight wealthy health care interest groups and help people who were really in need. And she saw no sign of it changing. "I was getting sick and burned out," she explained. She needed to find a new way to make a difference. After a lot of soul-searching, she found herself in London, at the helm of St. Bartholomew's, where she is working on health policy in a country that puts more emphasis on health care for the needy.

Trust. Trust is the bedrock of any successful relationship, whether it's professional or personal. When you know that you can rely on the people you surround yourself with, a world of possibilities opens up. That is not to say that to be trusting is to be naive. Sometimes relationships start with trust. Sometimes it has to be developed. But trust can never be missing from a solid relationship. We trust others when we know we can depend on them—and they can depend on us.

Gordon Gund, the former Owner of the Cleveland Cavaliers and Owner of Gund Investment Corporation, has to trust the people and organizations he invests in whether they're in sports, business, or health research. Trust has also had a lot to do with Gordon's personal relationships since losing his sight. When he's walking with someone, he has to know that person will watch out for him, let him know when a step or curb is coming up. "I remember when I first became blind, one of the basic things I had to come to terms with was the importance of trust—on a very deep level. And, in my case, that also means being willing to accept help from other people, which isn't easy when you're used to being independent. But it's a very important thing for all of us. And you learn that it can also mean a great deal to the people who are helping you. Whether you have a disability or not, the truth is that the most amazing friendships often get to be even stronger when we help each other. And that takes real trust."

Having Fun. It is impossible to succeed at something if you are not enjoying what you are doing. Some of us have gotten to take that enjoyment to an entirely new level.

Zip-A-Dee-Doo-Dah, born with the name Angelo Chianese, is a singing telegram artist who, as he describes it, "had quite a checkered past when it comes to my career; a real history of going from one thing to another, trying to find out what the heck works and what feels right." Before he started entertaining people at parties, he'd taught foreign languages, been an editor, and tried carpentry. Then one hot summer day, while sweating away as a roofer, he said, "It occurred to me that I was really, really miserable." He started climbing down the ladder, and when he got to the bottom, he said to his boss, "Anita, I'm giving notice. I won't be doing this much longer. I'm going to start my own company. I'm going to do singing telegrams." His boss asked, "Full-time? For a living?" And he said, "Wherever it goes. I know I can do this. I'm going to call it Zip-A-Dee-Doo-Dah Singing Telegram Company because that's my favorite song." Then he signed his boss up as his first client.

Being Open. We've found that people who can keep growing are open in two distinct ways. They are open to new experiences. And they are open to learning more about themselves. It turns out that being open themselves is how they open new doors. Libby Sartain is that kind of open. She's at the helm of human resources for Yahoo!, where she has made an incredible difference, though she may actually be better known for her 13 years at Southwest Airlines. "For me, leaving Southwest was like getting a divorce," she said. "It was horribly wrenching." When she decided to leave, she opened herself up to a whole new world of possibilities. Her openness helped her realize some very important things about herself and her options. Most important, she learned what was important to her.

Creativity. How do you think the world was created? The answer has a lot to do with who you are and what you believe. Creativity has to do with understanding our environment and transcending it. We have believed for a long time that there are two types of people in this world: those who create and those who criticize.

Creative people make things happen. And one of the most creative minds on this planet belongs to Michael Graves, who was hailed by *The New York Times* as "truly the most original voice American architecture has produced in some time." Michael said, "We are continually developing our curious minds, looking, analyzing, reflecting, then coming up with something different, something new. There is always that interest in continuing on to the next thing because there is always something new out there to learn."

Sometimes relationships start with trust. Sometimes it has to be developed. But trust can never be missing from a solid relationship.

Courage. Knowing the right thing to do is one thing; doing the right thing takes courage. Courage, it turns out, invariably involves fear. We often think of courageous people as being totally fearless. But courage really means overcoming fear. And doing what needs to be done. Courage can come through in many ways. It might be the courage to change jobs or get out of a negative relationship or start a business. Then again, there are people on this planet like Congressman John Lewis (D-GA), who take courage to a whole new level.

In the early 1960s, John Lewis was at the forefront of the Civil Rights Movement as a leader of the Student Nonviolent Coordinating Committee. He was beaten countless times and jailed 40 times. He said, "I'd been told over and over by my parents not to get in trouble. And here I was, getting in real trouble. But it was a good trouble. It was necessary trouble."

He was one of the planners and keynote speakers of the March on Washington in August 1963, the occasion of Dr. Martin Luther King, Jr.'s celebrated "I Have a Dream" speech. Then he led one of the most dramatic protests of the era. On March 7, 1965—a day that would become known as "Bloody Sunday"—he led over 600 marchers across the Edmund Pettus Bridge in Selma, Alabama. At the crest of the bridge, they were met by Alabama state troopers who charged the demonstrators, beating them with nightsticks. That evening, ABC news aired footage of people weeping, bleeding, and vomiting from the tear gas. Sheriff Jim Clark's voice could be heard clearly in the background, yelling, "Get those goddamned niggers." Men and horses were running right over fallen people. And viewers saw John, lying on the ground, struggling to get back on his feet. Then they saw him collapse, unconscious, his skull fractured.

A week after Bloody Sunday, President Johnson appeared before a joint session of Congress to insist on the passage of the Voting Rights Act, which enforced the voting rights of all Americans. Two decades later John ran for Congress and won. "You need to have the courage to stand up for issues that you will not compromise on. You need to have the courage to get in the way. To disturb the order of things. You have to say something and do something when you see things are wrong."

We hope this quick overview of 19 defining qualities will inspire you and also help you consider which quality or combination of qualities speaks to you.

Perhaps you are most drawn to courage or having fun or trusting others or knowing yourself. Maybe the quality that resonates with you most is self-discipline, integrity, or passion. Or are you more goal-oriented, persuasive, or competitive? Do you feel more optimistic, empathic, or confident? Are you patient? Or do you have a stronger need to get things done immediately? Is your strength reading others and tuning in to their needs? Are you able to handle rejection and bounce back with a stronger sense of purpose?

There is no right or wrong answer. There is only your answer.

Certainly, as we said before, your strengths could include a combination of these qualities.

In the following chapters, we will discuss these qualities in more depth and share with you some of the incredible stories we've discovered about people who have succeeded on their own terms by playing to their strengths.

Profiles of
Those Who Have
Succeeded on Their
Own Terms

CHAPTER

Perseverance

Samuel Pisar *survived the Holocaust by relying upon his instincts, determination, cunning and perseverance. In his new incarnation, Dr. Pisar went on to become a renowned international lawyer and author, counseling Presidents, Congressional Committees, United Nations Agencies, the International Olympic Committee and many Fortune 100 companies.*

Pushing Off the Bottom to Reach Unimaginable Heights

SAMUEL REMEMBERS HIS mother packing a little suitcase for him, folding his clothes as calmly and methodically as though she were sending him off to summer camp. Then she mused out loud, to him as well as herself, "Should you wear your short pants or your long pants?"

She hesitated, looked at him and at his little sister, and said, "If you wear short pants, they will let you go with Frida and me. If you wear your long pants, we'll probably be separated. You will go with the men, the laborers. You're a big boy now, maybe it would be better if. . . ."

Samuel was 13 years old at the time. His father, a few months before, had been tortured and executed by the Gestapo.

The next morning, the SS storm troopers forced open the door of the Pisar home. With the butts of their rifles and their vicious dogs, they drove Samuel, his sister and his mother, along with other Jewish families, out into the streets of Bialystok—his hometown in German-occupied Poland—to be deported to an unknown destination, and an unknown fate.

"And it *was* the way my mother had predicted," Samuel remembered. "They divided us into two columns. The women, the children,

41

the old and the sick were in one. The able-bodied men were in the other. I, with my long pants, ended up with the men. As we were ordered to march toward the cattle train, its doors gaping open to swallow us, I kept turning around to look at the other column. My little sister held on to my mother with one hand. In the other hand, she clutched her favorite doll. This is how they disappeared from my life forever."

Visibly affected by the memory, he added, "That moment pursues me to this day with its load of agony and guilt and unquenchable anger." He paused, then added, "It made something snap inside me. I think I became someone else."

At times, Samuel refers to himself as a man reincarnated. "Mine has been a twisted destiny," he said, in his polished, elegant voice. "I have known the worst and the best of what this world has to offer."

When we met at his Manhattan apartment overlooking Central Park, Dr. Samuel Pisar was at first reluctant to revisit the horrors of his childhood. "There are enough tragedies in our inflamed world already," he said. "I prefer to concentrate on the present and the future." Then, slowly, carefully, he began to open his memory, sharing with us scenes from a life that embodies hope, courage and triumph in the face of indescribable adversity.

"I survived at an age when—according to the Nazis—I had no right to live, by drawing upon the 'energy of despair,'" he said. Then he stopped to consider that phrase for a moment. "Despair, mixed with rage at the brutality of your enemies and at your own helplessness, can either devastate you immediately or fill you with energy and determination to resist and overcome. When you touch bottom, as I have, and give a hefty kick with everything you've got, you can sometimes return to the surface, and even beyond it. With every blow I received, I understood a little better that pain and suffering do not necessarily degrade or embitter you, that they can also energize, empower and even ennoble. This taught me many lessons that became extremely valuable later in life."

At times, when for him all hope seemed lost, Samuel would hear the voice of his mother, which told him to stop feeling sorry for himself and keep going. "I felt her presence at all times and her message to me was crystal clear. 'Try to survive, my son. Do it for me. Do it for all of us.'"

But how does one survive such a catastrophe, alone, at such a tender age?

"Frankly, even today this remains a mystery to me," he answered. "I guess that I learned, under extreme pressure, to improvise my own survival techniques. No doubt luck and perhaps divine providence also lent a hand."

Samuel paused, as he often did when recounting what happened to him and the insights he has gleaned along the way. Then he continued. "Certainly, before going off to die, my mother gave me a sense of mission and purpose. But soon, my fate was in my own hands. I realized very quickly that I was irrevocably alone and could no longer count on anyone else. I had to motivate myself, do my own thinking and make my own decisions. I could not afford to make any mistake. This compelled me to concentrate my limited mental and physical capacities in abnormal ways. So I gave it all I had—body and soul. In the process, I found within me resources I didn't know I possessed."

As details long forgotten began to flood his memory, Samuel veered between the past and the present, trying to connect the two. "I have come to believe that most people have precious inner resources they are not aware of, because they have had no imperative life-and-death need to use them."

Returning to his teenage memories, he added, "I had to put up with hunger, solitude, cruelty, fear, terror—you name it. Yet somehow I kept on pumping my adrenaline, day after day. This, I think, is how the child instantly became an adult, and how his traumas became a force of life."

> **"When you touch bottom, as I have, and give a hefty kick with everything you've got, you can sometimes return to the surface, and even beyond it."**

Still, it surpasses comprehension. It's too much for most of us to fathom. How did he endure all this for four long years? How did he cope when those around him were dying daily? What kept him from giving in?

"The truth is that we humans are more pliable than we think. Under the impact of dire necessity, we can adapt to almost anything. Maybe the best way to answer your questions is with a concrete example. My first death camp was Majdanek. It was almost as bad as Auschwitz, where I ended up much later," he recalled, shaking his head in disbelief. "The reason you have not heard much about Majdanek is that very few of its inmates survived."

When he arrived after a horrendous 72-hour cattle train journey from home, and the doors were flung open, blinding lights lit up the night. "A long line of SS men, dressed in black uniforms, each holding a restive police dog on a short leash, stood along the ramp," he recalled. "Then came an order, 'Everything out.' Dogs leapt into my car, tearing to pieces several of the half-conscious prisoners, and forcing the others to scramble toward the platform."

Samuel found himself surrounded by exhausted, starving, dehydrated people whose faces were literally blue, licking their own sweat. His first thought was that if he didn't have some water, he would die.

In the chaos, he dragged himself over to a guard who stood on the other side of a line of barbed wire encircling the station. The guard pointed his submachine gun. Samuel looked at him blankly, then pulled out his father's gold watch and chain, which his mother had given him just before their separation. Dangling them in front of the guard, he said, "Sir, could you please bring me a bottle of water?"

"The guard looked at the offering. He could have gunned me down right there and then, but he wouldn't have had the watch and chain because I was on the other side of the fence."

So the guard ordered, "Throw it to me."

"Wasser," Samuel replied. He had to have water.

"Throw it to me!"

"Wasser first," Samuel repeated.

He knew that for him this was a moment of truth. But he took the risk. He was negotiating on his own terms. Not getting the water first was a deal-breaker.

The guard disappeared and returned quickly with a bottle of water, which he pushed under the barbed wire. When Samuel had the bottle firmly in hand, he pushed his father's gold watch and chain under the wire fence.

"I put the bottle to my lips and took a long gulp. Then another. Then a third." Samuel said. "But before my thirst was slaked, there was a clamor and a dozen prisoners leapt at me, with outstretched hands. The bottle fell to the ground and broke. Some of the prisoners fell to their knees to lick up the moisture with their parched tongues, as it slowly seeped into the soil."

"I have always considered that the greatest negotiation of my life," he reflected. These are the words of a renowned international lawyer, who has negotiated on behalf of major chief executives that have put their company's fortunes on the table, relying upon his judgment and skill. "That deal was more important than anything else I have ever negotiated, or ever will."

Later that day, weak and hungry though he was, Samuel could not even look at, let alone eat, the putrid, watered-down soup that was poured into the rusty metal bowl he wore on his belt. "I figured I'd skip the first meal and try to get used to this repulsive diet the next day," he told us. "But an older prisoner, a total stranger, sitting opposite me on the floor tapped my clogs with his and said, 'Son, you listen. Do you want to eat that soup or croak? Your mother isn't here to make you pancakes. Eat or give it to me.' So, I closed my eyes, pinched my nose, and forced the stuff down my throat."

That effort was crucial in helping Samuel get over the first shock of his descent into hell. Only later, when he was crazed by persistent hunger, did he come to understand how a helping of stinking, lukewarm liquid can make one's body tremble in anticipation, and save one's life for yet another day.

The hunger was always there: haunting, relentless, obsessive. "All other sensations, even the feeling of pain or fear of death, became secondary," Samuel explained. "The animal instinct to eat, no matter what, no matter where, became a constant, predominant reality. That and the gas chambers spewing smoke and fire."

Majdenek was a place solely designed for human annihilation. "The only way out was through the chimney," he said, "which became in fact the exit for thousands of my fellow prisoners." It did not take Samuel long to figure out that whatever strength and cunning he possessed had to be devoted to dodging that fate.

How on earth did he manage to get out of Majdanek?

"One evening, after an endless roll call, the camp commander issued a very strange order: 'All who are tailors by trade remain standing; the others fall out.'"

Samuel figured, if they need tailors, they will keep them alive for a while. So he froze at attention. But his mind began to race. He remembered the tailor shop on the street where he grew up. How the huge buttonhole machine fascinated him. How he used to hang around the shop after school, and the tailor would let him push the pedal to punch out a few holes, because he was the landlord's son.

The Nazi officer looked down at Samuel with disdain and asked, "So, you think you are a tailor?"

"No, Sir, I am not," Samuel replied.

"Was your father a tailor, then?"

"'Yes, Sir,' I lied, aware that it was a trade handed down from father to son. 'And my grandfather as well, Sir. I was only the *Knopflochmachinist.*'"

"*Knopflochmachinist*, eh? What's that?"

"A buttonhole maker, Sir. To sew buttonholes on military uniforms by hand takes forever. But on a *Knopflochmachine* it takes only a few seconds."

His heart pounded before the verdict fell.

"The logic of my explanation—that wherever tailors are needed, buttonhole makers are needed, too—must have impressed the Kraut, because he waved me to the side of life. That's how I got out of Majdanek and landed in a hard labor camp."

Half a year later, Samuel found himself on another long cattle train. This time the destination was Auschwitz. "Once there, we were marched to a clearing and ordered to undress for a shower. I found myself in a long line approaching the infamous Dr. Joseph Mengele— the angel of death. Will he send me to the right or to the left? You watch the monster's eyes, his gestures, anything that might give you a clue as to whether you are about to die or live a little longer. A random puff on his cigarette might break the rhythm and send you one way instead of the other."

That time Samuel was waved to join those who would survive. But after a similar selection a few months later, he ended up among the condemned. For hours he stood with the other selected victims, huddled in dead silence. "I knew it was all over. Except for a slight sensation of nausea in the pit of my stomach, I felt almost reconciled to my fate," he said.

Then, as they were led through a long corridor toward the gas chamber, Samuel glimpsed a bucket of water and alongside it, a brush and a rag. Slowly, he bent down and crept sideways. The men whose legs he touched were too numb to notice him. Reaching the bucket, he wet the brush and the rag and began cleaning the floor.

On his knees, he scrubbed as hard as he could, then dried vigorously, going over one section thoroughly, then sliding down to the next, as if he had been assigned to perform that task. As he inched his way backward in the direction of the door through which his group had come in, one of the guards shouted, "Over here, you pig! This part is still dirty."

His pulse racing, he moved over and cleaned that area again. Then he continued slowly to work his way back, ever closer to the door. It seemed to take forever. At last, when he reached the exit and could see outside, he scrubbed the doorstep with all his might and dried it as though he wanted it to glow.

"Then and only then, did I allow myself to stand up and turn around. Carrying the pail, with the brush and rag inside, I walked through the door and out into the open. I fully expected to be stopped—to hear the bark of an order or receive a blow on the head. But there was nothing. With slow, measured steps, I made for the other barracks and lost myself in the anonymity of the camp."

Before sinking into sleep that night, Samuel summoned his mother's face and told her how he had defied death one more time.

"What I did on that occasion was not such a great feat of human intelligence," he said. "It was more like a nervous animal reflex in the face of imminent death."

He paused, reflected, then added, "In all honesty, I am not quite sure what others can learn from my experiences in that brutal world, where people much stronger and smarter than I were crushed every day. My experiences were too extreme, almost extra-terrestrial."

> **"I found myself in a long line approaching the infamous Dr. Joseph Mengele—the angel of death. Will he send me to the right or to the left? You watch the monster's eyes, his gestures, anything that might give you a clue as to whether you are about to die or live a little longer. A random puff on his cigarette might break the rhythm and send you one way instead of the other."**

Samuel was trapped in a savage wasteland, where predators preyed on him day and night. "Living between fear and hope, my constant preoccupation was how not to panic, how to identify the ever-present dangers around me and how to twist out of their clutches. While my life expectancy was close to zero, I made every possible effort to extend it, sometimes from minute to minute.

"This focused, all-consuming mindset gradually became second nature for me. I still rely on it at times, and find that it can be helpful in all kinds of difficult situations, even today when the stakes are not as great as they were then."

Returning to his nightmarish recollections, he said, "There were times when you felt you couldn't make it one step further. You thought 'To hell with it. Let them do with me what they will. What's the use of struggling on to get through yet another day when your days are numbered anyway?' It was so tempting, and would have been so easy, to put my hand on the electrified barbed wire and bring my misery to an end. Yet somehow, I forced myself up, stuck out my chin and vowed not to give in to the bastards—nor to myself."

As one day led to the next, he would sometimes think that there were no limits to what one can endure, or invent to save one's skin. The ability of a human being to withstand intolerable pain and suffering was to him mind-boggling.

Today, on the rare occasions when Samuel's mind becomes boggled, there is one other voice that helps to clear things up for him. It is the voice of that emaciated young boy with a shaved head, sunken eyes, and a number tattooed on his arm. Whenever he has to make a crucial choice in his life or his career, that young boy asks, "Are you sure it is for this that you were spared?"

"Yes, two different human beings cohabit within me," he said, smiling at the thought. "That little sub-human slave, gray like the color of the earth, and the modern, sophisticated man of affairs who lives and works in the glittering capitals of the world. Even today, the little one's instincts and intuitions remain pretty infallible. Better than mine," he says. "Much better than mine."

These instincts and intuitions, driven by rage and by hope, when everything around him seemed hopeless, helped Samuel overcome insurmountable odds, and in the end, to escape from his tormentors.

When the opportunity presented itself, he was able to reach deep inside himself and find the last reserves of strength and determination to make a break for freedom.

This came to pass in the Spring of 1945, as the Allied armies were closing in on the Third Reich from the East and the West. Samuel was almost 16 then, and in yet another hard labor camp, near Munich. One day, as the distant sound of Allied artillery became more and more audible, the Nazi guards started to panic. They ordered the prisoners to form two columns for immediate evacuation—Jews in one, non-Jews in the other.

Since he had picked up several languages by then, including fluent German, he decided to get into the safer non-Jewish line, and went undetected. But something began to gnaw at him. Overcome by an irresistible impulse, he darted back into the Jewish line to join his two inseparable friends—Niko and Ben—with whom he had struggled to survive throughout their interminable captivity.

"When I reached them, Niko knocked me to the ground with a powerful punch and called me an idiot. 'You could have lived, but now you're going to die with the rest of us,' he yelled. What I did was irrational, for sure. But a deep emotion had commanded me to stay with my friends. After everything we had been through together, I wasn't going to let them die alone. Nor was I going to deny my heritage," he said.

For three days and two nights they were marched towards Dachau, stopping only for meager rations of bread and water. In the late afternoon of the third day, several American fighter planes, mistaking them for a Wehrmacht column, swooped down to strafe them.

"Those bullets were God-sent. It was hope itself falling from the sky," said Samuel. "The SS guards flung themselves to the ground, their machine guns blazing wildly in all directions. Then, Niko shouted, 'Run for it!'"

Samuel, Niko, Ben and a few others made a dash for the forest. The guards couldn't pursue them because they were under attack themselves. "We ran and ran and ran, gasping for breath, until we could run no longer. But there was no sound of pursuit, only the thunder of our beating hearts," Samuel recalled.

"Did we plan the escape? No," he responded incredulously to his own question. "It was impossible. But, we were always obsessively scanning for a life-saving opportunity. When the planes swooped down, we saw our opening and went for it like a flash."

Figuring out the direction by the North Star, they made their way toward the Western front, moving by night, hiding by day. Once they almost blundered into an airstrip swarming with German troops. So they decided to look for a hiding place and wait until the Nazi's retreat had passed them by.

A few days later, Samuel heard a strange, humming, metallic sound. He peeked through a crack in the wooden slats of the barn where they were hiding and saw a huge tank lumbering across a field.

"I looked for the hateful swastika, but there wasn't one. Instead, I made out an unfamiliar emblem on its side. It was a five-pointed, white star. In an instant, I realized that I was actually beholding the insignia of the United States Army." His skull seemed to burst. With a wild roar, he broke through the thatched roof, leapt to the ground and ran toward the tank. A German machine gun opened fire. The tank stopped, its turret turned and the cannon fired back twice. Then all was quiet.

Samuel continued to run through the battlefield, waving his arms, oblivious to all danger. "At that moment, I felt immortal," he said, "and blissfully aware that the coveted, decisive miracle I had been waiting for was about to happen."

Suddenly, a tall GI climbed out from the hatch of an armored vehicle with pistol in hand, and motioned for Samuel to approach. As he moved closer, the GI carefully looked him over, as if to make sure he wasn't booby-trapped. To signal that he was harmless and in desperate need of help, Samuel dropped to his knees and wrapped his arms around the soldier's legs, repeating the few words of English he'd heard his mother whisper while she was praying for their deliverance: "God Bless America." The next thing Samuel remembers is being lifted up and eased through the vehicle's hatch—into what he called "the warm womb of life and freedom." Within minutes, Niko and Ben were also free.

After the Nazi surrender, the three of them—without a home or a family to return to—decided to stay in the area where they were liberated, roaming the Bavarian countryside on powerful motorcycles stolen from a German army depot. "The postwar scene was a lawless jungle, and our sense of right and wrong had also become somewhat impaired," Samuel reflected.

They had to let off their pent-up steam and breathe to the fullest their hard-won liberty.

"As for myself, in many ways I was a human wreck," Samuel said. "The wounds of my flesh healed quickly enough, but the wounds of my mind and my soul also needed healing before I could return to civilized society. That healing took much longer, until I started to ask myself, 'What will become of you? You know nothing. You have nothing. You are nothing. Wake up!'"

It was then that a Parisian aunt, his mother's sister, searching for family survivors, found him miraculously in the ruins of the American occupation zone of Germany. Shocked by the dangerous life he was leading, she talked him into coming with her to France. From there, she shipped him off to live with relatives in Australia, as far away as possible from war-torn Europe, with its constant reminders of what he had been through.

That was more than a turning point. Samuel called it a metamorphosis. In Australia, he understood that physical survival was not enough, that he needed to survive morally and intellectually as well. So, he set out to reconstruct himself from the ground up and began pumping his adrenaline once more, as if his life again depended on it. After six years of absence from a classroom, he quickly earned a high school diploma and enrolled at Melbourne University, from which he ultimately graduated with high honors.

In 1953, his teacher and mentor at the university, Sir Zelman Cowen, an eminent jurist and Oxford Don, who later became the Governor General of Australia, was appointed visiting Professor at Harvard. When Samuel heard the news, he had the "chutzpah," as he put it, to wonder if attending Harvard might not be a possibility for him as well. He immediately activated the professor to plead his cause there and threw himself into the application process. To his astonishment, he was not only accepted, but also given a full scholarship.

"When I arrived in Cambridge, Massachusetts, I got scared. There I was, among the best and brightest scholars in the world, cursing myself. 'You fool, now you have gone too far. You are completely out of your league in this place. The instincts and smarts you had developed to survive in the infernos of Europe are of no use to you here, where everything is of a higher order, where human combat is peaceful—mind against mind, idea against idea, talent against talent. It is ridiculous for you to try to compete here. You are playing to your weaknesses, not to your strengths.'"

But, of course, he wasn't out of his league, no matter how difficult the challenge or how disorienting the environment he was facing. "Mostly it was the distance," he reflected, "not geographically, but philosophically. Auschwitz and Harvard were light years away from one another. I cannot imagine two greater extremes. One, the ugliest symbol of human madness and evil; the other, the finest emblem of human enlightenment and culture. It was an enormous distance for me to cross. Fate had forged me for times and places of violence and mayhem, not for scholarly meditation in the world's most famous ivory tower. In short, I had to recycle myself once more."

After shaking off his doubts, Samuel poured himself into advanced study and research, first earning the senior degree of Master of Laws, then the Doctorate of Juridical Science—a kind of super Ph.D.—before earning another Doctorate from the Sorbonne in Paris. Now he was equipped with knowledge that was not only crudely intuitive, but also powerfully rational.

His prize-winning Harvard thesis, rooted in academic scholarship and convictions derived from war, genocide and terror, explored the prospects and processes of commerce between the communist East and the democratic West, whose growing animosity threatened thermonuclear doomsday.

At his graduation ceremony, Senator John F. Kennedy, who was present as a member of Harvard's Board of Overseers, told Samuel that one day he would welcome an opportunity to learn more about his ideas on these fundamental, existential issues.

In short order, Samuel was offered positions at major universities and top law firms. He was on the verge of accepting one of them when that inner voice tugged at him and asked, "Is this what you were spared for?"

So, he yielded to the little one, who wanted him to give something back to society, to think of public service, human rights, making a difference in the world. "Your mother would have liked that," murmured his inner voice, his conscience. Thus, at age 25, instead of accepting a lucrative job on Wall Street, he joined the United Nations in New York, then went on to UNESCO in Paris.

From horrors that no child should ever have to endure, to honors that most of us could never even dream of, he has come through with courage, perseverance and optimism.

But the brief encounter with the Junior Senator from Massachusetts never left his mind. A few years later, that encounter opened new doors to his future. He was invited to Washington to become a consultant to several Congressional Committees, an advisor to the State Department and, finally, a member of John F. Kennedy's Task Force on Foreign Economic Policy. Who would have believed? The child of war was becoming an architect of peace.

Then, in 1961, Samuel Pisar became a citizen of the United States in a most extraordinary way—by a special Act of Congress, unanimously voted by the Senate and the House of Representatives and promulgated by President Kennedy.

After his stint in the nation's capital, Samuel's career as a lawyer took off with such incredible force that even just mentioning its highlights sounds like a résumé of several phenomenally accomplished individuals.

From offices on both sides of the Atlantic, he would wind up as counsel to clients ranging from General Electric to Coca Cola, Henry Ford II to Steve Jobs, Elizabeth Taylor to Marlon Brando.

Beyond professional success, he found the time and energy to publish a number of influential books, including *Of Blood and Hope*, an autobiographical memoir written at mid-life, under the shock of Ben and Niko's untimely deaths. Translated into twenty languages, the book won worldwide acclaim. *Business Week* called it "a soaring triumph of the human spirit."

His seminal work, *Coexistence and Commerce*, was built on the premise that expanding economic and human contacts—country to country, company to company, individual to individual—can drain the venom from ideological, ethnic and religious conflicts, and channel their destructive fury into mutually advantageous peaceful relationships.

Written at the height of the Cold War, the book was informed by high-level scholarship, government service, and professional experience, as well as by wartime memories of a waif who had come back from the dead. "In our historic confrontation with Communism, the most powerful weapons we have are not only our military arsenals, but our superior capacity for economic progress, with the human freedoms and human rights that follow in its wake," he wrote two decades before the collapse of the Soviet Union. "It is with these 'weapons of peace' that we must engage our enemies. Our victory promises to be all the more peaceful, because deeply within them they wish it devoutly."

That weighty tome, which included an elaborate code of guidelines for expanded trade between the East and the West, sparked a vast international debate and became a centerpiece of Nixon-Kissinger diplomacy toward eastern Europe, Russia and China. Senator Edward Kennedy endorsed Samuel's policy proposals as "an enlightened course for the future of American and Western policy."

In the early seventies, Samuel was nominated and short-listed for the Nobel Peace Prize.

This extraordinary odyssey speaks to us of struggle, survival and redemption. At every stage of Samuel's young life, he was reborn from the ashes like a phoenix, with his faith in humanity intact. From horrors that no child should ever have to endure, to honors that most of us could never even dream of, he has come through with courage, perseverance and optimism.

"In the lowest valleys of human experience, and on a few of its summits, I seem to have forged a fairly serene and realistic perspective from which to respond to all strokes of bad and good fortune that came my way in buckets. But my most important achievement is not among the ones we discussed," he insisted. "It was bringing up, with Judith Pisar— my exquisite, sensitive and understanding partner—a brood of bright, educated and active children. This resurrection of a new family is the only, the sweetest vengeance over the past that I could ever imagine."

With an unerring sense of finality, he concluded, "To tell you the truth, I still don't know why, or for what purpose I was spared. All I can say is that something very powerful has pushed me to try to survive and then to give my survival some meaning, not only for my own sake, but for the sake of those I had lost. I have never forgotten that of my previous family and of the 500 children in my school, I was the only one to come out alive."

Samuel's intensely personal reflections on his loss were poured into "a dialogue with God," which he wrote at the request of his friend Maestro Leonard Bernstein for his famous symphony "Kaddish." Samuel performed this dramatic text with the Chicago Symphony Orchestra in 2003. In the coming years, he is scheduled to narrate it with the symphony orchestras of Philadelphia, Lucerne and Paris. Here is a short excerpt:

"To this day, I am haunted by guilt
for having survived,
when so many of mine were murdered . . .
As a living witness
to the greatest man-made catastrophe
that ever befell human civilization,
I feel that my life is no longer entirely my own.
Those who perished also live within me . . .
My duty today is not only to remember them,
but also to warn the living
against the risk
of similar catastrophes
that may yet lie ahead."

5

Goal-Oriented

Rebecca Stephens *on how climbing Mount Everest became her all-consuming purpose.*

Climbing Your Mountain

I-F TWO PEOPLE ARE CLIMBING a mountain together, what is the most important thing they need to get to the summit? Teamwork? Cooperation? The right equipment? Training? All those things are required. But what's most important is the mountain itself. You must have a goal.

Rebecca Stephens, the first British woman to climb Mount Everest, can tell you all about how a goal can become your main focus. And how it can change every aspect of your life.

How did her goal become to stand on the highest point in the world?

It started when she was sent to Tibet by the *Financial Times* to write an article about a group of climbers who were attempting to scale the northeast ridge of Mount Everest. At that time, she didn't know the first thing about mountain climbing, but the assignment captured her attention and fueled her imagination. As she explained, "What struck me most was that all the climbers had this passion to climb Everest. In every movement of their bodies, you could see how badly they wanted to conquer this mountain. I was intrigued by whatever was driving them to take such a risk."

The more she got into the story, the more important that question became.

She wired back to her editors that she thought there was a bigger story here. "I'd like to try to answer the question: 'Why do climbers

climb?'" Something inside Rebecca was taking her beyond her assignment and asking questions that would get to the heart of who she
really was.

At first she felt the climbers were "just the most singular individuals,
driven by something beyond understanding." Then she started to identify with them. Figuring out why climbers climb became more than just
an intriguing question—it became personal.

And her life changed.

She proposed to her editors that she climb to the first camp on the
northeast ridge and describe the effects of reaching that altitude. They
thought there was something intriguing about how she wanted to per-
sonalize the experience and take the story further.

But she was beyond just turning in an interesting story.

When she got to the first camp, she recalled, the sun was shining, the
sky was crystal, and it was beautiful. "I felt quite exhilarated," she told
us, "and I thought, what are they making such a fuss about? This is well
within my capabilities." Then the force of gravity, changes in barometric pressure, and the thin air started to take their tolls. The climbing got
harder and harder. As she climbed higher, the weather closed in so she
couldn't see more than 10 yards in front of her. In the background, she
could hear avalanches rumbling down the side of a mountain. "The
crescendo of thundering sounds just freezes you in your tracks," she
said. "It was a real awakening to the reality of that environment."

Finally she saw the little tent ahead at Camp One, and she managed
to reach it and collapse. She was exhausted and exhilarated at the same
time. She said, "I had to collect myself and look at where I was. The
view wasn't very clear, but I knew I had climbed a couple of thousand
feet. It was one of those moments when a combination of factors all
came into play. Physically, I had worked harder than ever before in my
life. I was very pleased with myself for having reached this point. I was
on a high ridge on the highest mountain in the world. And I was full of
awe. I went, 'Wow. What am I doing here?' It was just beautiful.
Exquisitely beautiful. All those little things together created an overwhelming emotion in me. It was so exciting that I couldn't contain
myself. I bubbled over with laughter. Then I understood: it's the intensity, the ultimate experience. That's why climbers climb."

She came back down the same day and filed her story, describing
how exhilarating the experience had been. Now, when she reflects back

on that moment on the ridge, she realizes that it was then that the germ of an idea started stirring in her head. "That was definitely the day," she said. "Not the day I really decided to do it. That took weeks. And months passed before I said it out loud. But that day there on the ridge, it came into my mind that climbing Mount Everest was something I wanted to do."

That was a turning point for Rebecca because, as she explained, "It was the first time in my life that I actually knew what I wanted to do. Before that I was drifting somewhat aimlessly. Not unhappily, mind you, but I was sort of a jack-of-all-trades and master of none because I hadn't really found my direction in life."

With climbing to the summit of Mount Everest as her goal, her life came into focus. "I had never sought out anything with such conviction as I did to climb Everest," she said. "For me the battle was already half won, if not more. Because once you have a clearly defined objective, everything else becomes a lot easier. You know where to channel your energy, and everything can go in that direction. You can see exactly where you need to go. Of course, there are going to be obstacles to your progress, but you will find a way around them or over them because you are so focused on where you want to be. I feel very strongly about that. While, in hindsight, climbing Everest might seem an unusual goal, it was the path that I had to follow. Sure, there were times when I could have gone many different ways, and I could have turned back any number of times. But it was possible for me to keep moving forward because I was so passionate about what I wanted to accomplish."

So she started training.

For the next four years.

Every weekend she caught a train to North Wales, one of the few mountainous areas in the British Isles, and she'd climb all weekend, then go back to her day job on Monday morning.

In the beginning, she was quite shy about voicing her ambition to climb Everest because she knew there was a traditional belief that you must have a lot of experience, live in an area with many opportunities for climbing, and should have been doing it from a very early age. For Brits, you needed to respect that tradition and build up slowly over an apprenticeship which involved up to two decades of training. But Rebecca was on another path. She wanted to climb as soon and as much as she could. And in doing that, she met like-minded people.

She learned that climbing has as much to do with your climbing skills and attitude as it does with your muscular fitness, lung capacity, red corpuscles, ability to stay nourished and protect yourself from the elements, your teammates, your respect for the mountain, fate, luck, and other such variables.

Does she remember when she first said out loud that she wanted to reach the summit of Everest?

> **"I had never sought out anything with such conviction as I did to climb Everest. For me the battle was already half won, if not more. Because once you have a clearly defined objective, everything else becomes a lot easier."**

A friend remembers her saying it as soon as she got back from writing the article. "It must be true," she said, though she thought it was much later. "By declaring your goal, you are telling other people that you are open to all the fears and, even more important, that you have made a commitment."

With four years of training under her belt, and after she and her team had scaled Mount McKinley, she knew she was ready to climb Mount Everest. For openers, the worst weather in 30 years forced Rebecca and her team to sit out a violent storm that lasted eight days. "Not to get dramatic about it," she said, "but a lot of people died while we were on McKinley."

There was no way to deny what she was facing. Still, she couldn't turn back.

In May of 1993, just before the monsoon season, Rebecca and her team set off to conquer the mountain. She was immediately faced with one of life's tests, which she passed with flying colors.

"My intention," she explained, "was to continue working for the magazine after I climbed Everest. It was like Everest was a hobby and I wanted to take a long holiday so I would have the time I needed to make the climb. But my superiors didn't see it that way. Because the state of the economy wasn't the healthiest at that time, they weren't in a position to give me the three-month extended leave I needed. Instead, they gave me a choice between keeping my job and climbing Mount Everest. At the time it was frightening because I wanted to just take a holiday, fulfill my dream, and then carry on working. So I gulped, accepted the situation, and submitted my letter of resignation. Since then, I've been freelancing. I haven't worked in the formal sense for a company for over a decade. At the time I had to make my decision, that mountain and the clarity of my goal helped make it easy for me."

It took seven weeks for Rebecca to get to the summit of Mount Everest.

During the ascent, one member of her team, a strong solo climber, went on ahead and made it to the top alone. Then he nearly died on his way down as he became snow-blinded, lost his way, and had to be rescued by two climbers from another group.

At that point, the rest of Rebecca's group realized that this was not their time.

The weather had made their decision. "It was atrocious," she said, succinctly.

So they started climbing back down. All but Rebecca. She waited overnight.

She was joined by two Sherpas, Ang Passang and Kami Tchering, who said they wanted to take a chance with her.

She called the leader of the expedition and reviewed the situation. If the weather forecast was accurate, there was no way they could get any higher. But there was a slim chance that the forecast could be wrong. It was a coin toss. They could be climbing into failure, or worse. Or they might, just might, make it.

The agony was in making that decision.

After a lengthy discussion and a long pause, her leader gave a hesitant nod. He said, "Go. But use your judgment and turn around if it gets any worse."

Rebecca remembered smiling as she heard his words. "That was liberating," she said. "While I was quite sure that we would need to turn back, I felt that if the weather stopped us, there was nothing we could do about that, and I would accept it. As long as I had done everything in my power, then whatever the outcome was, I could deal with that eventuality."

"At that time," she said, "there was a battle raging between my heart and my head. I felt an emotional drive to succeed, while my rational side was saying, 'This isn't really going to happen.' Which voice do you listen to?" Then she knew.

Rebecca and Ang and Kami napped for a few hours to restore their strength. When they woke up, there was no wind, which was entirely unexpected. Their tent stood absolutely motionless. They looked at each other, smiled, and then were off.

As they continued upward, Rebecca knew she was taking an enormous risk, but she felt prepared. And excited beyond all belief. As they trudged farther up the mountain, she recalled, "there was a sense of complete certainty that each one of us wanted to climb to the summit just as much as the other two. It meant the world to all of us. And we were in it together. Risks were all around us. But there was no way, and this was implicitly understood, that we could leave one person if he or she fell behind, because we were too high up and it was too dangerous."

They trudged on.

And the next day they reached the summit.

Rebecca said, "Now, I know lots of people had been there before me, but the illusion was that this mountain was completely ours. And on that day, it was. It was amazing. It was just a very magical feeling of solitude up there where everywhere you looked was this wilderness."

The summit itself is tiny. It's a point at which three ridges join. It's the size of a small room, 10 by 15 feet. That's all.

Rebecca said, "Yeah, it's very small. So you don't step back if you're taking a picture. And you're very aware it is the summit. There is no question you're there. On top of the world. On Everest, there's no confusion over that. And what was remarkable about being there, from my point of view, was that only at that point could I look down all the sides of the mountain, including the north side where my story had begun. It was exquisitely beautiful.

"And there we were. Neither Ang nor Kami had ever been there before either, so they were jumping up and down with excitement. They're very demonstrative, the Sherpa people. It was a magical time. But so short-lived."

How long did they stay?

"I don't think we were there more than 10 minutes," she said. "You're totally there, but you're also keenly aware that there is absolutely no time to waste. It was about half past twelve, so we had about six hours of daylight in which to make our descent back down the mountain. Also, when you're no longer actively climbing and just hanging around, the cold jolts you into taking action. We were getting very cold very quickly."

They made tracks back down the mountain after taking a couple of quick photographs.

Their focus was now on getting back down with maximum efficiency. Rebecca said, "I know this makes the whole thing sound a bit futile in a way. But you can only do it if you enjoy the journey. It sounds so clichéd, but it's also true. What is the point of being up there for 10 minutes if you don't enjoy the journey? It's like so many things in life. If you don't enjoy what you're doing, quite often you can find a better alternative. And yet I didn't feel the full exhilaration of having climbed that mountain until I got safely back down. Then I could relax and really know that we made it."

She said, at that point, her feelings were somewhat in conflict. "I felt this deep sense of satisfaction that we'd done it, along with an enormous sense of relief."

Relief that she'd achieved her goal?

"In all honesty, at first just relief that we were all safe. Then the whole concept of achieving my goal took over." She explained, "It doesn't hit you all at once. You get little dribbles of it as you come back down the mountain, and then have to get on with your life."

It all goes back to the beginning.

In Rebecca's decision to make the climb, she realized something about herself that she had never known before.

And it led her to standing on top of the world. For 10 minutes.

Along the way, it was invigorating—and clarifying.

Part of that realization had to do with her new definition of success.

For Rebecca, "Success is the achievement of whatever it is you set out to do. And no one else can make that decision for you. It's up to you to decide what your goal is. And once you've set your goal, the path also becomes yours. If you make it and learn a thing or two along the way, well, that's worth everything. It's not an easy definition, but success begins with knowing your goal and committing yourself to achieving it."

6

Self-Awareness

Ben Vereen *on how he continues to redefine himself and redis-cover what success means to him.*

Knowing What Drives You

SOME OF US ARE JUST NATURALLY introspective. We want to understand what drives us and how we affect others. And our reflections deepen our understanding of who we are. Then there are those of us who just race from point A to point B, always moving forward. Sometimes we glance around us, but we rarely look back unless we've just knocked something over.

Knowing yourself means taking the time to check your temperature and be aware of your internal barometric pressure. It allows you to travel at your own pace, charting your own course and determining your own direction—not just reacting to what is happening around you.

Ben Vereen, who has received the highest recognition for the parts he's played on Broadway, on television, and in the movies, is deeply reflective. This talented actor, singer, and dancer understands who he is and where he comes from. And he has an equally clear sense of where he is now and where he still hopes to go. With striking candor he shared insights about his mentors, his successes, his aspirations, his accident, and how, after his daughter died, he slowly, painfully picked up the pieces of his life and figured out how to carry on.

While growing up in Brooklyn, his dancing ability was recognized by the principal of his grammar school, who recommended he attend the High School of Performing Arts. That was when he started living in two worlds. There was his neighborhood, where church was the center, and his school, where Broadway was the aspiration.

"So the whole genre of arts was introduced to a child from what society calls *the ghetto*," Ben said, with a certain majestic flair. "I was plucked out of my regular world and plunked down in an alien world. Very alien. It seemed like these people were from another planet. They walked different. They talked different. You know, in my neighborhood we were *talkin' like this, you know what I'm sayin'? Yo, what's happenin'?*" he said, having fun with his deep, jive voice. "Then, all of a sudden, *I'm supposed to talk like this,*" he said, laughing at his impersonation of a highbrow British accent.

"So I was in this completely new world. You understand, when you were in the neighborhood, you talked about the events of the day. It wasn't about, 'Oh, we're going to strive to do this.' No, it was about just getting by, day by day. In the neighborhood we were in the *now*. This new place was talking about *the future.*"

The discrepancies surrounded him. It wasn't just the attitude. He also looked different. "I didn't have a dancer's body," he said.

What did he mean by that?

"A dancer's body. You know? They stand up straight. They walk with their feet out. Their butts in. They had no butts at all. And I had an Afro butt. And in those days there were no African-American dancers to emulate except Alvin Ailey, who was still trying to come up."

In some ways it felt like he needed a passport to get from where he lived to where he was going to school.

That got him thinking about aliens. "You know how in the movies the aliens always come to destroy the earth? Well, they don't always have to be the enemy. In my case, the aliens came to enhance and to bridge the communication between the world that I was living in and the world of opportunity."

When you're an artist, you have to express the spirit that comes from inside you as you try to interpret the world around you.

When did it occur to him that he was an artist?

"When you love what you're doing, you don't ask yourself, 'When did that moment happen?' It's an evolution. And along the way you develop the attributes and the tools you need to express yourself. In the meantime you are taken on this journey through all the ups and the downs, through all the pitfalls and the adversities in your life, but there is one constant, and that is the spirit that you bring and express."

"Because beyond the fear is your blessing. Beyond the fear is your flight."

After he graduated from high school, he worked in the mail room at United Artists, worked in a textile factory, and ran papers up and down Wall Street, all the time reading the trade publications and auditioning for parts.

"I couldn't audition to save my soul. I was nervous. I'd clam up. I couldn't remember anything I'd memorized. I was terrible," he confessed.

Ben Vereen lacked confidence?

It seems hard to believe.

He now teaches a course in auditioning in which he shows young aspiring actors how to prepare then forget it and just go out and do it.

What's his advice for dealing with nervousness?

"I still get nervous every time I go out on stage. If I didn't get nervous, I'd be concerned that I didn't really care. You have to learn to use that nervousness. You have to feel the fear and do it anyway. You learn to embrace it. Tackle it and let it tackle you. Because the nervousness can compel you to greater heights. It is there to speak through you. But we try to cancel it out. And when we worry about it and get uptight about it, it defeats us. Then we say, 'I'm too nervous, I can't do it,' instead of letting the nervousness come through for us. Most of us get stuck there. The important lesson is to move through it to get at who we really are. Because beyond the fear is your blessing. Beyond the fear is your flight," he said, sharing what he's learned along the way.

His first part after high school was in a theater in the basement of a church on 13th Street and Seventh Avenue. It was a part in a play called *The Prodigal Son* by Langston Hughes.

How many aspiring young artists were fortunate enough to have Langston Hughes as a mentor?

"He would take me to Harlem and talk to me about his journey, about his life, about the Harlem Renaissance, about his travels, and he opened my eyes to all kinds of possibilities. He talked to me about a world that I had no idea of. He talked about London and Paris, and he tantalized the taste in my mouth for Africa."

Then Ben and Bob Fosse met and formed their connection.

Can he explain how his personal style emerged from Fosse?

"Fosse was a style unto himself," he said. "Fosse and I merged styles. He saw me in *Jesus Christ Superstar*, where I played Judas and *The New York Times* reviewer said that I just tore up the scenery looking for Jesus. My energy was all over the place. And Fosse said, 'Now that you can let it all go, let me show you how to move within yourself. How to glide.' He gave me focus. He showed me less is more. He'd say to me, 'When the audience isn't there, don't go after them. Give less. If you're quiet for a moment, they will come to you.'"

Stand in the quiet. He added, "Now, when I do lectures, I will walk out and I'm quiet for a moment. And people will wonder what I'm going to do or say. Then I have them slightly off guard. And then, when I say something, they are ready to listen. That's why the opening of *Pippin* was so wonderful. The curtain went up, and you saw nothing but black. And then you saw these white hands. And you heard the voice. And everybody is going, 'What's happening?' Then all of a sudden a head pokes through the darkness. Whew! That grabs you. And we're ready to go. That was genius."

What does he think audiences want?

"They want to be fed. Audiences come to get away from their world, and they want to be fed something: information, entertainment, joy, life. And our job is to give them what they need," he said.

His first appearance in a big musical was on tour with the national company of *Sweet Charity*, which happened to be the first Broadway show he had ever seen. He said, "Fosse was the ultimate taskmaster. He'd work you incredibly hard to get the perfection of his work. He would drill us on one step all day; then we would go home and practice it and practice it and practice it. Because we all wanted to get it perfect for him. Perfection was the key for him. And I said to myself, 'I must work with a purpose that reaches that height.'"

In Bob Fosse's semiautobiographical movie *All That Jazz*, Ben plays a character standing between the door of life and death. He is a TV host moderator who could be the Devil, might be a saint, is clearly from another world, and leads Fosse through his journey. "Bob called me and said, 'I want you to do a little bit in this movie I've written about myself.' I said, 'Bob, I'll do anything you want.' Because he was my heart. And he said, 'I just need you for a day.' I came in, and we shot the first scene. Then he called me and said, 'I need you to come back.' And we came back, and I did the ending. He said, 'The important thing here is not to make yourself a hero.' He was telling the world, 'This part of my life is dead.' Incredible. How many of us could do that?"

How did Ben Vereen get to play the part of Chicken George in Alex Haley's *Roots*?

Back in 1972, he heard through the grapevine that ABC was considering a miniseries on Haley's search for his ancestors, which started with him returning to Africa, literally in the hull of a slave ship, so that he could get closer to their experience.

Ben said he wanted to be connected to the project in some way. But he was told he wasn't what they were looking for.

So he continued doing a one-man show based on a true story about a man of color who had to wear blackface in order to perform on an American stage. The role showed his pain and embarrassment at having to pretend to be someone other than who he was.

Then one night, one of the producers of *Roots*, showed up in Ben's dressing room and said, "I want you to be Chicken George." Ben was ecstatic. He said, "I told him, 'I want to be part of this. This is about the black experience. Sign me up.'" Two weeks later he got the script and discovered that Chicken George aged from 17 to 64 in the course of the series. "And I started thinking about my people coming to this country. In chains. Stuffed in ships like animals. Then our families were torn apart. And we were put on a block. Auctioned off as cargo. We came from royalty. And we were sold as slaves. That's our legacy. And I wanted to be part of the telling of it."

He became embedded in America's conscience.

Despite all of his incredible accomplishments, Ben Vereen's defining moment came out of the blue, turning his world upside down, shattering everything.

"Parents should never outlive their children," he said. "That's the law. And when a universal law is altered, and all control is lost, the lessons are hard and painful, and our world is torn asunder."

His life was shattered and put in a tailspin when his daughter died in a freak car accident because a truck driver made a stupid turn. The truck landed on top of the car his wife was driving. She was thrown free of the wreck, but their daughter was killed in the crash. "When I got the call, I just kept saying no, no, no. This isn't real. This is not happening. I'm going to wake up and she's going to come walking through the door. I can feel her. I know I'm going to go home and she is going to be there and when I go into her room she's going to be in her bed and she's going to look up at me and say, 'Hi, Daddy. How are you?' You keep going through this in your mind. You keep wanting her to be there. And she's not. I was filled with anger. I was angry at God for a long time. How dare He or She? To defy me? To do that? To take my child? I was so angry, I wanted to stand on a bridge and shoot every truck driver who came down the road.

"I was lost between anger, grief, and pain. Somehow I blocked it all out and gave my daughter's eulogy. Her friends at school planted a tree in her memory. The love that poured out was amazing. But the suffering was greater."

To make matters worse, Ben's marriage became so strained that he and his wife separated. She was feeling angry and guilty. He was full of anger and sorrow. Both were in great grief and couldn't connect with each other. "We never talked about it until about two years ago. It was the first time we sat and shared it. That's how long it took. The pain never goes away. You learn to live inside it and know that she is gone. Always. You come to the conclusion that the very breath I breathe is her. Whenever I take a step, she's with me. Everywhere I go she's with me," he said, then added, "People ask me how I recovered a few years later from being in an automobile accident where I broke my leg, had a tracheotomy, lost my spleen. And it was nothing. It doesn't compare to the pain of losing a child. People look at me and say, 'Oh, what a miracle. You're back on stage.' It's a miracle that I'm surviving the loss of my child. The only reason I'm on this planet is because I believe she would want me to be here. Through all my suffering and the dark shadows, she's always been there."

How do you get through losing a child?

"That's the ultimate question," he said, shaking his head, trying to make the pain go away.

"You have to go for the love. You cannot stay inside the pain."

"One day you're running down a mountain and you feel her breath just come through you. You go to sleep that night, and you have a dream. The dream is that she's going to summer camp, and she kisses your cheek and she says, 'Bye, Daddy.' And you say, 'Okay, baby, bye. You have a good time.' And she gets on a train, and you see her standing there looking at you as the train goes off. And you wake up. And somehow you get on with life. You get on with life. She's with me all the time. She's with me all the time, in everything I do. Still I suffer. Still I go through adversities. Still I go through anguish. And anger. And numbness. And somehow I got the message that I have to go on."

Is the suffering still greater than the love?

"It is. But you have to go for the love. You cannot stay inside the pain. Because if you stay in the suffering, she suffers. Someone told me this. As long as you grieve, she cannot go on with her existence in her next incarnation. And she is looking at you grieve, and so she's stuck. She's stuck. Because every time you go, 'Ohhhh!' or something, she is standing there watching you, going, 'Dad, I love you. Why are you doing this to yourself?'"

He added, "The only reason I'm here now, the only reason I'm free, is because she has freed me. She has taken the chains away from my heart. She showed me how to free myself. And it feels good. From within. Because it's all an inside job, isn't it? It's all an inside job."

What does he mean by "an inside job"?

"Everything comes from a thought or feeling inside of us. Nothing would exist without someone taking what's inside of him or her and making it occur here, now, so we can all experience it." He smiles that broad enigmatic smile that lights up a room, that changes everything around him, that contains sorrow and joy, that is welcoming and conveys a strange kind of comfort, acknowledging, "It's crazy. I know. But don't worry. Just leave your hat at the door. Everything is fine. We're all passing through this crazy journey together."

CHAPTER

Resilience

Muggsy Bogues *on how he defied countless critics and became the shortest NBA player of all time.*

Can You Bounce Back?

ONE OF THE QUALITIES that intrigue us the most is the way we handle rejection, defeat, or just the slings and arrows life has a habit of shooting our way.

More than four decades ago, Herb wrote about this quality of resilience, which psychologists call ego-strength, in an article in the *Harvard Business Review*. Essentially, individuals with a healthy, intact ego have a positive picture of themselves. This is the quality that enables us to brush ourselves off after getting knocked down and carry on with even more determination.

When all is said and done, this quality has a lot to do with defining who we are.

It is essential whether you are managing people, leading a company, selling a product or service, or just dealing with the setbacks of everyday life.

Everybody, no matter how successful, will fail, be rejected, and face personal defeats.

The question is: how did we deal with these situations?

Succeeding has a great deal to do with how we handle adversity. Do we shut down? Or open up? Do we put our heads down and just keep doing what we were doing before? Or do we look around and discover a new path?

The difference has to do with whether or not we succeed—and who we become in the process.

People with resilience—and it is difficult to succeed without it—all have this very unusual way of viewing rejection. They are able to learn from negative experiences and, in some cases, turn them into defining moments.

How does this happen?

First we have to recognize that most of us, when we are rejected, have enough common sense to say, "Well, that wasn't a whole lot of fun. I'm certainly not going to do that again."

We don't go out of our way to look for negative experiences.

But people with resilience demonstrate a unique approach toward dealing with situations that don't go their way. They feel the sting of being set back. They may even dwell on it and tend to be a little self-critical. But then they muster their determination, shake off any negative feelings, and learn what they need to do to carry on. It's like a voice in the back of their heads that says, "I'll show you," and then pushes them forward.

Essentially, individuals who have the talent and ambition to move ahead, yet who receive signals, whether subtle or overt, that others think they will not make the grade, use their resilience to fuel their ambition.

It's all a matter of whether we learn from our mistakes or repeat them. Do we internalize the rejection and accept it or challenge it and shake it off?

Succeeding has much to do with how we overcome negative experiences.

It's knowing that rejection is all just part of the game. Nothing personal.

People with ego-strength actually want to change the future and in the process erase the past. When things don't go their way, after catching their breath, they want to get back in the game. The negative experience propels them. They want to erase it. They want it gone. Out of their lives.

It's as if their minds are like tape recorders—and they want to tape over what didn't work out, replacing it with a successful outcome.

How we handle rejection—whether in sales, management, leadership, or any pursuit—has to do with how we succeed and who we become.

One of the people we met who bring this quality alive is Muggsy

Bogues, the shortest player in the history of the National Basketball Association. His story has to do with how he dealt with the doubt that constantly surrounded him. It seemed to come at him from every direction except from his parents.

Born Tyrone Bogues, Muggsy got his nickname when he was seven. He explains, "Growing up in the inner city of Baltimore, all of us had nicknames. The way I played the game of basketball, you know, was mugging everybody, stealing the ball. So a friend in the neighborhood actually gave me the name. We all had nicknames. Stealing the ball. That's what I was about. They were like, 'Oh, he's mugging everybody.' And it's been Muggsy ever since."

Two years before that he was shot in his neighborhood.

As he explained, "I was at the wrong place at the wrong time. This one night a fight broke out in the alley across the street, right behind my house. I decided to go take a peek, trying to be nosy. Well, a window was broken in a store. And the old gentleman who owned the store came out, went in his old shed, grabbed his double-barreled shotgun, and just started firing. And he hit me in my arm and my legs."

Luckily he was hit by pellets, not bullets.

What's it like for a five-year-old to be hit by a shotgun pellet?

"The lights went out for me," he said.

The next thing he remembered was waking up in the hospital. "It's a vague memory, but I definitely remember coming to," he said. "The way I looked at it, it was just another obstacle I had to overcome. Growing up where I grew up, in the inner city. Faced with those types of situations: violence, drugs. But who knows? I was a little kid in the wrong place at the wrong time, who didn't know any better."

This was a day in the life for Muggsy, growing up in the slums of Baltimore, in the Lafayette Court Housing Projects on Orleans Street. He was afraid to turn the lights on because he didn't want to see all the roaches and rats that would scurry around. As a kid, he even saw a man beaten to death with a baseball bat. "I'll never forget that scene," he said. "I can still see that guy swinging the bat with both hands. I can still hear the sound of that bat crushing the other guy's skull. It makes me feel sick inside, to this very day."

He also saw people with "swollen, puffy hands, feet, and legs." He said, "I thought they were from lifting weights, until I learned they were the signs of heroin use. There were loan sharks, and they were nastier than the dealers. They'd beat people to within an inch of their lives. There was a lot of drinking, gambling, pimping, stealing, everything."

He reflected, "That very easily could have been me. The difference between Muggsy Bogues, NBA player, and Muggsy Bogues, dead body, is so small. It scares me just to think about it."

So basketball became a safe haven for Muggsy. Basketball kept him off the streets, as his parents, teachers, and coaches helped him find a sense of self-confidence. "Growing up in the ghetto was often terrible," he said. "I can't lie about that. Life for us was never easy."

When Muggsy was 12 years old, his father was arrested for armed robbery. Muggsy remembered his mother gathering her children together one night and telling them that their father was going away for a long time. He was sentenced to 20 years.

Muggsy said he was very uncomfortable seeing his father behind bars. "Eventually, I kind of got over it," he said. But it took awhile. Over the years, he and his father developed a connection through basketball. "He liked how well I was doing at the game. So he started coaching in prison, and the guys in there would bring him the articles that appeared about me in the newspapers. And he was proud," Muggsy said.

"Basketball became something that we could build a relationship around," he said. "We learned to communicate our feelings through basketball."

He added, "Meanwhile, my mother got her GED so she could get herself off public assistance and get a nice job so she could provide for her kids." He remembered one time when he was crying to her that he wanted to be taller, and she said, "You'll do fine, Ty. God doesn't make mistakes."

"That was it. All the naysayers telling me I would never make it. All the folks saying, 'He's too small.' And here it is. I'm walking up there to accept my hat and shake Mr. Stern's hand. You know, five feet, three inches. I tell you, that was just amazing. The whole universe was just lifted off my shoulders. It was like, 'Hey, you finally made it. You're here! Your time has come!'"

He kept playing because he "knew ball would help me get a scholarship and that doors would be opened from there." He said, "I had moments where I lost focus. But basketball was always my savior. You know how a VCR always has to be on channel 3 to get a clear picture? Well, I was like a VCR: I had to be on the basketball channel to stay focused. If I switched to another channel, things got blurry."

He paid close attention to the coaches in school, who taught him the fundamentals of basketball. He learned how to shoot and pass, but, most important, how to understand the art of the game. Through elementary and junior high school, he kept playing. Then, when he got to play in high school, he said, "that was the ultimate." He was playing at Dunbar High School, and their team was number one in the country, according to *Basketball Weekly*. They won 58 games during his tenure, never losing.

Muggsy became known for changing the pace of the game. "I was a true point guard, passing first, shooting second. I was the type of guy who made the guys around me better. I was an extension of the coach on the basketball floor," he said.

Including Muggsy, there were four players from his high school team who eventually made it to the pros: David Wingate, Reggie Williams, and the late Reggie Lewis.

He earned a scholarship to Wake Forest, which he describes as "predominantly white, a school full of walking J. Crew models from the most exclusive prep schools in America."

Wake Forest was not a standout team, but playing there did get Muggsy the recognition he was seeking. It helped prepare him for the day, four years later, when he was a first-round draft choice in the National Basketball Association.

What does it feel like to be invited to your own dream?

"They invited the top 23 players at the time, the ones they felt were going to be selected," he explained. "So I got invited. I didn't know exactly where I was going to go. I knew Washington was interested. I knew New York was interested. And I knew Utah was interested. As the names got called, it came down to the twelfth pick. I watched the Bullets select Tyrone Muggsy Bogues. That was it. All the naysayers telling me I would never make it. All the folks saying, 'He's too small.' And here it is. I'm walking up there to accept my hat and shake Mr. Stern's hand. You know, five feet, three inches. I tell you, that was just amazing. The whole universe was just lifted off my shoulders. It was like, 'Hey, you finally made it. You're here! Your time has come!' It was just a matter of taking the necessary steps in order for it to come true. And it was a vision for me. I was a visionary. I definitely saw it. I saw it every step of the way. Now everyone has to believe in me."

One of the first things Muggsy did with his money was hire an attorney to help get his father out of jail. He had served almost 12 years in prison, and the lawyer was able to help get him paroled. A few days later, his father saw Muggsy play a professional basketball game in person for the first time. "He and my mom came to a Bullets pre-season game, and it was the best feeling I've ever had playing in a basketball game."

As it turned out, his first preseason game was against the Los Angeles Lakers, so Muggsy was going one-on-one with Magic Johnson. All six feet, nine inches of him was playing the same position as Muggsy. "So I said to myself, 'He's incredible. He makes all those fantastic passes. He uplifts his team. And that's exactly the same thing I can do. He's just a little taller. So here it is. Bam. We're about to play the Lakers, and Muggsy Bogues is about to face Magic Johnson.'"

Muggsy remembered Magic saying, "Damn, I didn't know you were that small." "So there it was," Muggsy said. "The adrenaline. The butterflies. And I couldn't wait."

How do you play against Magic Johnson?

"Well, when he first put the ball down on the floor, I just took it from him. And then I took it from him one more time. And then I took it from him again. Of course, Magic realized, 'Hey, this little guy is nothing but trouble. I have to have somebody else bring the ball up court.' It was too much energy to fight me to bring the ball up and down the court. So he'd throw it to someone else to bring it down, then he'd post it and try to pass it and do whatever he was going to do. But at least I made him change his game."

After the game, Magic Johnson said, "I'll tell you one thing: if you let Muggsy get beside you, forget it. He's gone. The little guy is quick. No one will get it up the floor faster. He changes the whole game when he comes in."

At the end of his first year, Muggsy was traded to the Charlotte Hornets, an expansion team, where he spent most of his 14-year NBA career.

From the time he started playing basketball on lots in Baltimore's projects through high school, college, and the NBA, Muggsy said what drove him was that "I always wanted to prove them wrong. Where does that come from? I don't know. Genetic? My background? I just had that belief in me. I always had that belief in me—that I could overcome anyone's doubts. People kept saying, 'Muggsy, you're too short to play basketball.' And it would make me feel bad, but I would never let them know it. I might go home and tell my mom when I was younger. I remember once she said, 'Baby, don't worry about it. Nobody can be an expert on your life. No one knows what your capabilities are. No one knows the potential of you. You can be whatever you want.' And I was like, 'Yeah, all right, Mom, okay.'"

He said, "All the folks saying, 'He's too small.' They said it when I was in grammar school, then junior high, then high school, then college, then the pros. And in one sense it was in and out. You know, in one ear and out the other. But it hurt. So in another sense it was just another measuring stick as far as proving them wrong. And then it gets to the point where it's even more important than just proving them wrong."

Here's a guy who knows where rejection belongs. And that attitude helped him overcome the most incredible odds.

"I think one of the main keys to my success is that I use negative emotions as internal motivation," he said.

When he was a kid, Muggsy played from the time he got home from school until his mother would call him in. On weekends, he started practicing right after breakfast. "I knew I had a passion to play basketball. And it was something that no one could take away from me. I studied the craft, and I learned it to the point where it enabled me to get a lot more from it than just basketball. It gave me an education. It gave me a way of providing for my family. It gave me an opportunity to meet other individuals and build relationships. I got to see other countries. It just did enormous things for me. And I thank the Man every day for putting me in that position because he could have chosen anyone. He could have chosen someone else besides me, the kid that's from the inner city in Baltimore, Maryland. He could have chosen another five foot, three inch guy from Lithuania, or from the Bronx. Who knows? But it was me. He chose me." He paused and then added, "Of course, I also know I had a lot to do with it as well."

Just recently he became the head coach of the WNBA's Charlotte Sting. And he has also been running summer camps in Winston-Salem and Charlotte, North Carolina. "I'm there all day, every day," he said, "making the rounds to different teaching stations and giving pointers, coaching teams in games, refereeing; sometimes I even play. The kids really enjoy that, and believe me, they do everything to try to show me up."

What advice does he like to leave them with?

"I let them know that we all encounter a lot of negativity through life," he said. "But my life proves that anyone can overcome negativity. You can do anything you want to do in life if you have a fierce belief in yourself, a strong will, a big heart, and some role models to inspire you."

Willingness to Take a Risk

Senator Barbara Boxer *on the importance of fighting for what you believe in, even when you know you're going to lose.*

Putting It All on the Line

FOR SOME PEOPLE THE VERY thought of taking a risk can be paralyzing. Others take risks like vitamins—at least once a day.

To help them feel a little less risky, risk takers are prone to using the word *calculated* beforehand.

Somehow, being a calculated risk taker makes them seem less reckless. And we're not just talking about skydivers.

But the truth of the matter is that without taking a risk, or a leap of faith, very little happens. And even for those who prefer to be cautious, risk can never be avoided.

The world has a way of sending floods, hurricanes, and locusts our way when we least expect it. We run a risk just by going about our business: driving to work, getting on an airplane, swimming in the ocean.

There's no way to avoid risk. (Besides, if you don't take a chance now and then, life can get pretty boring.) So, you might as well take your risks on purpose.

Senator Barbara Boxer (D-CA), one of President Bush's most vocal critics, has always been one to seize the moment. And the longer she's been on this planet, the more confident she's become in her risk-taking ability. Senator Hillary Rodham Clinton cites Senator Boxer as an heir apparent in the noble line of societal reformers stretching back to Abigail Adams, Elizabeth Cady Stanton, and Eleanor Roosevelt.

The risks she's taken have enabled her to win her third term as a U.S. senator after serving for 10 years in the House of Representatives. The more risks she takes, the more sure and strong her voice becomes.

But, she said, you have to realize that the risks along the way were not taken to fulfill some sort of childhood dream. "Looking back to when I was a kid, there was no clue that I ever wanted to get into politics," she said. "You have to remember, the only female senator at that time was Margaret Chase Smith. My mother would talk about her with great admiration. But basically the message was that she was an anomaly, that she was extraordinary. And there was no way the rest of us mortals could aspire to such heights. So there weren't really role models for any of us to emulate. Girls and young women were not really allowed that kind of dream when I was growing up." She paused, then added, "But my election and the election of several other women to the Senate is the fulfillment of an American dream previously reserved for American men."

The *Congressional Quarterly* describes Senator Boxer as "an ardent feminist, a defender of environmental regulation and an enemy of the National Rifle Association." She was drawn into politics in the 1960s as a young Vietnam War protester, and while she is not completely against the use of military force, Senator Boxer voted against both the 1991 Persian Gulf resolution sought by the senior George Bush and the younger Bush's 2002 use-of-force request against Iraq. She offers no apologies for her passions and her bold style. "My political style is to be extremely candid and straight from the shoulders and not to be mealy-mouthed or waffle," she said. "When I believe in something, I believe in it strongly."

She is known for impassioned, uncompromising speeches, providing her with countless press clippings and a strong following, but few ceremonial pens from the signings of bills she has sponsored. Some have said her convictions can get in the way of her reaching across the aisle and compromising.

She explained, "My view is that, in any negotiation, you will always have people who are going to stick to their position and stake it out. And if you don't have people who stake out a position, there never will be compromise. I mean, if everybody walks in and gives in immediately, you're lost. So what I've done over my career is, on vital issues, to say,

'Look, this is my position. And that's it.' You have to be tough in certain regards. In other words, if we have a Clean Air Act, for example, that is functioning right and it's saving people from getting asthma, how do you compromise and say, 'Well, it's okay if some people get asthma'? My view is that someone else can do that. But not me. If you have veterans returning home and they need mental health care, which we know happens after every war, I'm not going to say, 'You know, let's just compromise so 10 percent of them don't get it.' Maybe somebody else wants to say that, but it's not going to be me. So, as I've said many, many times, there is no center if there is no left and right. There is no moderate if there aren't liberals and conservatives. So my function in a lot of the debates has been to say, 'This is a place where I'm drawing a line in the sand.' Now, there are other times when there is room to move. For example, on a highway funding bill where I'm arguing for money for bridges and things like that. Yes, we can talk about how to move certain funding around a little bit.

"So I'll compromise on the small stuff. But not the major issues. On the important issues, I'm very consistent. I'm not the type of person who changes views on the basis of polls or the way the wind is blowing."

On a wall of her Capitol Hill office hangs a picture of her as a House member, leading six other female representatives up the steps of the Senate in October of 1991 to demand public hearings on law professor Anita Hill's allegations of sexual harassment against Supreme Court nominee Clarence Thomas.

You have to keep in mind that, according to *US News & World Report* polling data at that time, only 24 percent of the women in the United States believed Anita Hill, whereas 60 percent believed Clarence Thomas. Barbara's own pollster confirmed those findings, but that didn't sit right with Barbara. In her book *Strangers in the Senate*, she asked, "Why would women react in such a forceful way against Anita Hill after all the years of the women's movement and the fight for equal pay for equal work and the fight for choice and equality?"

She believed there was more to the story, and she was stunned that the Senate Judiciary Committee would not air the sexual harassment charges.

So she and six other women leaders of the House of Representatives marched over to the U.S. Senate to ask the senators to reconsider Anita Hill's charges. "We didn't know if we were doing a popular thing or an unpopular thing; we didn't know whether it would make any difference whatsoever. We only knew that we were uneasy, so uneasy that we were willing to break the unwritten—but strict—rules of the U.S. Senate and demand that we be heard. We were unladylike about it, and we were not sweet about it. We couldn't be."

In retrospect, she said, "It has always fascinated me that when women do things like this, we are seen as 'strident,' while men are 'strong'; we're often 'loud,' while men are 'forceful'; we are 'opinionated,' while men are 'smart.'"

In terms of the style of women leaders, she said, "I think women do have a little bit of a different way of leading. I think we try to be more inclusive. We try to bring people along with us, if it's possible. But if that's not working, then we know how to shift gears and be tough."

> **"My view is that you can't be afraid,
> because you are going through this
> world in such a short amount of time.
> You are just here for the blink of an eye.
> And we are all here for a reason."**

In the book *Nine and Counting: The Women of the Senate*, she noted, "There was an article in *Ms.* magazine when I was first running for office, which said that the biggest difference between men and women was that men could just go out there time and time again. Losing doesn't destroy them. Women have tended to take losing more personally. But I think as we grew up more, in terms of our political toughness and our understanding, we're learning that it's not personal. People say they hate you, but they've never met you. There's a lot of passionate expression in politics. But really, it's not you as much as it's your positions they're attacking. Once you realize that, it makes losing a lot easier to handle. The first time I lost an election, which was for supervisor, I felt shredded. I was depressed. I couldn't look in the mirror. But now I've been through the wars. I can take it on the chin."

After serving five terms in the House of Representatives, Barbara considered a run for the Senate. She described a conversation she had with Senator Barbara Mikulski (D-MD), who she had worked alongside in the House.

Mikulski got straight to the point. "How old are you, Babs?" she asked.

"Almost 50."

"Go for it," the Senator urged. But she also provided a caveat: "If you're ready to leave the House of Representatives, and never look back, and never regret it, then I'd say 50 is the perfect time. You can do more here. You can be heard here. It'll be worth the fight you'll have to wage. And it will be a fight."

So she risked a sure seat in the House of Representatives for a long shot at the Senate. She ended up in a fight for her political life.

In 1992, California already had a female, Diane Feinstein, running a successful senate race and Barbara, who was considered a long-shot running for the other senate seat, would hear, "California will never elect two women. And certainly not two Jewish women." Often during the campaign, she would note, "nobody made an issue over electing two Protestant men."

During the toughest part of the campaign she decided she had to pull out of the race. She was spending most of her time raising money, and there didn't seem to be enough money to get her message across effectively in the huge state of California. Her opponent's campaign seemed well-oiled. They were spreading messages about her that weren't true, but she didn't have the resources to counter. Three months before the election, she called her husband and told him about her decision to drop out of the race. When she got home, her two adult children were there unexpectedly. When they heard what she was thinking, they pulled out a copy of a children's book she used to read to them as they were growing up. It was Dr. Seuss's *Oh, the Places You'll Go!* She particularly remembers, "Wherever you go, you'll top all the rest. Except when you don't. Because sometimes you won't."

Then her daughter Nicole said, "Mom, this election isn't just about you. There's no way you can drop out. What will that tell the world about women? That we can't take the heat? That we let the polls and the press push us out?" Then Nicole added, "Women are counting on you to be tough, and your toughness will give them strength. But you can't fight for the people if you can't fight for yourself."

Barbara reflected, "At that point, no one thought that I could win. So I figured I might as well do my best and come as close as I could."

The election evening was a blur until, at two in the morning, her opponent conceded in a telephone call. "Then I really believed it had happened," the new senator said.

Now she keeps that Dr. Seuss phrase in mind whenever she loses a vote.

"It helps me focus on what I can do, not what I fail to do. It keeps me coming back to try again."

What is it like to be a member of the U.S. Senate?

"My friend Patty Murray (D-WA), who is serving her third term in the U.S. Senate, says that being a kindergarten teacher was the best training for being a senator. The point is, nothing changes. It's the same dynamics, just a different setting," Barbara said.

In truth, the qualities that make her an effective spokesperson for liberal ideals also make her a top target when she faces re-election. But that doesn't daunt her.

She remains very open about her pro-choice views at a time when almost every other elected official in Washington is trying to soften, if not distance, his or her stance. "I view reproductive choice as a freedom issue in addition to being a woman's issue. We must make sure that the right to choose remains an individual woman's choice rather than that of the government, the judiciary, the religious right—or the members of a violent mob outside a clinic," she explained, succinctly and unequivocally.

She speaks with the same forthrightness about protecting the environment and opposing the war in Iraq.

Ultimately, she said, "My view is that you can't be afraid because you are going through this world in such a short amount of time. You are just here for the blink of an eye. And we are all here for a reason. I am very spiritual about that. So if you are not going to do what you think is right and you're not going to be brave, then you don't deserve trust. So when I stand alone or with just a few of my colleagues, I'm just doing what I have to do, what needs to be done. It's not about being brave to take the kind of risks I'm taking. How does what I'm doing compare to what our soldiers are facing? How does what I'm doing compare to what Martin Luther King faced? I understand the perspective. I know what I'm doing is important. But it is not on that level. What I'm doing is trying to come through for people who are thirsting for straightforward representation. I'm not going to be dissuaded from doing my work because I'm fearful of being called a lightning rod or because I'm fearful of losing my position. I'm willing to take that risk. I'm here to be who I am. And I couldn't care less about all the reasons why I should hold back a little. A lot of people will tone down their message because they're afraid of how they're coming across. But all that stuff doesn't really matter. Not if you really care about what you're doing and what you stand for," she said. Then she added, "You know, a lot of that, for me, was coming to the realization that if everyone loves you every single day of your life, then you really aren't standing for much. If all you do is take the path of least resistance, because you're afraid of not being loved, then you don't really stand for much. If I've learned anything, that's it."

She didn't hesitate to be the only senator to stand with the Black Congressional Caucus to challenge the results of the 2004 presidential election. Four years before, when the black members of the House stood up to protest the results, pleading for a senator to join their objections, none did. Senator Boxer said that in retrospect "it was a mistake not to object then."

She is keenly aware of her place and time in history.

As she said, with a wry smile, "My husband thought he married Debbie Reynolds, and he woke up with Eleanor Roosevelt." She knows all too well that women in America were not allowed to vote until 1920, when the Nineteenth Amendment to the Constitution was passed. No doubt, somewhere in the back of her mind is an image of Susan B. Anthony, who was arrested and fined $100 for voting—before women's suffrage had been established—in the 1872 presidential election.

So, the risks Senator Boxer takes are not just for her, but, as her daughter reminded her, for women—and, in fact, for all of us.

Thriving on Pressure

Roger Staubach, *who led the Dallas Cowboys to two Super Bowl victories, on why the best comes through in the final two minutes of the game.*

How's Your Hail Mary Pass?

GRACE UNDER PRESSURE is one thing. It's when the Space Shuttle is on the verge of a catastrophe and an engineer is at the controls, analyzing the situation, making adjustments, and just starting to perspire as he implements a solution moments before time runs out, avoiding certain disaster.

Most of us wish we could be that cool under pressure.

But thriving on pressure. That's quite another thing.

When Roger Staubach was leading the Dallas Cowboys in their dynasty decade in the 1970s, including playing in four Super Bowls and winning two of them, it was the pressure that pushed him forward.

Sure, he was an inspiring and commanding leader the rest of the time. But "Captain Comeback," as he was known, became one of history's best quarterbacks when the clock was ticking. Loudly. It was as though he needed the pressure to bring out the best in him.

When everything was on the line, others could get flustered and make mistakes, but for Roger, that was when it all kicked in. He became even more focused and astonishing. He would call up something inside of himself that even he didn't know he had. And become better because of it.

Twenty-three times he led the Cowboys to victory from fourth-quarter deficits. On 14 of those occasions, he pulled it off with less than two minutes remaining, or in overtime.

That was when his confidence really turned on. And he showed that confidence was contagious as his teammates came to believe more and more in him—and in themselves.

One of the most memorable instances of winning a game with virtually no time left on the clock, against all odds, was Roger's go-for-broke, hope-and-pray throw, which has now entered the vernacular as the Hail Mary pass.

When everything was on the line, others could get flustered and make mistakes, but for Roger, that was when it all kicked in.

Although it occurred more than three decades ago, that phrase still sends uncontrollable spasms up the spine of any diehard Minnesota Vikings fan. It was an incredibly close game, when, with less than two minutes remaining, Fran Tarkenton's Vikings capped a drive with a touchdown, putting them ahead 14 to 10. It looked certain that the Vikings were on their way to a third consecutive Super Bowl.

That was when Roger kicked into a whole new gear. He moved the Cowboys to midfield in nine plays. The cold Minnesota winter wind made everything seem even more difficult. Dallas was out of time-outs, and there was less than 30 seconds left on the game clock.

The Cowboys lined up again in their familiar shotgun formation. Roger took the snap, pump-faked left, then turned to his right and fired the ball deep down the field in desperation, aiming for his wide receiver Drew Pearson, who was completely shadowed by a Viking defender. Roger was hit immediately and didn't see it, but Drew made an incredible catch, and, with the ball lodged snugly between Drew's right elbow and right hip, he ran into the end zone to score the winning touchdown.

After the game, a reporter asked Roger how it happened. Roger replied, "I closed my eyes and said a Hail Mary."

From that moment, the phrase "What we need now is a Hail Mary pass" has gone on to become part of our everyday speech in situations where it seems that all hope is lost.

What was it like for Roger being inside that moment?

"Well, it comes down to confidence. You have to believe in yourself, especially when you're the quarterback and people are looking to you to pull them together. They want to believe in you, so you've got to be there for them," he said. "Once you've done it the first time, it gets easier afterward. It's just a matter of being prepared, then letting it happen. We would prepare for those last two minutes all week long. That was our drill, with the clock running. But you never know what's going to happen until you're in the game."

Interviewing Roger about such moments, it's hard to get at what he was really feeling. He is a natural leader, but is extremely modest. And he deflects praise, preferring to give credit to others or to the team as a whole. As far as he's concerned, he said, "I just want to be remembered as a darn consistent quarterback."

Frank Deford, the *Sports Illustrated* editor and a regular columnist on National Public Radio, counts Roger among the game's top three quarterbacks, along with Johnny Unitas and Joe Montana.

To get a real sense of what drives Roger, interviewing him and assessing his personality profile provides key insights. But with someone like Roger, maybe all you've got to do is review the game tapes to get a real sense of what he is all about.

The Dallas Cowboys' coach at that time, Tom Landry, explained, "In Roger's case, it was a matter of believing in himself. He knew he could get the job done, regardless of what the circumstances were. This made Roger special. He made the great difference. There wasn't a player on the Cowboys who didn't look at him and think, 'As long as we have Roger, we have a chance to win.' Even when a lot of us were maybe losing a little faith in a ball game, in any tough situation, he seemed to always be the one to pull us through. The Hail Mary pass was one example of that. We were playing a great team like Minnesota—probably one of the best teams—and they had everything going their way to win the ball game. I think most of us felt like it was slipping away. Yet Roger came in with Drew Pearson and made the plays that were necessary to make it happen."

Recalling that long, unbelievable pass in the final seconds of the game, Coach Landry added, "It wasn't so much the play, but the quality of the players involved and their attitude in the situation. A player with character looks at the best side in every situation. There's always hope, even though the clock is running out. That attitude is the difference, and it has won a lot of games for us."

Sounds unbelievable?

Add to it that Roger joined the Dallas Cowboys in 1969 as a 27-year-old rookie. Most of his incredible accomplishments on the field didn't occur until after he turned 29, when he became the starting quarterback. That's a time when most professional athletes have gone on to something else and are hardly even remembered by their fans.

It took that long for Roger to enter the pros because, even though he won the Heisman Trophy as a junior, he was playing for Navy and had a four-year military commitment after graduating from the academy. That turned most recruiters off. He ended up being a throwaway draft pick in the tenth round.

When you look at the game films of Roger with the Cowboys, you can't help being impressed by his incredible footwork. He could avoid tacklers and somehow wait for just the right moment—that split second—to throw or run. It was impressive. Unless you were his coach, Tom Landry. "Coach Landry wasn't happy with my scrambling," Roger admitted. "It caused a running feud between us. But I put up with his play calling, and he put up with my scrambling."

Roger's scrambling probably started in high school, when he was a running back and a tight end. Then, in his senior year, Roger's coach switched him to the quarterback position. Roger felt awkward about it at the time because there was a friend of his who had been groomed for the position that year. He asked his coach why he was making the switch. The coach responded, "Because the other players listen to you." That's where leadership starts. When we're doing what we want to do and others start to pay attention to us.

"I can't thank Coach Jim McCarthy enough," Roger said. "If he hadn't switched me to quarterback, I probably would have gone on to become a decent player in college. But I wouldn't have been given the shot to go on to the pros."

In the pros, however, Roger was prone to getting hurt because of his scrambling. As Coach Landry was keenly aware, that could cost the team dearly. In a preseason game in August of 1972 against the Los Angeles Rams, Roger faded to pass, then saw an opening and took off for the goal line. Instead of stepping out of bounds or falling after making the first down, Roger ducked his head like a fullback and tried to run through a tackler. Roger said that before he even hit the ground, he felt a burning sensation in his right shoulder. After he was escorted off the field, his badly separated shoulder required surgery.

The coach could talk until he was blue in the face. Roger had a mind of his own and in a preseason game had risked it all.

Fortunately, he recovered and was able to lead his team to four Super Bowls, two of which were victories.

What was it like to win his first Super Bowl game?

"It was something that . . ." He paused, then said, "It's hard to describe. It was our goal all year long. And we got it. And no one can take it away from you. We were the best. As a team, it creates a special bond. We all did it. Together. It does stay with you."

After 11 years at the top of his game, Roger decided to retire at the end of the 1979 season. It was his call. He had just spent another season as the league's best passer. The doctors indicated that there might be some neurological changes on the left side of his brain, resulting from injuries, and it was possible further damage could occur if he received more concussions. His style threatened to become dangerous to his health.

Roger bowed out gracefully and shifted comfortably into the business world. He had become involved in real estate shortly after moving to Dallas because, as he explained, "Back in 1969, when I was a rookie with the Cowboys, I had a wife and children, and they didn't pay quarterbacks what they do today. I was earning $25,000 a year. So I was looking to work in the off-season, and someone at the Naval Academy introduced me to Henry S. Miller, Jr., who ran, and still runs, a successful real estate company." Henry wasn't thrilled with the idea that Roger was only going to work in the off-season, but they got along well, and the quarterback became a part-time real estate salesperson. "It turned out to be a job I could deal with because I was on commission. So I could work when I wanted and not feel guilty," he explained. As it turned out, Mr. Miller became Roger's mentor and later he decided to form his own company.

Now The Staubach Company, with over 1,200 people, is an enormously successful commercial real estate enterprise, with over 60 offices. "I spend my time on the strategic part of the business," Roger said. "I focus on where we are today and where we need to be tomorrow. I also spend time in the field offices with our people and current customers, while also looking to attract new customers."

He also connects with his people in a very real, personal way.

While we were waiting to see him, he walked by, greeted us, and said he'd be just a minute. Then he said hello to the company's receptionist, who he calls the "Director of First Impressions," and she responded with, "How are you doing, Coach?"

When we asked why she called him "Coach," she said, "Because Roger coaches and assists everyone at The Staubach Company." When she started working for the company she had no idea that Roger had played professional football. She quickly got to know the man, his character and his integrity. Relating her own experience with Roger, she said, "I was home sleeping when a storm split a tree and it fell on my house, starting a fire. The next thing I knew, firefighters were all around as I saw all my worldly possessions go up in flames. Fortunately, everyone in my family got out okay. When I called the office to say I wouldn't be in that day, 'Coach' called back on my cell phone five minutes later and offered to take care of everything." Everything included offering her family the Staubach home to stay in.

Stories like that abound in Roger's company, though he'd be the last person to tell you about them. They show he is a deeply principled man with a huge heart, who thrives even under someone else's pressure. A man who lives and breathes his faith.

You realize that business, like sports, like everything in life, is personal to Roger. There are no dividing lines.

When it comes to business, the corporate world is replete with sports analogies. Which ones make the most sense to him?

"Competition is certainly important. Being clear about your goals is crucial," he said. "But for me, the key to developing a successful organization is all about team building. It's all about the people you surround yourself with. Succeeding in business, in sports, in your life, is a matter of pulling together people you can trust, who are honest, who have their priorities in line, who have the talent, ambition, and desire to reach beyond themselves and make something really big happen—particularly when the pressure's on."

CHAPTER

Optimism

Janet Lasley *on how she stays positive, even when it appears all hope is gone.*

Beating the Odds

DOES THE WAY WE VIEW the world make a difference to anyone but ourselves? Can our attitudes affect other people or change the way things turn out?
Here's a little test:

If something negative happens, say, you ask someone to dance with you and your request is turned down, do you think it is because

(a) the other person doesn't feel like dancing

(b) you are not a good enough dancer

If something positive happens, say, you win a race, do you think it was because

(a) you tried hard

(b) your rival had an off day

Whether we view what we do and what happens to us as being permanent or temporary has a lot to do with whether we are optimistic.
Optimists view a negative event as temporary, one of those things which just happens. They know it will pass and tomorrow will be a new day.
On the other hand, optimists view positive events as the result of something inside of them that is permanent, according to Martin E. P.

Seligman, Ph.D. In his book *Learned Optimism*, Seligman explains that positive events cause optimistic people to try even harder the next time. Optimists believe that events that turn out as they wish enhance everything they do.

In contrast, people who are not optimistic see temporary reasons (e.g., my rival got tired) for positive events. As a result, they may give up even after they succeed, believing their success was nothing more than a fluke.

Another distinction is that optimists believe events that don't turn out as they wish have specific causes. They want to understand what happened, know what to do about the situation so they can change it next time, then move on. Failure can make all of us feel, at least momentarily, helpless. It hurts, but the hurt goes away—and for optimists it goes away quickly. Optimists persist in the face of routine setbacks and even major failures. In difficult situations, at crucial junctures, optimists persevere through the sheer force of will.

In his book *Optimism: The Biology of Hope*, Lionel Tiger argues that as a species, humans have been selected by evolution because of our collective optimistic illusions about reality. How else could a species have evolved that plants seeds in April and holds on through drought and famine in anticipation of an October harvest? What else but optimism could keep you standing alone before charging mastodons, waving nothing more than sticks? Or how can you explain a species that commences to build cathedrals that will take several lifetimes to complete? The optimism to act on the belief that reality will turn out better than it usually does inspires such courageous, or foolhardy, behavior.

How much can optimistic individuals change their world and the world around them?

Ask Janet Lasley, whose construction company has received countless awards and distinctions for creating innovative renovations and building new homes.

Seven years ago Janet listened to a doctor at Memorial Sloan-Kettering Cancer Center in New York City explain that her death would be painless, like falling asleep.

"I was thinking, 'What are you talking about?'" she said. "I have two young children!" Then she tried to catch her breath. It was as if she'd been kicked in the stomach. As she scanned the doctor's office trying to refocus, a belief in her swelled. "This is not *freaking* going to happen to me," she vowed. "I'm not going down this way."

As she walked out of that doctor's office, her journey, ultimately testing what she was made of, began.

The cancer she has—leiomyosarcoma—is a very rare cancer of the soft muscle tissue of the body, and the chances of recovery are slim. Very slim. She was told that people usually live just two to three years with this particular cancer.

How did she face such a prognosis?

"I went through all kinds of emotions," she said. "At first it was grim. It was very hard in the beginning." After surgery to remove the tumor, she believed for a few months that she was fine. "That was 'my brush with death,'" she said. Then the cancer came back, and she was angry: "I was so enraged. I kept thinking, Why wasn't it one of those shitheads out there who got this? Why was it me?"

In the eight years since Janet's diagnosis, she has undergone six surgeries and six rounds of chemotherapy. She is scanned regularly to monitor what are now two tumors in her liver that seem to periodically disappear, then return.

Eight years. With other cancers, if a patient goes seven years without a flare-up, the patient is considered to be in remission. That's the stage where you can sigh. "But I'm not really in remission," she explained. "I like to believe I am, and sometimes I pretend I am because the tumors don't seem to be growing. I sometimes just use the word 'remission' because it helps me get through the day," she said.

Part of what has gotten her through it all, she's convinced, is her optimism. "My husband reminds me that I can take seemingly bad things and, after a period of mourning or anger or whatever I go through, turn it around into something positive. It's the only way I can deal with life," she said. "Part of my optimism might even border on being delusional," she added, smiling. "But there's no question that optimism has carried me through this."

While she was being treated for cancer, Janet began making decisions that were as creative as they were difficult. She decided to make a video for her children, with her talking about who she was, what she had done, what was important to her, her hopes and dreams for herself and each of them, and maybe to anticipate and answer some difficult questions she thought they might have about their mother who left them too soon. Caylin, who is now 12 years old, was 4 when her mother was told she had cancer and had just a few years to live. And

Charlie, who is now eight, was just seven months old when his mom got the news.

"If I wasn't going to be there with them, through their individual joys, sorrows, disappointments, and accomplishments, then I wanted to leave them a legacy. I wanted them to know that they could do anything they wanted in their lives. And I wanted them to have a sense of who I was. The good and the bad. I wanted them to have access to all of it so that they had a full idea of who I was. So many times when someone dies early, particularly a parent, that person becomes an angel. Those people become perfect bigger-than-life human beings. You know, they become the photograph that never changes. So I wanted to be sure that didn't happen." She didn't want them to see her as some perfect image which they could never be able to live up to.

So she sat down with a friend who had a video camera, and he started asking her questions. "At first it seemed awkward, and I thought, 'This isn't a good idea. I don't have anything to say. Maybe we should just forget about it.' Then I burst into tears and talked for three hours. I just looked at him and pretended he was my kids, and I tried to tell him everything I could think of that I wanted them to know," she said.

What were some of the things on the film? What did Janet feel she needed to say?

"I told them that when I worked at United Parcel Service, I had 27 accidents and I had to do a lot of maneuvering to keep myself from getting fired. I told them about the time I was arrested for protesting the Vietnam War. There are plenty of other things. But I'm not going to talk to you about those things now, because now that I'm going to live, I don't think my children will have to see the video—at least not for a long time."

That's intriguing.

We view our lives differently when we're facing death than we do when we're not, or at least when we're not immediately aware that we are.

Why doesn't she want to show her children the video she made for them when she thought she wasn't going to be around?

"Now that I'm here, I want to live in the present. I want to be here for them, to help in whatever way I can, to try to guide them as much as possible as they maneuver through their own complicated journeys," she explained. Her advice comes subtly, when she's cooking dinner and talking with her children about the events of their day, rather than beaming from a projector, coming from a disconnected time in some far-off place. When she was making the video, she had to imagine who Caylin and Charlie might be. Now she knows. The video had to do with who they might become without her. Her conversations with them now are about who they all are, individually and together.

"Our discussions now can be about little things, which is terrific," she added.

When her prognosis was grim, Janet also decided to do as much as she possibly could with her children in what appeared to be her limited time on this planet. She would take them out of school and go on spontaneous day trips with them. They also planned trips to Costa Rica, Bali, and England. Those are all memories she looks back on with great fondness, and that probably wouldn't have existed if she had been focused on other aspects of her life.

Janet also keeps a journal of all the wonderful little things that happen to her and her family "and the cute things each of them say," she said.

When it seemed she had a very limited time left, Janet accepted it in the most optimistic way anyone could. She faced the likelihood that she wasn't going to be here much longer. Then she made something of it. She created a video for her children; she started writing for them. She said, "Okay. If this is my lot in life, I'm going to accept it, but my way."

But then things started changing. She seemed to be getting better. Could she think the thought? Dare to say it out loud?

"It was an enormous change," she explained. "*And* it was gradual." She paused, then added, "It was fostered by the wonderful things that started to happen to me as I fought the disease. I was very lucky. I responded well to my treatments, and I was very aware that most leiomyosarcoma patients don't respond."

Initially she accepted her prognosis.

"I assumed that I would do poorly, like most people do. So I did some other things that I am very happy about. For instance, I took my daughter out of school more than 30 days that first year. And we did wonderful things together. We would go to the park, or we would go on a trip. I just never thought twice about whether it was more important for her to be in school. And she was only in the first grade. At one point I said to her teacher, 'I would like an award from the school for my daughter missing the most days of any other child here.'" She laughed and then added, "I'm not sure that the teacher shared my sense of humor. But it didn't matter in the entire scheme of things. My daughter didn't seem to be suffering academically by spending more time with me than she was in the classroom. And we did wonderful things together. We still do."

She added, "I lived every day as if it was my last. And I was really sick. So there were times when I couldn't do that because I would be in bed for days and days at a time, recovering from the chemotherapy. The chemo was tough. It was horrible. And the surgeries were very difficult to recover from. I've had 60 percent of my liver removed. I've done some very, very aggressive things."

Did she know she was recovering?

"Not really," she said. "The only time I felt ill was from the chemotherapy. I never felt ill because of the tumors. I wouldn't know I was actually getting better until the tests came back. I mean, I was hopeful, and I did a lot of positive imaging. But I didn't really know. I was always white-knuckled about how the tests would come out."

The waiting is the hardest part.

"But gradually, things started to happen. And I started to picture myself as a fox. All I was doing," Janet said, "was running for the next forest to keep myself from the dogs that were baying at my heels. I didn't feel like I had to conquer the disease totally. I didn't have to do anything that seemed unreasonable or unrealistic. I just had to stay ahead. So I kept running. And things opened up. One time I had a tumor that was getting out of hand, and the doctor at Sloan-Kettering said, 'They have a new chemo they're introducing at four o'clock this afternoon.' And it was what I needed. So I got another couple of months. Then another year."

> **"Part of my optimism might even border
> on being delusional," she added, smiling.
> "But there's no question that optimism
> has carried me through this."**

At that point a transition was taking place. The fox was leading the way. It seemed like she might be able to beat this thing.

Her optimism in the face of death was turning into optimism in the possibility of life. How did she make that transition?

"It wasn't like one day I realized I was out of the woods. I just kept running," she said. "I was the fox. And I was running. Every now and then I would look back, and the dogs would be farther behind. Then they were an entire field behind me, nearly out of sight. And I sighed an enormous sigh of relief." That didn't mean the tumors were not inside her anymore. But they were behaving, and her thinking could shift. Could she say it out loud now? Could Janet go from fearing death to embracing life?

In each of the stages of treatment, her optimism was her constant.

It wasn't denial. In Janet's case, she had enormous determination and was very involved in her own recovery, constantly.

Her optimism allowed her to make the best of whatever the situation was. Her optimism let her accept her situation as a baseline, but kept her from giving in or giving up. She always pushed for change. She always left a door of hope slightly open. And when it seemed to slide a bit, she pushed it for all she was worth.

If she heard that a new chemotherapy was working for only one person out of a hundred, that was good enough for her. She assumed she'd be part of that one percent. Did she want to find out who that person was and talk with him or her? "No" she said. "I just liked knowing that they were doing fine. That someone else was making it too."

"All I wanted to do," she said, with enormous candor, realism, and optimism, "was tip the scales in my favor."

Through it all, she said, "It's amazing that my construction company and I both survived."

Lasley Construction was having its own transformational dramas. When word got out that Janet was ill, assignments became fewer and fewer. Like so many entrepreneurs, she had built the business on the basis of her personal vision and involvement. As a direct result, her clients wanted to be sure they would be working with Janet. And in the beginning, when she was undergoing chemotherapy, she had no choice but to disappear. She didn't work for almost a year.

During that time, her husband, Marc, an architect, tried to hold it together.

These days, Lasley Brahaney Architecture and Construction, as the company is known, is thriving, with projects such as a new private residence designed by the architect Michael Graves. She said she's now comfortable knowing that she doesn't have to be there all the time and that the company can succeed without her being directly involved in each and every project. In terms of managing the company, her personality, she notes, balances nicely with her husband's. "He is steady, like a barge," she said, "chugging down the middle of the river. And I'm like a sailboat, zipping around."

Now a healthy entrepreneur and mother, she knows what is most important, what she will be remembered for when she's no longer here. Spending time with her children is what Janet is mainly about these days. "We only have so much time for that," she was quick to acknowledge. "It's fleeting. There's no question," she added, "that I'm a better mother because of all I've been through." She described herself as "less hurried, less harried, more in the here and now." The possibility of having less time has allowed her to find more time for what is important. She said, "Now I know that time disappears. And I have to take it for all it's worth. I have to take the time to go to all the people I really care about and tell them exactly how much they mean to me."

"Every day, sometimes several times a day," Janet said, "I think, 'If this were my last day on earth, how would I want to spend it?'" She recalled one day when she kept Charlie out of school because she was having a particularly rough day. "I was getting ready to go for a CT scan and I was scared, so I wanted to spend the day with love." That day they went to the pool, and he learned to swim. "It's just part of my soul, of my very bones, to quickly think about what I can do to make things different. It's up to me, along with my doctors, to beat this thing. It's up to me to swim every day so I stay healthy. It's up to me to fill my heart with laughter and joy so I stay alive."

Janet is keenly aware that many people she knew, "some absolutely remarkable people," got the exact same disease and fought it with everything they had, but didn't do as well.

"Even though I wouldn't wish cancer on anyone—and if I could do it over again, I wish I didn't have it," she concluded, "I have learned so many wonderful things from having it, from facing my own mortality, from realizing who I am and what I want to leave behind."

Empathy

Claude Grunitzky *on transcending boundaries and becoming a global citizen.*

Do You Understand the World Around You?

HOW DO WE TUNE IN TO others and understand where they're coming from? Can we connect in a way that is meaningful? Or do we just skim the surface? Empathy is the starting place for succeeding in virtually every relationship—on a professional level as well as in our personal lives.

Having assessed the potential and motivation of more than two million individuals, we have found that empathy is actually rarer than you might think.

Most of us get stuck interpreting the world from our own narrow point of view. And that can be very limiting, particularly as the world becomes smaller, communication happens faster and connections are made—or missed.

We all can express sympathy. When we hear of someone's misfortune, we can say, "Sorry about that." But, as Herb pointed out in the *Harvard Business Review*, true empathy starts with making a genuine connection and really being able to feel as another person does. Someone with real empathy is able to get others to open up and share things about themselves in a way that they might not ordinarily.

It's not just asking "How are you?" It's asking the question in a way that expresses real interest and genuine caring, so the answer becomes deeper than "Fine. How are you?" More important than the words that are spoken is the meaning that is conveyed.

Someone with real empathy is able to make the walls between us crumble. It's authentic. And it all starts with being interested in and caring about others.

Claude Grunitzky gets it.

He's the Chairman and Editor in Chief of *Trace*, an avant-garde magazine devoted to capturing the young energy of the streets and uncovering transcendent styles and ideas emanating from Tokyo to Rio de Janeiro, London to Paris, Mexico City to New York, Amsterdam to Johannesburg. Claude said his vision was and still is "to open a path for communication and collaboration between music and fashion, between high culture and street energy, and particularly between first-world and third-world communities." Not bad for a guy who started the magazine out of his bedroom in London in 1996.

After graduating from London University, Claude worked as a music journalist, but felt frustrated because he couldn't find a publication "that was really going deep into the emerging youth culture from a global perspective," the way he felt it should be done.

So this son of a Togolese ambassador to the United States, who speaks six languages, carries two passports, and grew up between the small African country of Togo, Washington, DC, Paris, and London, created his own underground publication. "I wanted to have a voice and be able to write for an audience that didn't have a venue," he explained.

"The most important thing I learned was to question everything I was being taught."

Moving between countries and cultures shaped his "transcultural" philosophy and fueled the creative energy that drives his ventures. "Growing up, I was always the new kid on the block. It gave me incredible opportunities to meet all kinds of people from all over the world and attend schools that were truly international. So I experienced different cultures, languages, and ways of thinking," he said.

Togo, which was once a French colony, had been a vibrant and peaceful tourist destination, but is now a tiny, poor country on the western coast of Africa. "It is currently being torn apart by tribal fighting,"

Claude explained wistfully, "and has lost the three major things that make people free: freedom of speech, access to education, and proper health care."

As a young child in school, Claude learned a combination of French and African history, and it wasn't uncommon for those versions of the truth to collide with each other. "It was very confusing," he said, "so the most important thing I learned was to question everything I was being taught." His confusion about what really happened in history became even more pronounced as he started going to school in America.

Claude says, "Moving from the sandy streets of Lomé, Togo, to the curvy tree-lined roads of Washington, DC's, Rock Creek Park neighborhood was a real awakening." As a seven-year old, he said half jokingly, "I inhaled America's culture from cartoons like *The Flintstones* and sitcoms like *Charlie's Angels*. And on weekends we were driven to other African embassies in a merry-go-round of African civility, but I was always asking for permission to sleep over at the house of my school friends Rodrigo Herrera-Vegas (from Argentina), Anthony O'Sullivan (from Ireland), and Amadou Thiam (from Senegal)."

All along, he kept questioning the official record and searching for his own way to explain the truth of what he saw happening around him.

That questioning led to his philosophy of transculturalism, which focuses on the qualities and accomplishments of certain people who manage to transcend their culture of birth. "It has to do with an openness and a desire to really learn from and become enriched by people from other cultures," Claude explained. "For individuals who are genuinely interested in people from other walks of life, this world has limitless possibilities."

As a result, his take on the world is slightly different from that of most executives in the communication business. In getting messages across to an audience, Claude explained, "age and attitude are what's important. What country someone is from doesn't matter as much. Their race and gender are becoming less important. Instead, mind-set and culture outweigh all those differences. And it's happening all over the world. In the future it will become increasingly difficult to identify and separate people according to previously accepted delineations."

He points out that many of our ways of describing the world are stuck in the past. Concepts such as nationalities, ethnicity, race, and minority group are becoming outmoded as, in his vision, he tries to uncover the connections and communicate in an authentic way beyond those outdated categories.

Claude's personal quest and professional goals are entirely in sync. "When I started this magazine, my mission—it seemed crazy at the time—was to reunite the seemingly conflicting cultures within my transcontinental travels. What that meant was that, for instance, Parisian photographers would be asked to shoot New York rappers of Caribbean descent while they were interviewed by British Pakistani writers." He was convinced this cross-cultural connection of the youth culture—with hip-hop as its driving force—would prove inspirational when presented to an international audience in a style that *The New York Times* called "visually striking and frighteningly cool."

This niche positioning of his magazine created opportunities that Claude had never even dreamed of. For starters, advertisers in his magazine came to him and asked if he could create marketing campaigns that would reflect the images and messages being conveyed by the magazine.

He figured, "Why not?" At first it was just an added revenue stream. Claude and his team would create visually stunning posters and then hang them up in unexpected places along the streets. They introduced these nontraditional guerrilla campaigns for Nike, Levi's, and Adidas.

That led to his starting a boutique advertising agency he called True, where he formed an alliance with Omnicom. One of their breakthrough campaigns was called Theater Jam; it was so unique that CNN covered it as a news item. Claude explained the concept: "When the movie *The Matrix* came out, we decided to plant actors in a theater and have them interact with the action on the screen. This was for our client, Nissan. So we had a woman on the screen say, 'Who are you?' Then an actor in the theater would stand up, maybe right next to you, and shout, 'I'm a meteor in the red hot sky!' Then the woman on the screen would say, 'What?' and another actor would pop up and scream something else outlandish. It would happen one more time, then on the screen would appear Nissan's logo with the phrase 'Shift Expectations.' It was a very, very different Nissan commercial, relying on call-and-response theater—and catching people unaware. It created a real buzz for our client, and we became known as a very different kind of agency.

We designed it for a client who was willing to take chances because they were trying to get back on the map and align with the type of person who was willing to take risks."

"To create compelling messages that resonate with your audience, you have to first empathize with them."

The ability to break through and connect with people in a way that they're not expecting takes exceptional empathy. Claude's varied life experiences helped develop his strong ability to read situations and understand other people's mind-sets. He explains, "In every country I've moved to, I went in as an outsider, but I always became an insider. The key is empathizing with the local cultures, understanding and appreciating their mentalities and habits. When you come to a new country and discover a new and different culinary tradition, musical culture, or fashion trend, you need to be open and accepting. And once you make that effort, people accept you more readily because they feel that you've gone out of your way to embrace their culture. And that's pretty much been the story of my life. I've always embraced new cultures, not just to try to fit in, but to really understand why people are different and, along with the differences, to find the commonalities between us." That is at the root of transculturalism itself.

What intrigues Claude most about advertising is blurring the line between what's real and what's not. "Most advertising campaigns seem disconnected from reality, created by people who live in a vacuum. We're not interested in creating ads that look like ads," he explained. "Audiences sense a fake a mile away, and most advertising is fake. To create compelling messages that resonate with your audience, you have to first empathize with them."

Throughout his travels, Claude has found that being empathetic is at the heart of being able to transcend cultures. It's one thing to empathize with your next-door neighbors about how their kids are doing in school. It's quite another to be able to understand what other people are feeling when you don't speak their language and are confused by their culture. That's when you find out how much empathy you really have.

"If you are genuine," Claude added, "people want to identify with you. You can feel that empathy with, say, Bob Marley. Even though he's been dead for a quarter of a century, he is still very current. His influence is immense. His identity is so strong that it transcends culture."

In many ways Claude is his father's son: an ambassador trying to create connections between disparate cultures.

He is searching for universal truths. Whether in music, film, fashion, or art, he is identifying styles, statements, and trends that are "unique, genuine, an authentic expression of identity," as he explained.

An authentic expression of identity. That's what transcends boundaries. And holds the hope of connecting us all.

CHAPTER

Competitiveness

Geoffrey Bodine, *winner of the Daytona 500, on coming back after a near-fatal crash because he didn't want to be replaced.*

Giving It Everything You've Got

COMPETITIVENESS IS ONE of those concepts we all grow up with. After all, who doesn't want to win?

Certainly that's what Vince Lombardi was all about when he declared, "Winning isn't everything; it's the only thing."

Ultimately, records are only broken during the heat of important competitions. Nobody gives their best performance when they're in training. Training just gets them ready for the arena.

But who are we really competing with? The current champ we'd like to replace? Ourselves? The ghost of someone who is there only vaguely, somewhere in the back of our minds?

Who do we need to beat? And what happens if we win? Is the competition ever over?

Ask Geoffrey Bodine, who has been honored as one of NASCAR's 50 greatest drivers.

He and Dale Earnhardt, Sr., two fierce competitors in the late 1980s and early '90s, had characters loosely based on their antics in the film *Days of Thunder*, starring Tom Cruise. We asked Geoffrey how that came about. "Well," he recalled, "Paul Newman, a racing enthusiast in private life, wanted to drive around the Daytona track in a stock car. He came by with this young actor he was mentoring named Tom Cruise. They both took my Grand National car around the track. Then we went out for dinner, and they said they were interested in making a movie about racing. They got me to tell a lot of stories and had me introduce them to other drivers and crew chiefs. We all had a great time. Then they asked if they could send some writers down to interview us. And we said, 'Why not?' Some of the movie ended up being based on the rivalry between Dale and me, but they also turned my character into a more attractive playboy kind of guy. Of course, the writers glamorize things."

At that time Dale and Geoffrey were drawing a lot of people into the stands who hoped to see those two aggressive drivers turn the race into a contact sport. "NASCAR didn't like the controversy that was brewing around us," Geoffrey said. "But the racetrack owners and promoters loved it."

Geoffrey shared one of his stories about the rivalry that made it into the movie.

"Dale wrecked me during a Sunday race at Charlotte, and the next day we each got a call from the head office at NASCAR, saying they wanted to see both of us immediately. We got our butts chewed out, and after the meeting one of the officials threw us a set of car keys and said, 'You two need to ride together to where we're going to have dinner. And by the time we get there, you better have worked things out.' Well, we were driving behind the NASCAR officials. I was behind the wheel, and Dale said to me, 'Go ahead. Give 'em a shot.' He was laughing his head off at the idea. He wanted me to bump into their car. I said, 'Are you crazy? We're in enough trouble. If *you* want to do it, I'll pull over and let you drive.' Then he calmed down and said, 'No. That's all right.'"

"Well," he continued, "the writers took that story and gave it their own twist. They put Dale and me in separate cars, and on the way to this dinner we started bumping each other until it escalated and we had completely wrecked each other's cars by the time we reached the restaurant."

That's celluloid.

In real life, on February 18, 2000, Geoffrey narrowly escaped a fiery nine-vehicle wreck in Daytona when his truck hit the wall at about 185 miles per hour and cartwheeled down the track in flames. The top of his vehicle was sheared off, the engine rolled down the straight away, pieces flew into the stands, and the truck's metal disintegrated until about all that was left of it was a roll cage—before it was hit again. And again. And again. On a video replay of the accident, even in slow motion, you can't count how many times that vehicle flipped over. The announcer assumed that Geoffrey was no longer with us.

In fact, Geoffrey had what he described as an out-of-body experience. He heard the first-aid medics trying to get him out of the vehicle. Then he had a vision of his father, who had died three years earlier. "He looked great and all that, and I said, 'Dad, I'm coming to see you.' And he said, 'No, it's not time. You have more to do.' And then he disappeared."

Geoffrey paused, then added, "So I was close. I was very close to not coming back." He smiled and shook his head, then said, "I really don't believe I spoke with my father."

No?

"I just believe this is how God speaks to us when he needs to. He uses someone you are familiar with and a voice you know. We don't know what God looks like, so he comes to us in a form we will recognize and tells us what we need to hear. So I clearly must have more to do."

Two months after the accident, Geoffrey was back behind the wheel. Why? What drives this guy?

His first explanation was, "I'm just competitive."

Okay, wait a minute. We've met chess players who are competitive. But they don't challenge death. Clearly, Geoffrey's got something else going on. What is it? Racing is one of the few sports in which competitiveness can be a matter of life or death. Isn't he afraid of death?

"No. I've been this close to death before," he said, holding his thumb and index finger about an inch apart. "I'm not afraid of dying. I believe we're all going to a better place eventually. I don't know what it is or where it is. But I'm okay with that. I've been in several accidents. You'd think they would have knocked some sense into me. But, chances are, I'll probably be in an accident again. Those are just the odds. It's just part of the game. You just can't let your fear slow you down. It's not like I'm out here challenging death. I don't want to die. But I'm not afraid of dying, either."

The top of his vehicle was sheared off, the engine rolled down the straight away, pieces flew into the stands, and the truck's metal disintegrated until about all that was left of it was a roll cage—before it was hit again.

What is it that keeps him going back?

He paused, then said, "I didn't want to be replaced."

What does he mean by that?

"That's my fear," Geoffrey explained. "Look, if you're off the circuit for two months, they'll find somebody to take your place. And that somebody could take your place permanently. So, yeah, you're in a hurry to get back in that seat so nobody else gets in it. That's the real fear for race drivers. That's why we'll drive even when we're hurt. We do that a lot. I've done it throughout my whole career. Just about every race driver can tell you, 'Yeah, I've driven with a broken this or a torn that.' We drive hurt all the time. I know eventually I'll be replaced, but I didn't want it to happen just yet."

So he got back behind the wheel even though he knew his equilibrium and peripheral vision weren't what they should be. If he moved his head quickly from side to side or up and down, it took a while for his eyes to catch up. But he also knew how to bluff his way past the doctors. "I wasn't fully recovered from the accident for about a year," he admitted.

When we met Geoffrey, the 57-year-old driver was at the Pocono Raceway, qualifying for an upcoming race.

Despite his calm, you could feel his excitement as the sound of revving engines became deafening.

"Right before a trial, I'm thinking about the track. I try to visualize going around the track, making whatever adjustments the car might call for," he said.

What could be wrong?

"At this point, even slight adjustments can make all the difference. There could be something wrong with the car's handling. The back end might not be gripping the track right, so you can't get the speed you need."

Today he will qualify based on time. It's just him and the car, the track and the clock. Tomorrow he will face the competition.

"A lot of people think that going around in circles is easy," he said. "But qualifying in a NASCAR cup race is one of the hardest things you'll ever do in your life."

How does the team fit into all this?

"The team and the car are one," he said. "Then the driver is out there by himself. While the driver gets the ultimate credit or blame, the car is actually more important than the driver. I can only work with the machine I have.

"For the driver," Geoffrey said, "it comes down to controlling your adrenaline. If you let your adrenaline take over, then you'll make mistakes. The driver has to keep everything under control, because mistakes change everything on the track. You need the adrenaline," he emphasized, "but you can't let it take over. To compete at this level, you've got to control your adrenaline."

For now, Geoffrey has to figure out if he can make the transition from driver to mentor. Life continues to challenge him. "I need to compete," he mused. "I want to be involved in racing in some capacity. Maybe it's time I helped other people who want to become drivers. Or maybe it will be something else with this sport. Or another sport."

Actually, he has already designed and financed the bobsled that is being used by the U.S. Olympic teams, an improvement which helped both the men's and women's teams win their first medals in that sport since 1957.

For Geoffrey the race goes on.

Always.

CHAPTER

Patience

Daisy Myers *on standing up to the Ku Klux Klan when they threatened her family.*

The Strength to Wait It Out

SOMETIMES THE WAITING is the hardest part.

It's usually easier to do something—*anything*. The sound of the clock ticking can drive you crazy. But, there are times, after you've done everything you can, when patience becomes the wisest course of action. And sometimes wisdom prevails.

It can remind you of Atticus Finch, the wise lawyer and father in *To Kill a Mockingbird*, who, after "unhitching his watch and chain," delivers his compelling closing argument, "walking up and down in front of the jury," and then "takes out his handkerchief and wipes his glasses," considering all the options as he patiently waits for the all-white male jury to return with its verdict and hopefully catch up with history and for justice to overcome centuries of prejudice and prevail. Then, even after the verdict doesn't turn out as he'd hoped, by the end of the novel, as he tucks the covers around his daughter, he is able to assure her, "Most people are real nice, Scout, when you finally see them."

Often after we've done everything we can to change a situation, patience is all we have left. By waiting for the tide to recede or for fate to play its hand, patience can sometimes change the course of human events.

Just ask Daisy Myers, whose family made history in 1957 by being the first people of color to move into Levittown, Pennsylvania. The Ku Klux Klan burned crosses, blasted racist music, picketed their house, threw rocks through her front window, and threatened her children for months even though the state police were sent in to protect them.

Daisy says the major quality that kept her and her family going through that ordeal was patience. "I'd wait for the night to become daylight because they were only brave when it was dark. Then we'd wait to see if they would be there again the next night. Throughout it, we just had to be patient. Just believe that everything would work out, sit tight, believe, and have a little patience," she explained.

That was not what Daisy and her husband, Bill, expected on August 13 when they moved into 43 Deepgreen Lane in the Dogwood Hollow section of Levittown, Pennsylvania. The family had outgrown their house in Bloomsdale, an integrated neighborhood less than a mile from their new home. They needed another room for their daughter, Lynda, who was just a month old, and their two sons, four-year-old William III and three-year-old Stephen.

They had no idea they would become part of history.

As Daisy explained, "We honestly thought that very little in our lives would change. We would still patronize the Levittown Shop-a-Rama for most of our purchases. We just needed a slightly larger place. Bill was particularly happy about the new garage. We never had one before. We also had a laundry room, another good feature for a family with three small children." She knew her husband would make the yard attractive and the children, who had been cramped by the small yard in Bloomsdale, would enjoy the ample play space.

They were moving less than a mile away, but they found it was really a completely different world.

It wasn't that Daisy and her family were totally unaware of the prejudice that surrounded them. They knew that being the first family of color to move into Levittown would cause a stir. "But to tell you the truth, we thought it would be more or less a neighborhood kind of thing. You know, like the neighbor across the street might not speak to you, or perhaps the family next door, or something like that. We had no idea it would become national news," she said.

But in that community of unassuming ranch houses that looked so much alike, many of the residents were afraid of change. "It was just some kind of psyche they built up within themselves that this was a white community and they wanted it to stay white. You know? And nobody challenged it," Daisy said. "It's like sometimes people make up in their minds that something is going to be this way, and it's going to stay this way because I say so. And I'm going to keep it this way, you know?"

Much of that attitude was perpetuated by William Levitt, the builder of the community, according to Daisy. She explained, "We knew, as everyone else did, that this new suburb called Levittown had been described as, 'the most perfectly planned community in America,' and was supposed to be lily-white. And, as far as we could tell, the builder, Levitt & Sons, intended to keep it that way. They made no secret of their policy of selling their new homes to whites only. Lawsuits had already been lost by families of color trying to buy new homes in both the New York and Pennsylvania Levittowns. But we also knew that in theory, if not in fact, as Americans we were free to purchase a home anywhere we wanted as long as we could pay the purchase price."

Between 1951 and 1957 Levitt & Sons built over 17,000 modestly-priced homes on eight square miles of Bucks County farmland. Levittown consisted of 27 sections with woodsy names like Dogwood Hollow, Indian Creek, and Vermillion Lane. As the local newspaper described it, "there were sparkling public swimming pools, steepled churches, large shopping centers, nice schools and ball fields, backyard barbecue parties and very little crime."

Levitt said his policy of refusing to sell to people of color was not a reflection of personal prejudice. In the local newspaper he said he was dealing with the realities of the housing market; selling to people of color would drive most of his white customers away. "This is their attitude, not ours," he said in 1954, three years before Daisy and her family moved into Levittown.

So the stage, or at least the mind-set, was set.

As Daisy and her husband were moving furniture into their new home, there was a knock at the door. It was the mailman, who asked, "May I speak to the owner?" Daisy replied, "I am the owner." She still recalls the look of fright on his face, "as if he had seen a ghost," she said. Then he handed her a letter, which was not registered, so there was no need for it to be hand-delivered. Crowds soon gathered across the street. Daisy noticed a man going from house to house with a paper in his hand, which she assumed was a petition.

Within an hour, she said, automobiles were creeping bumper to bumper down the street in front of their house. "I'd never seen anything like it, except maybe for rush hour on a busy New York street or a crowd leaving a ballpark," she said. "Brakes screeched frightfully. Drivers, moving slowly, stopped suddenly to stare and jammed traffic behind them. The crowds grew larger and larger. And, as they moved closer, tempers rose and we could hear their rumbling voices through our open windows.

"We telephoned the local police, the township manager, and the Pennsylvania state police again and again," Daisy said. "The state police said, 'It's up to the local police.' The local police said, 'The situation is being taken care of.' But it wasn't."

A photograph in the local newspaper showed a crowd of more than 200 people surrounding Daisy's house that night. One man had a bull-horn, some were waving their arms wildly, others waved Confederate flags, and most appeared to be jeering. Somebody in the mob hurled a rock that broke Daisy's picture window.

Finally, local police dispersed the crowd, arresting five people for disorderly conduct. One of those arrested shouted, "These niggers must have good lawyers to have the cops protect them."

For weeks after Daisy and her family moved in, the newspaper reported, "insurrection followed." The Bucks County sheriff cabled to the governor, "The citizens of Levittown are out of control." As the news-paper reported, "Levittown appears to be headed toward a race riot."

> **"Darkness seemed to make them feel stronger. Maybe they figured they could hide in the dark. I don't know. There was something in the darkness that made them fearless. Night was when they became most dangerous. They had to have darkness to hide behind."**

Daisy and her husband then decided to take their two sons to his parents' home in York because of a bomb threat. Since their baby was so young, they decided to keep her with them in what had become their new, and certainly dangerous, home. "If we were killed in the house," Daisy said, "at least Lynda would be too young to know." Then she paused and added, "I'd never thought much about my mortality, but here I was being forced to examine the meaning of life and death."

Throughout the next week the mob grew larger and larger. Daisy's phone rang constantly, even though her number was unlisted. Many of the callers were supportive, but some were threatening, like the one who asked if she knew what a Molotov cocktail was.

While the mob remained outside her house, Daisy and her family also made many new friends who would stay with them through the terrifying evenings.

On each side of Daisy and her family were two completely different groups. There were people who were supportive, and there were those who wanted them to leave. People were either with them or against them. There was a dividing line. And at that point in history, Daisy and her family became that dividing line.

The following week, Daisy's husband was approached on his job by the Bucks County assistant district attorney, who, Daisy said, "proposed to give us $15,000 for the house. That would have been a $3,000 profit. The man said that he represented a few interested people and that it could be a quiet deal. He said it would be best for all concerned if we accepted the proposition and moved away. The offer was presented in the tone of a mild threat, but Bill said 'no' firmly." By that time, Daisy said, the house had taken on a whole different meaning. It was like a fortress with people who were with them inside and those who were against them outside.

From time to time during the struggle, however, Daisy said, she and her husband thought about that offer to buy their house. "It took a lot of determination for us to stay there. I'll tell you that. A lot of determination. Because we were used to being just a quiet couple, focused on our family. You know? There wasn't anything outstanding, anything unusual about us. But we just finally said, 'We're going to stick it out.' There were a lot of people on our side who would come to our house every night. They would bring food and sit and talk and pray, and sometimes we would sing. One time our washing machine broke, and the next thing I knew, it was replaced. To this day I don't know who did it. They were just good, caring people. So how could we turn our backs on them after they did so much for us?"

Still, Daisy recalled, "My husband and I would sit on the side of our bed every night and talk about the very real possibility that we might not wake up in the morning. That was something to think about. You just didn't know. You didn't know if you would make it from one day to the next. You just hoped and prayed you would."

This was about the time when the chief of police suggested that they had communist backing, according to Daisy. This was while crosses were burned in front of the homes of neighbors who had befriended Daisy and her family and "KKK" was painted on the house of Daisy's next-door neighbor. Ku Klux Klan literature was being printed and distributed by members of a group that called itself the Levittown Betterment Committee. One of the leaflets had an illustration of a white woman being kissed by a dark, badly drawn Cro-Magnon man, with the headline "The Kiss of Death: Segregate the Negro or Lose the White Blood Forever," and another poster said, "Save Our Land for God and Country" and told people how to join the Klan.

Then a group that called itself the Dogwood Hollow Social Club rented a vacant house behind Daisy's and raised a Confederate flag on top of the roof. "They made as much noise as they could by blowing a bugle or singing, yelling, clapping, and playing records of 'Dixie,' 'Old Black Joe,' and 'Old Man River' at top volume," according to Daisy. "Newspaper reports estimated that 100 people frequented the house, including the mailman who had been so shocked to face me the day we moved in," she added.

Finally, on October eighteenth, two full months after Daisy and her family moved in, an impasse was broken. A man was arrested for painting "KKK" on the side of Daisy's neighbor's house. In court testimony later he said he had drawn lots with four other unidentified men to do the job. Then two more men were arrested and charged with conspiracy for making and transporting a cross that had been burned on the lawn of one of Daisy's neighbors. A week later the Pennsylvania state police filed a petition for an injunction, naming eight Levittown residents who had played key roles in the disturbances.

Their trial began on January 31, 1958.

Daisy said, "When we met those fanatical bigots face to face for the first time in the hallways of the courthouse, they appeared cowardly and retreating. Closing my eyes momentarily, I could see them in previous days and nights as frightening monsters. But in the courthouse they became trapped mice seeking the nearest hole in which to hide." During the hearing it was disclosed that 1,200 Levittown residents had paid a dollar each to join the Levittown Betterment Committee.

Although that first trial was declared a mistrial, a permanent injunction was finally granted on August 15, 1958—a year and two days after it all started. Daisy recalled, "We were finally assured a peaceful life in Levittown."

Thinking back on that long year so many years ago, Daisy shared, "You know, they didn't bother us during the daylight, and they'd leave us alone on Sundays. It was just when it started to get dark. Everything got worse at night. At night they'd come out. That's when they'd throw things at police officers. Paint the 'KKK' sign. Honk their horns. Do anything to create a disturbance. Darkness seemed to make them feel stronger. Maybe they figured they could hide in the dark. I don't know. There was something in the darkness that made them fearless. Night was when they became most dangerous. They had to have darkness to hide behind."

Through the darkness, you can imagine Daisy and her husband "just trying to stick it out," as she said. The courage and patience it took. How easy it would have been to do something. To strike back. To take the money they'd been offered and go someplace where they were welcome. But once they decided that this house meant something more to them, that they were involved in something bigger than themselves, that they were going to make a stand, Daisy and her husband had to find the strength inside themselves to wait for justice to prevail.

What surprised her most about herself during that long year?

"How patient I could be," Daisy said. "I never particularly considered myself as being patient before. But we learned how to sit tight, believe, and be patient. That's what got us through." They would wait for the night to become daylight because the mob was brave only when its members could hide in the dark. Then she waited for one day to become the next. That was how Daisy Myers and her family became a small but important piece of our history.

Daisy and her family stayed in their pink rancher in Levittown for five years. In 1962 her husband got a job as superintendent of the state finance building in Harrisburg, and they moved back to central Pennsylvania. He retired in 1986 and died of lung cancer a year later. "He was my best friend, and I miss him every day," Daisy said. Daisy went into guidance counseling and then into administration. By the time she retired from the York City school system in 1979, she was the principal of Ferguson Elementary School. Her children, she said, are all grown and successful and "have very few memories of what happened in Levittown."

Persuasiveness

David Oreck, *inventor of the famous lightweight vacuum cleaner, on bringing people around to your point of view.*

Getting Others to Buy In

PERSUADING INVOLVES TWO completely different strengths, which have to work together simultaneously. First there's empathy: the ability to tune in to someone else's perspective. Then there's *ego-drive*: a term Herb first used in an article he coauthored in the *Harvard Business Review* in 1964. The way Herb describes it, ego-drive is the motivation to get someone else to agree with you, to say "yes" to whatever it is you're selling or proposing.

To persuade others or win them over to your point of view, you have to first understand their particular perspective. Understanding where people are coming from can help you bring them along willingly, rather than by pushing them. If you start pushing, they'll either push back or you'll just push them away.

Persuading starts with listening. Not with what you want to say. True persuasion is different from the debates you see on Sunday morning talk shows when a liberal and a conservative banter back and forth about their take on some issue, person, or event. Most of the time, they're not even listening to each other. They're just waiting for a pause so they can jump in with their own point of view.

We'd be floored if the liberal on such a show paused and said, "You know, you've convinced me. I never thought of it that way before. I've changed my mind. I'm going to be a compassionate conservative from now on."

That's not what's going on. They're not even trying to persuade each other. They're debating.

Debating is not persuading. Persuading begins with an understanding of someone else's needs, particularly the unspoken ones. From there you can help that person see something in a different way—through his or her own eyes, not yours.

Persuasion is an art. Those who are best at it pull it off with great aplomb, providing solid information and real engagement.

One of the most persuasive people we've met is David Oreck. You undoubtedly recognize David from his ubiquitous infomercials where he tells us all how unseen germs in our houses can spread and cause illness; then he urges us to clean up our environment and protect our families with his incredibly light vacuum cleaner.

David believes that the three most wonderful words in the English language are "I'll buy it."

His approach to selling starts with listening to his customers. One recently asked him, "How can I get my teenager to clean his room?" At first David just laughed, but then he thought about it and designed an upright vacuum cleaner with an FM radio and headphones in the handle.

David started out selling RCA radios, phonographs, and televisions door to door. He rose very quickly through the ranks and was asked to accompany RCA's founder, David Sarnoff, to Washington, DC, where congressional hearings on setting technical standards for color television were being held.

He might have continued at RCA with enormous success, but David soon realized that he needed to be on his own.

In 1963 he established Oreck Corporation, based on his innovative breakthrough: the lightweight vacuum cleaner. However, from the start he had trouble breaking into the consumer market. There just was not any demand for a light vacuum cleaner at the time. In fact, back then he had to overcome the perception that heaviness meant cleanliness. Established brands made it difficult for him to crack that marketplace. Some distributors, while agreeing that his product was superior, suggested he make the vacuum just a little heavier so it would seem more substantial.

Instead, David took a backdoor approach.

He introduced his lightweight vacuum cleaner to premium hotels, where it made the jobs of people who were cleaning room after room all day long much easier. Then he began advertising directly to consumers, highlighting the fact that his lightweight vacuum cleaner was already being used to keep some of the finest hotels in the country clean. He said, "I could honestly say that my vacuum cleaner was being used in hotels where people were paying hundreds of dollars a night to stay." That tactic not only made the transition to the consumer marketplace easier, it also provided him with a unique positioning in the marketplace.

Around the time he was starting out, there was a company in Chicago called Ozite that was also introducing a new product: indoor-outdoor carpeting. It could be used almost anywhere you might imagine: on your porch, in a walkway, in a child's room—you name it. Once it was glued down, it was very durable. It could even be hosed down without damaging it. "But dirt clung to it like Velcro," David said. "It was a great innovation, but you couldn't really clean it."

David then explained, in great detail, why most vacuum cleaners require forcing air through the carpet to dislodge the dirt.

"But my vacuum cleaner, beyond being so light and easy to use," David explained, "works on a completely different principle. It only works as a vacuum in the space of a few inches, and then it becomes a dirt pump. And that is still one of its distinctions."

With enormous enthusiasm, he covered all the intricacies of cleaning a carpet. David takes cleaning very seriously. And when he gets going, there's no stopping him.

"Our vacuum had a very high brush speed, which I knew was needed to properly clean this new indoor-outdoor carpeting." So he went to Ozite unannounced, with his vacuum cleaner tucked under his arm.

"I walked up to the receptionist, whose desk was prominently placed on a dirty Ozite carpet, and said, 'Can I see the president?' And she asked, 'Do you have an appointment?' 'No, I don't.' 'Well, you can't see him.' 'Very well,' I said. 'Can I see the sales manager?' 'Do you have an appointment?' 'Nope.' 'You can't see him.' So I said, 'Well, then, do you mind if I show you my product?' She said, 'Have at it. Who cares?'"

At that point, we couldn't help asking if he pulled the old routine where the vacuum cleaner salesperson throws dirt all over somebody's carpet and then puts on a dazzling display of cleaning it up.

"No. No. I just cleaned the dirt that was already there," David assured us. "I just plugged the little thing in, and, in no time at all, I cleaned that carpet and got out dirt they didn't even realize was there. Well, the receptionist then excused herself for a moment, and damn if it wasn't long before the president came out with the vice president and the sales manager. They knew immediately that this was what they needed; I had solved the problem that was holding back their sales. They asked, 'Will you do a mailing to all of our distributors around the country and tell them about your incredible vacuum cleaner?' And I said, 'Would I? Sure!'"

That is the way it went at first, according to David.

The key was convincing people that they needed his product, but just didn't know it yet.

"Who are you? Who needs you? Eight pounds. Are you kidding? Get your toy out of here! I've got a business to run. And blah, blah, blah!" as David recapped, laughing at his beginnings.

For David, it was all about getting that first "yes."

"Whether you are offering a product or a service," he said, "success is all about persuading. You have to be able to sell your ideas—usually to people who haven't the faintest idea that they need them. Never underestimate the power of ideas. Ideas have started religions and nations." Then he added, "We've all heard that if you build a better mousetrap, the world will beat a path to your door. But that isn't true. The world has to first get the message."

David often is invited to speak at universities around the country, where he shares what he's learned over the past four decades, through trial and error, about entrepreneurship, brand building, marketing, and sales.

> **His advice to entrepreneurs is to identify a niche that plays to their strengths and is distinct from that of everyone else in the marketplace. Then own that. Bring everything you have to bear on that single point.**

He tells students that today, more than ever, many companies try to increase sales the quick and easy way; simply by cutting the price.

In David's opinion, this is an enormous mistake.

"First and foremost, you have to understand the worth you bring to your customers," he said. "This is not as simple as it sounds. It has little to do with price and everything to do with value."

How does he differentiate between price and value?

"Let me share some quick thoughts on pricing," he said. "The fact is, the prices of most similar products are usually not that far apart. And how can anybody make a profit if competitors merely undercut each other's prices? If your competitor drops his price, then you have to drop yours. After you've both done that a few times, you'll both be selling below cost. And then it's just a race to see who will go bankrupt first."

"A much better way," he added, "is to build a brand based on the superior benefits your customers receive: the best service, the most dependable parts, the strongest warranty, and that you stand behind what you deliver. That's what determines real value. And that value creates the best kinds of customer relationships, because they are based on trust."

This man, who has sold millions of vacuum cleaners, started his business in New Orleans after taking a flight from Chicago in the middle of one of the worst winters the Midwest had ever experienced. After landing in "this place with palm trees, a great breeze, and 72 degrees, I said to myself, 'I could live here.'"

He started the company regionally and built it market by market on the strength of his product and sales.

"I remember I had one salesman, besides me, who had the entire United States as his territory. He was a great guy, Bob Miller, who eventually retired with us. Anyway, the business grew a little bit, so I figured, well, we need another salesman. So I said, 'Bob, we're going to have to cut your territory. You'll have half the country, and the other guy will have the other half.' And Bob said, 'You're kidding me.' I said, 'I'll tell you what I'll do, Bob. I'll guarantee that with just half of the United States as your territory you will make at least the same amount of money, if not more, than you were making before. I guarantee you.' So he trusted me and said that was okay. And over the years, as the company kept growing, we would have the same conversation until he finally ended up with Cleveland. But every time I cut his territory and added a man, I said, 'I guarantee you'll make as much money if not more.' And he always did."

David is incapable of talking about his company without selling. It's just part of who he is. He can't help himself.

As he looks to the future, is he concerned that the company might not be able to grow beyond his image?

David said, "I was giving a lecture at the University of Georgia the other day, and I said to the students, 'Ask me anything. At my age you can't embarrass me. I'm more than willing to share with you anything I know. So just ask.' Well, one student hesitantly began, 'Well, you're in your eighties. And you are the sole spokesperson for the company. . . .' 'Let me help you,' I said. 'I think I know where you're going.' Then I said, 'I was a little concerned about that until a friend of mine, a biblical scholar, reminded me that Abraham lived to be 175. So, I figure, what do I have to worry about? I'm only middle-aged.'

"The fact of the matter is, yes, we have a persona, and yes, I am the spokesperson. But don't forget, we provide a phenomenal product with excellent service. I'm constantly hearing from customers about how pleased they are with every aspect of our company. And we work hard to maintain that consistently high level of quality. So, for now, I'll continue to be the person who speaks for the company. But I know the company is much bigger than me and is well positioned to carry on without me."

His overriding concern, and part of what he would like his legacy to be about, is overcoming the pervasive idea that dropping prices will somehow make selling easier. There is a point, he emphasized, of no return. "In today's throw-away society," David said, "you cannot compete by providing less value at less cost. That formula doesn't work anymore, particularly now that products and services are being built in and delivered from the far corners of this planet."

His advice to entrepreneurs is to identify a niche that plays to their strengths and is distinct from that of everyone else in the marketplace. Then *own* that. Bring everything you have to bear on that single point.

At the same time, his advice to consumers is to purchase on the basis of value.

But as the world becomes more global and quality and prices keep hitting record lows, there is that lingering feeling that David's advice might be a little out of sync with the swirl of forces that seem to be changing the world's economy.

He shrugs off such thoughts.

"There will always be consumers who want to have their expectations exceeded," David responded.

Then, without missing a beat, he added, with the certainty and ease of someone who knows why he's succeeded, "The fundamental things—value, service, and focusing on what you're good at—will always apply as time goes by."

CHAPTER

Confidence

Jeffrey Lurie, *Owner of the Philadelphia Eagles, on the attitude of a winner.*

Start by Acting Like a Winner

"CONFIDENCE IS THE BRIDGE connecting expectations with performance," according to Rosabeth Moss Kanter, a professor at the Harvard Business School and the former editor of the *Harvard Business Review*. In her book *Confidence* she noted that individuals with confidence view a loss as a "crossroads, not a cliff." Confident individuals make mistakes and encounter troubles all the time, without falling off the edge. Then, when they have winning streaks, their confidence grows and helps propel a tradition of success.

In the decade since Jeffrey Lurie bought the Philadelphia Eagles for $185 million, at that time the most anyone had ever paid for a professional football franchise, he has taken the Eagles from mediocrity to being Super Bowl contenders.

In the early years the mayor often criticized him, the fans were merciless, and *The Wall Street Journal* said he was making the biggest mistake of his life. Still, he promised change, installed a dynamic team, built a new state-of-the-art workplace and stadium, hired a new head coach, boosted the team's self-esteem, signed a new quarterback, gained the trust of the fans, and, ultimately, created a world-class team. Amid all the criticism and changes, the only thing that remained constant was Jeffrey's confidence.

So, where did this guy come from?

"I grew up in the entertainment business," he told us. "My family operated movie theaters and was also involved in publishing. At the time, we had the largest theater chain in the country and all of this expanded into other areas." His family was from Boston but moved to Los Angeles to produce movies and look for acquisition opportunities.

When Jeffrey turned 40, he started looking at the possibility of acquiring a professional football team. He said, "I definitely saw professional sports as a major part of the entertainment world and looked at owning a team as an investment opportunity, a chance to combine my business acumen, my knowledge of the entertainment industry, and my enthusiasm for sports. I understood the television business, and it seemed to me that broadcasting football games was like producing a hit movie every single weekend. And I felt this was just the tip of the iceberg in terms of the value of supplying a television network with hit programming."

First he tried to purchase the New England Patriots, which seemed like a natural, since he was from Boston. But that deal fell through. So he went after the Philadelphia Eagles and made a deal that held.

The very next day a front-page article in *The Wall Street Journal* said that Jeffrey had bought the Eagles on an emotional rebound from not getting the Patriots. Now, how many of us have had the Journal declare that one of our proudest moments was a colossal mistake? What kind of confidence does it take to shrug off something like that?

In the first few years Jeffrey had the fans and even the mayor challenging him on every decision. There were doubters everywhere. Some people even thought he was just waiting for the right moment to relocate the team to Los Angeles, since he had lived there and that city was without a professional football team. He assured everyone that he was staying in Philadelphia to create a Super Bowl team.

Most people just laughed.

"Everyone thought I was pipe-dreaming," he said, smiling. He paused, then said, "And at the time I was. But I just assured them and said, 'We've got to start by acting like a winner.'"

Back then the Eagles had a dismal stadium, conflicts with the city, and needed a new coach and a new quarterback. Somehow he had to convince the fans that the Eagles were no longer just another team that achieves mediocrity.

How many of us have had The Wall Street Journal declare that one of our proudest moments was a colossal mistake?

One of the first things Jeffrey realized was that the team needed a new stadium. "Veterans Stadium was probably the worst facility in the NFL," he said. "There were no windows, rats ran across the floors, the sidelines were poor, the elevators only worked occasionally, and there was no place for the head coach to meet with all 53 of his players at once." To many people, Jeffrey's calling for a new stadium seemed superfluous. To him, it was essential to attract a new head coach who would see that the franchise was serious.

Under Jeffrey's leadership, a new vision was being realized. A new training facility and headquarters for the Eagles, designed by Michael Graves, opened in March 2001. And a new $500 million stadium opened in 2003. These are a testament to the game, the team, the future, and Jeffrey's vision.

While the stadium planning was in full force, he hired Andy Reid as the team's new head coach. That choice was somewhat controversial because Andy was a little-known assistant coach from the Green Bay Packers. But Jeffrey and the Eagles president, Joe Banner, saw real leadership potential in the team's new head coach. Then, in a move that proved to be even more controversial, Jeffrey and his leadership team selected Donovan McNabb to be their quarterback in the 1999 NFL draft. The mayor even introduced a resolution in the city council to have the Eagles draft Ricky Williams from Texas instead of McNabb. Fans called radio stations and the Eagles' switchboard to express similar feelings. But Jeffrey, Andy, and the management team saw Donovan as a franchise quarterback, with the character, the maturity, and the steadiness needed to inspire their team.

The new stadium, the new coach, and the new quarterback all proved to be key points in the Eagle's turnaround. But none of them were popular decisions—quite the opposite.

"I wasn't aspiring to be the most popular owner. My goal was to build a winning franchise," Jeffrey said.

The business world is full of sports analogies about team building and coaching and the idea of winning. The analogies that make the most sense to Jeffrey concern team building. He explained, "I surround myself with people who are intent on achieving in whatever they're doing. I'm not interested in yes-people. This is not a game of follow the leader. I'm only successful when I am surrounded by a core group of high-achieving individuals who can focus all their energy and attention on the same goal. Then, together, we can defy the odds."

How did Jeffrey Lurie get to be so confident?

"That's a question that gets at the heart of who I am," he said. "The truth of the matter is that much of who I am has to do with the fact that my father died when I was very young. And he's the one who taught me the game of football."

Jeffrey was nine years old when his father passed away after a bout with kidney cancer. His father was one of the first experimental chemotherapy patients in the United States. "They did everything they could," he explained, "but there was no turning it around."

Growing up in the shadow of his father was "a complicated situation," as Jeffrey described it. "I was the oldest child, with a younger sister and an autistic brother. My mother had her hands full. For me, it was difficult to be the oldest male in the family at the age of nine. So I think what happened to me is that on the one hand I felt a heavy sense of responsibility, and on the other hand I felt a need for an escape. So I would try to be around for my mother. Then I would delve into sports and movies as my escape. In fact, my favorite movie of all time is *The Great Escape*, starring Steve McQueen."

There he was, nine years old, trying to be responsible and, at the same time, escape. "I turned my escapes into the dreams I wanted to fulfill," he said.

"From the age of nine on, you know, I've always valued life more because of what happened," Jeffrey explained. "When you see your father deteriorate and die so young, you are thankful just to be alive. And then you take your own life very seriously."

Jeffrey continued, "I grew up feeling certain about some things, but puzzled by others.

"Why did my talented, handsome, vibrant young father die so early? I still wrestle with that huge question. Yet there was no denying that he was no longer with us. That everything had changed."

He wanted to be there for his mother while, deep down, there was a longing to disappear into the movies he was watching. What kept him going?

Jeffrey sighed and said, "You know, part of my motivation—and maybe this is a partial answer, or maybe it's just a neurosis, who knows—but I really wanted to do something special to honor my father, whose life was cut so short, as well as acknowledge how great my mom was. I thought if I could be really successful, that would be a living testimonial to both of them. That's really been a driving force for me. It's like I've always imagined someday winning a championship. Personally I'd be thrilled beyond belief, but I'd also be grateful for the opportunity to fully credit my father and my mother for all they've done for me.

"The biggest challenge for me is to find and appreciate the balance," Jeffrey said. "No question. I'm sure my life could have gone in the opposite direction. When something as devastating as losing your father occurs, you can see yourself as a victim and expect that bad things are always going to happen. Or you can redirect your energy . . . you can take what happened and create something wonderful because of it. The loss of my father gave me an appreciation of the fragility of life. That is one of life's most important lessons. Part of my confidence and optimism is a direct result of the lessons I've learned from adversity. I know how short life can be, and that propels me."

CHAPTER

Passion

João Carlos Martins *on how, after losing the use of one of his hands, he still went on to perform a landmark Bach recital at Carnegie Hall.*

Sharing Your Intensity

WHEN YOU'RE IN THE PRESENCE of individuals who are passionate about what they are doing, you find yourself caught up in their intensity. They have an undeniable energy that fills a room. The fire ignited inside them catches on. And sparks fly.

Individuals with passion for what they are doing stand out because they are surrounded by people who are just getting by, putting in their time, feeling flat and not really committed to what they are doing.

Passion, which we identify with exuberance, comes, ironically, from *passio*, which means "suffering." Our passion comes from a depth of understanding of life's joys and sorrows and an appreciation that between our births and our deaths we each have, if we take advantage of it, a chance to make a difference.

Consider João Carlos Martins.

The last time João Carlos played a Bach concert at Carnegie Hall, *The New York Times* said there were fireworks in all directions. His passion for interpreting Johann Sebastian Bach was rushing through his entire body, his head shooting back, his hands flying off the keyboard, his audience in rapture. They even put 500 seats on the stage.

"I played as I never played in my life," he said. "Any time I go to the stage, I have to perform as if it were the last concert of my life. I have to play with all my passion. It's the only way I know how."

129

At the time of that last Carnegie Hall performance, João Carlos was regaining the use of one of his hands.

His story is about arguing with fate, abandoning his talent, and then embracing music with more passion than ever before.

In the early 1960s, when João Carlos Martins's first recordings of Bach became available, he was challenging the classical music world. His refreshing originality, daring technique, and youthful joyousness engaged many but offended others.

His energy captured the expanse of Bach's expressive heights and depths, conveying unbridled joy as well as debilitating sorrow. For conscientious clinical conservatory players, João Carlos was nothing less than shocking. He was coming into prominence on the heels of Glenn Gould, the enormously popular and deeply eccentric interpreter of Bach. Martins's and Gould's interpretations of Bach were so strikingly different that some referred to it as a Latin Bach and a Lutheran Bach. João Carlos explained, "I am from the south. My Bach is of crowds, warmth, pleasure, and virtuosity. Gould's is a northern Bach, one of intellectuality, solitude, but also ecstasy. Gould and I meet there. We are both ecstatics."

> **"Any time I go to the stage, I have to perform as if it were the last concert of my life. I have to play with all my passion. It's the only way I know how."**

As one of the foremost interpreters of Bach, João Carlos has a passion for the master that comes out as soon as he mentions his name. "Although Bach had hardly any formal education," he said, "I'm convinced that he had the highest human intelligence ever attained in any field and without the burden of translation." When he talks of Bach, time becomes suspended. For young musicians, João Carlos blazed a path to a new freedom in playing Bach, tapping into each interpreter's passion. "Instead of a trip back to the eighteenth century, I invite Bach on a trip to our century. So I play my personal way, but, of course, always respecting the text."

By the time he was 21 years old João Carlos knew by heart every note Bach had ever written for the keyboard. "If I were to start playing his complete works for you now . . . let's see, it is two o'clock on Thursday. I would finish at four o'clock in the morning on Saturday."

When did he know that Bach was his passion?

It all started when he was six years old. He had surgery on his neck, but it didn't heal correctly, so he withdrew and became reclusive. His father bought a piano to see if he might be interested in learning music. From that moment on, all he wanted to do was play the piano. Six months later, João Carlos won first prize in a Bach competition. A decade later, he attended the Pablo Casals Festival in Puerto Rico and was selected to perform the prize-winning recital in Washington, DC.

Flash forward 10 years. "When I was 26 years old," he said, "my life was better than any dream I could possibly imagine." He had just performed at Carnegie Hall to rave reviews. While he was there, Brazil's top soccer team was in New York for a competition. He got together with the team and trained with them in Central Park. "Every young Brazilian wants to be a professional soccer player," he explained. "And here I was, fulfilling two childhood dreams at the same time."

Then he fell.

"One morning we were practicing, and I slipped. So I threw my arm back to break my fall," he explained.

And he landed the wrong way. He ruptured a nerve and lost the movement of the fingers in his right hand.

Surgery and physical therapy could only help a little.

"I was so angry," he said. "At myself. At the world. At life. At God. Why did I have to play so hard with Brazil's professional soccer team? What was I trying to prove? That I was invincible?"

At that point, he couldn't even look at a piano.

"I fought with everything and everyone. I got divorced. My life was a mess," he recalled sadly.

Then he sold every one of his pianos. And didn't play another note.

He couldn't even be around a keyboard. "If I went to a bar and a pianist was playing, I'd just walk out," he said.

Still, there were times when he couldn't go to sleep because he knew something was missing from his life.

He entered the world of boxing and became a manager. Then one of his fighters, at the age of 37, won back a title he had previously held and something in João Carlos clicked. "If he could do that, so could I," he said, at first just to himself.

He bought a piano and started practicing again with his usual ferocity—after being away for seven years.

As he started to regain his agility and his confidence, João Carlos called his former manager, who was more than a little surprised to hear from him, and said, "Get me Carnegie Hall, because I want do to Book I of the *Well-Tempered Clavier.*" His manager was encouraging, but suggested they take it one step at a time.

One year later, João Carlos was backstage at the great hall.

"It was the night of my life, and I played as I had never played before," he said with an enthusiasm that filled the room. The audience applauded for 12 minutes after he was done. Then the lights blinked to indicate the concert was over.

"I love challenges, and if I'm challenged, I have to do a killing. Like a matador in the bull ring," he said.

That night he decided to record everything Bach had written for the keyboard. But he knew he had to pace himself.

"I gave only a few concerts from 1979 until 1985," he said, "but every concert had a certain kind of drama and passion. I performed several times at Carnegie and Avery Fisher Hall. I never went for small change. I always went into the mouth of the lion."

For six years, he was reaching deep inside himself and interpreting Bach on a heightened level of exaltation.

Then he started to lose mobility in his fingers again. From the years of playing 8 to 12 hours a day, João Carlos had developed repetitive strain injury.

He had no choice but to slow his pace and undergo more physical therapy. His hands could no longer keep up with his thoughts: The connection was gone. He couldn't play at the level he was used to. "I just couldn't control my hands," he said. He stopped playing . . . again. For what became another seven years. He figured his life had to go on, so he started a construction company, which became very successful.

It looked as though his project of recording the entire Bach literature would have to fade away. It was the second time in his life he had abandoned music.

Then he was mugged in Sofia, Bulgaria. "I was hit with an iron bar and suffered a brain hematoma. My right hand was paralyzed, along with the entire right side of my body. I was in total despair," he said.

But he said to himself, "I will not stop this time."

"I felt I needed to return to music. For my soul," he explained.

For eight months he stayed at one of the most sophisticated computerized biofeedback labs in the world, where he worked 16 hours a day to regain his grace, speed, and agility. "I was driven to return to the stage and perform again," he told us. "And I had to complete my recording project."

"In order to play the piano again, I had to make certain tough choices," he said. "For instance, rather than work on the muscles that would allow me to hold a fork or a cup of coffee, I focused on those which enabled me to play the piano with full force. That was my trade-off. But it was an easy decision because of my overriding passion to return to playing Bach."

However, while his proficiency at the piano was improving, his health was failing. "It was getting so bad," he said, "that they told me I had to make a decision. You can either have quality in your life or you can play the piano, then simply stay in bed and recover."

So, he thought about it, then said, "Let me finish recording all the Bach keyboard works," which he did. "Then," he added, "I want to have one farewell concert," which he did with the Royal Philharmonic Orchestra in London.

As soon as he finished the concert, he took a plane to Miami, where surgeons cut the nerve that was causing him such pain. "And then I knew I could never ever play again, at least not with my right hand. Because with the nerve cut, although I no longer have the unbearable pain, I still have the spasm."

So he has a spasm in his right hand, but not the pain.

Still, he has come to the realization that he will never abandon music again.

"When I count everything, I have been out of music for a total of 16 years," he said. "Those are years I can never retrieve. But they have somehow also helped to make me who I am."

Shortly after his last operation he decided to continue his recording and performance career, playing with just his left hand. His projects included, of course, finishing the complete works of Bach. He even recorded a CD called *For the Left Hand Only*.

"What drives my passion?" He paused, then said, "I believe I have a debt with God. Why? Because God gave me a talent. And early on it was too easy for me. But I didn't have the right to abandon the piano just because it became tough." Now when he plays, he sees that it is even more of an inspiration for people. "They are touched in a very real way because of all I've been through. We can all relate to that. And celebrate the passion to persevere," he said.

"I approach Bach with such passion because, to me, he is life. While his work is full of mathematical aspects, he is a true romantic. And throughout my life he has taught me that I should never again abandon my talent. Whatever happens, I will never again abandon music. I walked away twice and wasted too much time. Now I have the courage and maturity not to give up my art. I know it is worth pursuing with all I have, with every ounce of my passion. How could I give anything less?"

When he plays, the passion flows through his entire body. His long hair flows from side to side, his shoulders undulate, and his hands fly across the keys. His story of public acclaim and private tragedy, of traumatic injury and obstinate recovery, is an astounding triumph over adversity, the ultimate test of who he is and what he is made of.

If Bach indeed touches the divine, then João Carlos, through his endurance, fortitude, and passion, gets us all a little closer.

Just listen.

Integrity

Connie Jackson *on finally hearing her own voice.*

Are You True to Yourself?

HOW HONEST AND TRUE we are with ourselves gets at the very essence of who we are. But, it is one of the most difficult challenges we'll ever face, because there are no road maps. We only have our own internal compass, and we can fool ourselves very easily.

First of all, there are those little tapes we play inside our heads. They have messages that someone else might have put there purposely or accidentally when we were kids. Or they may be tapes we've created for ourselves that have gotten us through certain situations but no longer get us where we need to be.

Can we sort through all those dissonant voices to get at the heart of who we really are?

The psychoanalyst Erik Erikson considered integrity to be the ulti-mate stage of identity. He defined it as "the quality of being complete or whole."

That sounds like the end of the journey, but it's really the beginning. It's the place we all want to get to in order to succeed on our journeys.

We often find out about our integrity when it is tested. Those tests get at the very heart of who we are.

Discovering whether we have any cracks in our integrity starts with being open to asking ourselves some very tough questions.

Can we really be honest with ourselves? That's probably part of the eternal appeal of Shakespeare's Hamlet. It's his search to uncover the truth, his ceaseless questioning, that may, in fact, be driving him mad.

Do we have the courage to question who we are, what we are doing, and where we are going?

Can we ask those questions without letting ourselves off the hook? Are we willing to take a risk and do something completely different with our lives because we've discovered something about ourselves that we didn't know before?

Thoreau told us that we have to examine these things. But it's easier to have one of his phrases knitted on a pillow than it is to really question who we are.

How do we get at those questions? Know which ones to ask? And answer them honestly?

For some of us, it takes having our world turned upside down in order for us to ask ourselves the tough questions. For others, we are able to ask them first and then turn our world upside down. The best way to start is to pay attention to the quiet voice that whispers something incomprehensible just before we fall asleep.

Connie Jackson knows about the questions and about her world being turned upside down.

When she was heading up a health care clinic in Chicago, Connie realized she was becoming disillusioned by politicians who were unwilling to fight wealthy health care interest groups and help people who were really in need. No, she wasn't just disillusioned—she was starting to get ticked off about it. She'd find herself talking about the nation's need to reform health care even if she and a friend were having a conversation about the transit system or the weather. Her passion was driving her, but as she said, "I was getting sick and burned out because I saw no signs of change." She needed to find a new way to make a difference.

Connie's story is about discovering who she was, questioning whether she was just doing what she thought someone else wanted her to do, then finding a way to carve her own path and be true to herself.

Are we willing to take a risk and do something completely different with our lives because we've discovered something about ourselves that we didn't know before?

It begins with her working on Wall Street at a two-year position with Credit Suisse First Boston. Even before she started, she had a solid game plan to go on and obtain an MBA from Harvard. "I was a classic overachiever," she said, thinking back. "Work always, always came first. I remember once when my mother came to New York for a conference. She was in town three days, and I didn't see her until the last one. We talked on the phone every day, but I didn't see her until she was leaving. She actually came by my office. And then we went to dinner and I took her to the airport." She paused, then added, "I would never do anything like that now because you just can't take for granted that you'll see your mother next time. I know now that life doesn't always work that way."

Her plans seemed to be working out, as she was accepted to Harvard.

She was doing very well, on track for her next career move, when in her last semester, while she and her husband weren't necessarily planning it, she became pregnant.

Then her pregnancy became complicated. Connie found herself in the hospital, fighting for her own life, losing the baby. That's when her world was turned upside down.

During the six weeks in which she recovered from the emergency, she realized she had to drop out of the program at Harvard. There was just no way for her to make up the case method work. And as tragedies sometimes have a way of getting worse before they get better, she and her husband decided to divorce.

Everything in her world had changed.

"It was the worst I could imagine," she said, then added, "Actually, I never imagined anything that bad. And it all crashed in at once."

She decided she needed to change her landscape.

She moved back to Chicago, where she had grown up, to sort things out, to rethink everything.

Connie knew she wanted to go back to school, but she needed some time. She also knew she did *not* want to go back to Wall Street. "While I loved the work, I didn't like what it was doing to me, who I had become," she said.

She wound up working in local government for The City of Chicago before returning to Harvard to finish the MBA program. She also spent several years working on partnerships in both government

and the private sector, and served as Finance Director for Carol Mose-
ley-Braun when she was a senator from Illinois.

It was during that time that Connie became more focused on the
health-care crisis. And when she became ill, as an aide to a senator, she
was even more certain that the solution was unlikely to come from the
highest elected officials in Washington, DC.

"The representatives in Congress will never understand how people
in need feel about health care," she said, "because our representatives
are completely insulated from the problem. They have an unbelievably
generous health plan themselves, so they're never going to get it in the
way it needs to be understood. That understanding is where change
begins."

Connie had a personal experience that brought that point home. "I
got sick once at a staff meeting, in the office, and they whisked me down
to the infirmary, where two people met me and checked my vital signs
before the ambulance arrived and whisked me off to the medical center
at George Washington University. And the head of the emergency
room met me while I was still in the ambulance and personally super-
vised the care of my illness, which turned out to be a chest infection. It
was nice to be treated so special, but my condition didn't warrant that
kind of attention. I only received it because I worked for a senator."

Shortly afterward, Connie headed up The Clinic in Altgeld, a social
service organization that her mother, a physician in Chicago, founded
to provide health care to people in several public housing develop-
ments. Connie said that taking that position represented her coming
full circle. "It was actually the complete antithesis of what anybody who
knew me thought I would ever end up doing," she explained. Everybody who knew her thought of her as a financial type, but she was moving beyond that, completely changing direction. "What I learned is that
money isn't everything. It took me a while to get that," she said, "which
is kind of funny, because I was raised with solid, progressive values. My
parents would never cross a picket line. They were very focused on
social concerns, very left of center. And here I was, definitely right of
center, as a young woman, thinking things like, 'Those poor people; it's
their own fault.' I guess you always have to break away from your parents to forge your own ideas, then come back and take the things that
work for you and go forward."

For a while, heading up the center was challenging and fulfilling. She was introducing new technology, moving to a new building, creating new systems for patient management, and delivering more services to the patients.

But the constant struggle to keep things going was exhausting. Clinics everywhere were caring for more and more patients with fewer and fewer resources. All around her the signs were bleak. Several hospitals in Chicago had to file for bankruptcy protection. Still, no one was promoting a comprehensive plan to provide health care for people in need. And she saw that need growing daily, with no end in sight.

Connie felt trapped in a maze, trying to find a solution, suspecting there wasn't one.

It started to feel like she was just "shuffling deck chairs on the *Titanic*," Connie said. If she had little faith in the system changing when she was working for a progressive senator, she had absolutely no reason to believe that the current conservative administration would look twice at people in need of health care.

Then, rushing back to Chicago after attending a conference, Connie collapsed in the St. Thomas airport. Fortunately it wasn't anything serious, but it made her pause and think about her life and where she was heading.

Connie said, "I was turning 40 and realized I needed a break." No, not just a break, or even a long vacation. A total change. "Like many firstborn children, there were many times in my life when I've done things that people thought I should do, instead of what I really wanted to do. In many cases I even lied to myself, saying, 'Well, why not? It's probably a good idea. I guess I should do this, whatever.' During the first half of my career work had always been the most important thing in my life. My life was completely out of balance."

Then she started asking herself questions: "What do I really want to do?" "Where do I want to do it?" and "Were there decisions I've made that I wish I could reverse?"

She had completed a graduate program at the London School of Economics after graduating from college. She recalled wanting to stay in London after the program, but she had a job and a fiancé waiting back in the States. A voice inside her said it was time to get serious and responsible. But where was that voice coming from? Was it hers? Her parents's? A teacher's? Or just something in the air? What did it sound like, this adult voice of reason, which, at the time she didn't even consider arguing with?

Finally, Connie thought about it. "Why didn't I just stay in London back then? How would my life have been different if I'd listened to myself? Listened to what I really wanted to do?"

She couldn't go back in time, but she could go back to London.

This new voice—she knew was hers. It wasn't the voice that said, "You better get home if you don't know what you're going to do. You need a plan, Connie. Where's your plan?"

"So," Connie explained, "I took a sabbatical to think about it." She was awarded a mid-career fellowship to finance her year in London, where she did independent research in health care policy.

"It was really about following my instincts and trying to stay grounded in myself, which was something that I thought I knew but had never really done before. A lot of times you don't listen to your own voice because the people you respect say things that seem to make a lot of sense, and you say, 'Well, they care about me. They're smart. What they're saying makes sense. I guess I should do that—whatever "that" is.' But I came to realize, for the first time in my life, that nobody can make a better decision for you than you. Even if it's the wrong decision, it's still your decision."

Connie added, "I needed to sort through those voices and figure out which one was mine before I took my next job." It was tough, she confided. A lot of people who cared about her kept asking, "What are you doing? How much longer are you going to be there? What are you going to do next?"

And she'd simply say, "I don't know."

Connie remembers telling her mother, "I'm going to renew and reflect and see where the road leads. I can't tell you anything more than that. And I hope you will not ask me this question anymore until I know where I'm going, because you are making me nervous."

In her book *Working Identity: Unconventional Strategies for Reinventing Your Career*, Herminia Ibarra, a Harvard professor, conducted a study of people making major career changes. She found it usually takes between two and five years from the time people get a nagging feeling that they're not doing the right thing until they make a major change.

A lot of those changes come after major life events such as the death of a parent, turning 40, and divorce.

For Connie it took only 18 months. Always the overachiever.

She reflected, "There were times when I thought, 'This is the stupidest thing I have ever done.' Particularly as I watched my bank balance go down and down. I was living in a glorified dormitory and walking down the hall to an unheated shower in order to afford to live in London. But I am so glad I did it. I am very glad about the choices I made. What I learned was to listen to myself and to recognize my authentic voice. So I was glad that I was brave. But it was scary. At times, very scary.

"Obviously the whole thing could have gone pear-shaped," she said hesitantly. "But it didn't. My backup plan was to go home. I mean, what's the worst thing that could happen? It's not like I was going to be homeless or whatever. I knew I could always go home. So the risk was to discover and be sure of my own voice."

Connie is now sure that the experience not only helped her get in touch with herself but helped her become a better leader. "I think one of the most important things about leading is that after considering all the options and listening to all the opinions, you still have to follow your own voice. And you have to know your voice. A lot of time leadership means going where no one has gone before. It takes stepping out there and following what you think is the right path," she said.

That path led her to become the Chief Executive of St. Bartholomew's and the Royal London Charitable Foundation. In this position she manages the charitable assets of three of the oldest hospitals in London, dating back to 1123.

"It's very interesting because half of my job is very corporate, investing approximately £200 million in assets. And the other half of my job is to give between £10 million and £15 million of income away to the hospitals and organizations that care for the hospital's patients, which is very fulfilling," she explained.

Her past and her present have come together in London, which, for her, is the crossroads of the world's eastern and western hemispheres. She appreciates the city's outward-looking view. But her journey there was made through her own inward view.

For young women in particular, Connie said, "I think one of the most important lessons is learning to know themselves. I think it's unfortunate that often we don't really know who we are until much later on in our lives, primarily in our thirties. And we wind up interviewing with companies and taking jobs in our twenties, where we let them interview us. We don't interview them. I know I worked for two companies where it was a total mismatch, but I didn't understand it initially, and so I was trying to fit in. This was back in the era of floppy bow ties and starched shirts. And a lot of us were trying to turn ourselves inside out to fit in. I was so busy thinking, 'Will they want me?' instead of 'Do I want them?'"

She paused, then added, "The important thing is to get more in touch with who you are and stop trying to change yourself to fit into someone else's mold. That's the lesson that took me so long to learn. That succeeding has to do with being true to yourself."

Trust

Gordon Gund, *the Founder of Gund Investment Corporation,*
on losing his sight and finding trust.

Putting Your Faith in Others

TRUST IS AT THE HEART of any relationship that is working. Can you depend on someone? If you were in a tough spot, would
that person be there for you? You might trust someone's ability, but do
you trust that that person would keep your confidence? That he or she
would back you, no matter what?

Trust removes all doubt in a relationship.

Gordon Gund, the former Owner of the Cleveland Cavaliers and the
Owner of Gund Investment Corporation, has to trust the people and
organizations he invests in whether they're in sports, business, health
research, or his personal relationships.

He has given a great deal of thought to the importance of trust since
losing his sight at age 31. Now, just going for a walk involves trusting
someone. He's trusting that person to be his eyes. Will that person
watch out for him? Let him know when he's approaching a step? Make
sure he doesn't trip over a curb? Or bump into a wall? Will he or she
pay close enough attention to keep him from getting hurt?

"I remember when I first became blind, one of the basic things I had
to come to terms with was the importance of trust—on a very deep level.
And, in my case, that also means being willing to accept help from other
people, which isn't easy when you're used to being independent. It took a
long time for me to let down my guard and allow others to help me. But
it's a very important thing for all of us. And you learn that it can also mean
a great deal to the people who are helping you. Whether you have a dis-

ability or not, the truth is that the most amazing friendships often get to be even stronger when we help each other. And that takes real trust."

Gordon's lessons about trust abound. They include trusting his instincts about people, trusting doctors to find cures, trusting researchers to break new ground, and, most of all, trusting his friends to understand.

Trust, he's learned time and time again, is at the center of any real relationship, business or personal.

Gordon's trust was shaken when he learned after graduating from Harvard, where he played hockey, after serving as an officer in the U.S. Navy, and while then working as a bank loan officer that he was losing his sight. He had absolutely no idea he had a hereditary condition that was affecting his vision. "I thought my peripheral vision might be fading, but I wasn't sure, because we only know what we see. We don't have anything to compare it to. Particularly the way they used to test your eyesight, with a chart across the room. You know, asking, 'How many lines can you read?' And my vision was very good in the central acuity sense."

Then he started to lose his night vision, and he had to give up driving after dark.

At that time he was a lending officer at Chase. "I really enjoyed meeting entrepreneurs and learning how they thought and deciding whether we wanted to invest in their projects," he said. He remembers the time he was taking a customer out to dinner, and when he walked into the dim restaurant, his eyes could not adapt to the lack of light. "All of a sudden I was blinded," he said. "And I bumped into a waitress, who was carrying a tray full of food." He paused, then added, "That was embarrassing. But it made me realize I had a problem." During the day he could still drive an automobile and even fly a plane, but he knew something wasn't right.

He went to his family doctor, who sent him to an ophthalmologist. Then he discovered that he had retinitis pigmentosa, an incurable hereditary disease in which the retina slowly loses the ability to transmit images.

> **"Whether you have a disability or not, the truth is that the most amazing friendships often get to be even stronger when we help each other. And that takes real trust."**

Five years after the diagnosis his vision started to fade quickly. "You could almost see it getting worse," Gordon said. He had visited all kinds of specialists, but none held out any hope. Then he heard about an experimental treatment in Russia that didn't have much of a scientific basis but offered a glimmer of hope. "I figured it couldn't hurt, and I might as well try everything," he said.

That was in 1970, at the height of the Cold War. As one last hope, he had to place his trust in the unknown. He was trusting in a medical procedure from a country that our country didn't trust.

He got a visa and with his useful vision gone by then, he went off on a final hope of regaining his sight.

One of his brothers, who is an architect, had been over to Russia the summer before, so he accompanied Gordon on the way over. But his brother could only stay a week. This was in November. By that time Gordon's sight, which had been rapidly closing in, went from a narrow tunnel vision to no vision at all.

They flew into Moscow, then went inland to Odessa on the Black Sea, where one of that country's top eye institutions claimed to be having success treating Gordon's disease.

He thought he would be there only a few days, then head back with his brother. As it turned out, he stayed six weeks as a patient in the hospital, where no one else spoke English and he didn't speak a word of Russian. His brother had to get back. But Gordon trusted that it would be worth it to stay for this one last chance.

"In this run-down, decrepit old mansion," he said, "I received 10 to 12 daily injections, sometimes in my temples. Most of my family and friends couldn't understand why the dickens I was over there," he said. "There was a lot of suspicion because it was at the height of the Cold War. But I stayed."

As it turned out, the treatment didn't make a bit of difference to his sight.

What it did do was allow him to hit rock bottom in a foreign land. "I had nobody around who knew me, and that was probably a good thing. There was no one for me to complain or whine to. I really just had myself to talk with about it—and to figure out what the rest of my life meant. So this time, by myself, surrounded by people who couldn't understand or help me in any way, turned out to be really important to me," he said.

He was completely alone in the dead of winter, in one of the coldest places on earth. A stranger in a very strange land. And his world had changed completely. Now absolutely nothing, was familiar. No one could understand him and he couldn't understand them. "I couldn't even get anybody to tell me where the bathroom was—or to understand what I was asking," he said.

For six long and lonely weeks, he struggled to come to terms with the realization that there was no longer anything he could do about losing his sight. His fight was over. "I had to get basic with myself. As hard as that was, I attribute it to changing my life," he said.

What could have been going through his head all that time?

He allowed himself to feel sorrow. And anger. And to ask questions that had no answers, such as "Why?" He would never be able to see a sunrise or a sunset again. Or see his children as they grew up. Or move about independently. "It is very frustrating and traumatic to lose your sight," he said. "And it was a drawn-out kind of thing where I didn't know from day-to-day if I'd wake up and not be able to see. I didn't know how long this gradual-to-total loss would go on. I remember finally saying, 'Let's get this over with so I can get on with the rest of my life.' It wasn't that I wanted to lose my sight. I just couldn't take this prolonged agony."

Then, in that very distant, cold, foreign place, he said, "I finally got it. I realized what mattered most to me—and that's the people I love. My family. My wife and our sons in particular. And my friends." He and his wife Lulie were married four years earlier. "She hadn't bargained for this," he said. "Here it was, at the tail end of 1970, and we had two young sons. One was only two-and-a-half years old, and the other was only a couple of weeks old. I saw our youngest child in the delivery room and then for a week or so later. I could scan him with my tube sight, just before I could no longer see. But that's very important to both of us, that we saw each other. Then what really became clear was that I also believed that I wanted to contribute in a real, meaningful way. I came to terms with the fact that my life wasn't going to be like I thought it would be. But that didn't mean I couldn't still be who I was. I couldn't see, but otherwise nothing was wrong with me. Sure, it was going to require some different ways of doing things. What mattered, though, was that more than anything else I wanted to be there for my wife and my children."

Although the treatment in Russia didn't restore his eyesight, Gordon said, "It was really, for me, very important that I ended up there. I came back with a sense that I really had a lot to live for. And I wanted to."

"I had to get basic with myself. As hard as that was, I attribute it to changing my life."

What Gordon has learned about trust also informs the decisions he makes at the helm of Gund Investment Corporation, where he does "venturing, more or less on an ad hoc basis," as he explained with characteristic modesty. Among his more notable investments have been the Cleveland Cavaliers and the Minnesota North Stars. "Unlike other venture firms, we don't raise huge pools of funds. Instead, the source of our funds is money I've made through the years. This way, we keep it a small operation, but I'm happy to say we have seen some very nice successes by taking only a few investments and being actively involved in them."

Another venture capital company that he and his wife helped to begin is the Foundation Fighting Blindness, "which invests in researchers who have new ideas and provides seed money so that if and when the idea shows sufficient progress, the National Eye Institute might pick it up," he explained. He is particularly enthused about some of the new discoveries coming out of the laboratories that the Foundation Fighting Blindness has had a part in funding, which, he said, "have reached a proof of principle, though they are a long way from actually being made commercially available." Still he cautions, "You have to keep in mind that for every 100 sound approaches that come out of the lab, maybe five will make it into clinical trials and maybe one of those will make it all the way to the marketplace. So the risks are huge." Right now the Foundation is funding several laboratories that are taking very diverse approaches to curing different forms of blindness.

"Finding a cure for blindness," Gordon said, "is the most significant thing I am involved in, because if, as I believe we will be, we are successful, it can really change the face of the world. For all time. This is extremely important for me."

Does he think any of these possible cures could help him?

"While I don't dwell on it, I still harbor hope for myself," he said. "I think the retinal chip could help once it is improved and becomes safe.

There are also groups working on brain implants, which allow images to be beamed in electronically, directly to the brain's vision center. And there are also some exciting gene therapies emerging. It is really a great time for research."

Gordon has learned to take trust to an entirely new level: on top of ski slopes. Before he lost his sight, in 1965, he drove across the country, stopped in Aspen for a month, and learned to ski.

Then, after he became blind, he decided he didn't want to give up skiing. "I had to prove to myself that I could do it. I needed to push myself like I never had before. It was like learning to ski all over again. I can't tell you how nervous I was the first time," he said.

Ever since, he's been skiing with the same instructor, Dave Elston. "When we start a run, Dave will brief me on the snow conditions and tell me how crowded the trail is," Gordon said. "Then I just point the skis downhill and go. And I get to feel it. I can feel the mountain. While we're skiing, he's about five feet behind me, and he'll say, 'Go,' every few seconds just so we're in touch. If I'm getting a little off, he'll just say, 'Hold right or hold left.' But he doesn't tell me when to turn—only if there is an obstacle or someone in my way. Within a certain envelope of space, I can be free and do my own thing. For me, skiing is one of the few times I don't have to hold on to anyone. I can move *fast*, unimpeded. It's an incredible sense of freedom." His smile kept growing as he reflected, "I ski better now than before I lost my sight. Without sight, you develop a keener sense of touch and feel. You have to rely on your other senses. And you also need to have more trust in yourself. Being blind has really taught me how to trust—on so many levels. And that is really the ultimate freedom." He paused, then added, "I love moving through the air and feeling the sun on my face: all the things I took for granted before I lost my sight."

CHAPTER

Having Fun

Angelo Chianese, *the Owner of Zip-A-Dee-Doo-Dah Singing Telegram Company, on how freeing it can be to realize that everything is just temporary.*

Enjoying What You're Doing

FOR SOME PEOPLE WORK is just a j-o-b. Something that fills the hours from nine to five and lets you collect a paycheck before lunch on Friday. And that is a sure way to go about wasting your time on this planet.

In contrast, if you're interested in doing something meaningful, you've got to start asking yourself a few questions. Like, what do you really enjoy?

If you flinch whenever the word *work* is mentioned, this might sound like a crazy concept. But one thing we've learned from assessing and interviewing people who succeed is that they really like what they are doing.

There's one guy who really gets this. He also happens to be one of the most naturally funny people we've ever met. There's just something about his energy that cracks us up.

He takes the concept of enjoying work to a whole new level. He not only gets a kick out of what he does, he also makes other people laugh while he's at it.

He was born Angelo Chianese, but he adopted the moniker Zip-A-Dee-Doo-Dah when he started his own business: delivering singing telegrams.

So how did he start doing singing telegrams? Was it just a lark?

"Well, no, it wasn't," he said, his deep voice resonating. "The decision was really well thought out. The idea of doing that for a profession came to me on the top of a house in the middle of a roofing job I was doing in Morrisville, Pennsylvania. I was really, *really* miserable in that particular field. I just fell into it while slipping out of something else. I've got quite a checkered past when it comes to my career, a real history of going from one thing to another, trying to find out what the heck works and what feels right. Anyway, the singing telegram thing occurred to me up on a roof. In the hot sun."

What exactly occurred to him?

"Well, a few months earlier I had been in this workshop that was supposed to help people discover their potential. You know, in two weekends. And I was hoping to really, at age, whatever I was, 36 or so, find what felt good in work and in my life. All I knew was that I was not a happy camper with the things I had tried so far. And I had been racking my brain, asking all my friends, 'What am I going to do?' Then, suddenly, here I am, a few months later, up on this roof, and it hits me. It sort of cracked me up. I started laughing and said, 'Wait a minute. I don't like being here.'"

He continued, "See, I hadn't thought about it at the time, but as I was sitting up there on that roof, it came back to me. As fate would have it, on my lunch break during that workshop, somebody had come into the delicatessen where I was getting a sandwich, and she got in line right next to me, and she's wearing this bright red bellhop costume. It says on the shoulder 'Philadelphia Singing Telegram Company.' And I asked, 'Do you do that *for a living*?' And she looked at me and said, 'Sure. It's great. I love it. In fact, let me sing you a song. You'll love it, and it will be great for business.' And she just burst out in one of her stock songs. Bam! And the whole place is looking at her, and she is having a great time, and I'm just speechless. My chin just dropped to the floor. And I loved it."

Who would have imagined the effect that would have on him? He could have just thought, "Well, that was fun" and left it at that. But it led to something much bigger.

"It took a while to sink in," he admitted. "I don't know, I might even have been dreaming about it. But I do know that on that day in May up on a roof, everything changed.

"I remember climbing down off the roof and saying to my boss, 'Anita, I'm giving notice. I won't be doing this kind of work much longer. I'm going to start my own company. I'm going to do singing telegrams.' After a pause, she asked, 'Full-time? For a living?' 'I'll take it wherever it goes,' I said. 'I want to do this. I know I can do this. I'm going to call it Zip-A-Dee-Doo-Dah Singing Telegram Company because that's my favorite song. I love that song.' Then Anita asked, 'Do you think you can make a living at that?' I told her, 'I'm not sure. But I'll find out.' I think everybody has something to communicate, something they're dying to deliver to someone else. Maybe all they lack is the vehicle. I can be that vehicle. Why not? I've written songs all my life. I just make them up. And I'm good at it. If I have an interesting experience, I can rhyme it. No sweat. It can come out in just a few minutes. I write it down, and there it is—ba-boom."

"Then I said to her, 'I'll bet there's somebody you'd like to send a message to, isn't there?' 'Oh, yes,' she told me. 'There's a guy I'm trying to sell a piece of property to, an architect right here in Princeton. Could you make up a singing telegram for me and deliver it to him?' 'Sure,' I said. 'I'll do that. I'll deliver it in a tuxedo and a straw hat, playing a ukulele.' So I gave her a price and told her, 'If he buys that property, you can double my fee and take me to dinner.' And she said, 'Deal.' That was my first gig, right there on Nassau Street in May 1980, and it just kept going from there."

So did it work? Did he buy the land?

"Yes, eventually," he said. "Anita told me when she came to my one-man, off-Broadway show, *Ange Chianese Does Singing Telegrams*. I congratulated her, then asked, 'Are you ready to fulfill our contract?' And she did."

The day Angelo Chianese went up the ladder to that rooftop and Zip-A-Dee-Doo-Dah came back down, everything changed.

"My business grew organically," he said. "I was fortunate that I wasn't under a great deal of stress or obligation, financially. At the time, I was single. And my mortgage payment was very small. I just ran around telling everybody I knew that I had quit my job and was out on my own, delivering singing telegrams. 'You're doing what?' they'd ask. 'Really?' 'Yes, really,' I would say. 'And it's a lot of fun.' And, as luck would have it, it was then less than a week until Mother's Day."

There are supposed to be more telephone calls made on Mother's Day than on any other day of the year. "People really want to reach out to their moms," said Zip-A-Dee. Father's Day, on the other hand, is something like twelfth or fourteenth on the list. So starting his business a few days before Mother's Day was a stroke of good fortune.

"The next thing I knew, many of the friends I had spread the news to were signing me up to perform special singing telegrams for their mothers on Sunday."

One song led to the next. Sometimes the person who asked him to deliver the singing telegram was there. Sometimes the customers sent him because they couldn't be there.

What would happen once anyone observed something like this, which was a completely unexpected, inspired moment, was that new possibilities would arise.

He would learn about who he was delivering the telegram to and then sometimes write things out ahead of time and perform them. Other times he would memorize them. "And sometimes, which is my favorite, I just improvise because I might be late or I got the request on short notice. Those can be the most inspired because deep inside I know I can pull it off, I'm just not sure how. That's living on the edge. Testing yourself. And I know it's going to be a rush in terms of excitement because I'm thrilled with what happens. I don't know what's going to come out, not consciously. And the rhymes, of course, have always been real easy for me. So I know it's probably going to rhyme through most of the sonnet or whatever it turns out to be. And it's probably going to be humorous. Who knows? I take what's available. I've done that in schools when they ask me to appear during their career days. I love to demonstrate what is possible. Because, you know, children, they're totally alive and awake and present."

"That's why I love clowning," he said. As it turned out, his company didn't limit itself solely to singing telegrams very long. "Other sorts of things started creeping in," he explained. "Performers would ask me if I could find a need for their juggling. And I'd say, 'Sure, fine. Let's make a need.' Other singers would come and say, 'Can I audition?' And I'd say, 'Why not?' Then other companies would sometimes call and say, 'Look, we can't cover this thing. Could you do it?' And I'd say, 'No problem.' I don't consider anybody competition. We're all in this crazy game together."

That's true on so many levels.

From a certain angle, somebody might look like your competition. But then when you get to know that person, you realize that your differences make you interesting and you really have much more in common than you thought.

Before coming up with a rhyming career, Zip-A-Dee had tried teaching French and Italian, editing, carpentry, and—the straw that broke the camel's back—roofing.

Sometimes you have to go a long way out of your way to find your direction.

When he got down off that hot roof, he knew he wanted to start something of his own. What was it inside him that made him do that?

"Maybe it has to do with timing in your life, where you are," Zip-A-Dee pondered. "Luck is certainly part of it. The other part of it was the frustration of not being fulfilled in my work. That was a big part. But that took a few months to sink in: from the time I met the young woman singing telegrams until I realized that I needed to do that. It wasn't immediate. I didn't know when I listened to her that I could or wanted to do this. In fact, I was not feeling very confident about myself in general. You know, there's the saying, 'When the student is ready, the teacher will appear.' Well, my internal teacher was working. It was at work up on the roof with me. And all of a sudden I'm chuckling rather than cursing, saying, 'This is temporary. I'm going to be doing something that I really love in a very short time. I've got an idea here.' And I knew it could work. It's all about being in the moment. Improvising is not thinking ahead about what you're going to do. It's just bringing forth whatever you are. Who you are. Right there."

Here's a guy who takes having fun seriously.

"Zip-A-Dee-Doo-Dah." That's it. Sing along. "Zip-A-Dee-Ay." You're there. "My, oh my, what a wonderful day." You got it. "Plenty of sunshine headed my way." One more time. "Zip-A-Dee-Doo-Dah." Now the big finale: "Zip-A-Dee-Ay!"

20

Being Open

Libby Sartain, *Senior Vice President of Human Resources at Yahoo!, on knowing when it is time to leave and go after a new opportunity.*

Finding New Possibilities

AS COMPANIES MERGE and jobs disappear, it might be tempting to just play it safe, keeping your head low, doing the best you can. But in today's job market that approach can be fatal.

We recently asked over 200 presidents of companies, "What are the key qualities you would like all your employees to possess?"

Among the top answers were "being versatile, being adept at solving problems, and being open to new possibilities."

What those employers were telling us is that when they hire individuals, particularly for key positions, they are not just thinking about whether they can succeed in that particular job. They want to know that their top employees can outgrow their current roles and step into a higher challenge—one that may even be unforeseen. They want them to grow with the company.

We've found that individuals who can keep growing share two distinct qualities: they are open to new experiences. And they are also open to learning more about themselves.

It turns out that being open in these ways is how they open new doors.

Libby Sartain is that kind of open. She's the Senior Vice President of Human Resources and Chief People Yahoo at Yahoo! (We wouldn't kid you, that's really her title, though we're not sure anyone actually calls her that. Apparently, they just seem to have fun with titles there. But then, what else would you expect at a place called Yahoo!?)

Libby entered the field of Human Resources before it was acknowledged as a strategic key to distinguishing a company's success. Along the way she's learned how to elevate her profession by getting, "a seat at the table," and she's used that opportunity to help the companies she's worked for gain recognition as great places to be employed.

"Most CEOs don't really understand the value Human Resources can bring to their organizations," Libby admitted. "But CEOs will freely tell you they spend most of their time on 'people issues' such as: Can we attract the talent we need to grow? Why isn't our customer satisfaction rating higher? Do we have the right mix of talent for the future? Why aren't two key executives seeing eye to eye? Is our leadership team capable of moving to the next level? What's the best way to help our people implement our new strategic plans? And where can we find the leaders we need?"

So early in her career Libby learned that her success was directly connected to how well she understood and focused on what the CEO needs. "When you think about it," she said, "what CEO can get excited about such mundane matters as overseeing employee records, the handbook, the policies, the discipline and termination procedure, the interviewing process, the new hire orientation, the performance evaluation form, or the details of the latest merit increase program?"

The eyes of most CEOs glaze over when they hear that sort of language.

"What they care about are solutions that take major concerns off their plate," she said. "My advice is to always be working on three or four key projects that you know are important to your CEO. It's all about prioritizing and delivering on projects that will have a real impact. Then you should celebrate your successes, catch your breath, and go on to the next three or four key projects."

"Today's success currency isn't about what you've achieved in the past; it's about your capacity to learn and grow in the immediate future. And if you think you've done all you can in your current company," she added, "I hate to be the one to tell you this: It's probably time to move on."

Although she is now a major player at Yahoo!, Libby said she is probably best known for her 13 years at Southwest Airlines. "For me, leaving Southwest was like getting a divorce," she said. "It was horribly wrenching." Both her personal and professional identities were very connected to the airline. She remembers going to the weddings of some of her colleagues' sons and daughters, who were young children when she started at the airline. And the human resources department she was at the helm of, with a staff of 300, was making great strides. Southwest was well on its way to making *Fortune*'s list of "100 Best Companies to Work For" five years in a row. The airline was known as much for its people as for its outstanding customer service ratings and on-time records. And Libby, who was also Chair of the Society for Human Resources Management, was constantly being invited to speak at companies all over the country, helping other practitioners in her field elevate the status of their profession.

So why leave?

Libby explained it this way, "There comes a time when you have to ask yourself some very tough questions. If you're not growing and learning every year, if you're not having fun, if you no longer have the ability to be the change agent you need to be, and if there is no prospect for additional progress in the future, then it's time to get the word out to headhunters that you're receptive to their phone calls."

That was her answer on one level. Then she paused and added, "My husband said that I had outgrown Southwest. And at first, I told him that just sounded arrogant. Then, as I thought about it, I realized that Southwest and I had probably outgrown each other. I believed that their rush to innovate had slowed. And, as I expressed my feelings, it was clear that I was becoming an irritant to them."

So she forfeited her seat on what was considered one of the best-run airlines in the country.

Libby was very close to her boss, and together they developed an exit strategy. Libby would officially step down at the end of June, then spend the summer looking elsewhere. As it turned out, she also was stepping down as Chair of the Society for Human Resources Management. It was a time of endings and beginnings.

She worked on the speech she was going to give at the association's annual convention. Her theme was "No Limits." A speechwriter who was working with her advised, "You have to tell your audience that you're also leaving Southwest." But Libby felt uncomfortable about doing that. She saw the speech and her stepping down from Southwest as two separate events. And, she still felt a bit uncomfortable saying out loud what she was about to do. The more she thought about it, though, the more it made sense to tie her personal story into her overall message. So Libby ended up sharing with an audience of 13,000 of her professional colleagues that she was leaving Southwest, with no idea of where she would land. And it was very freeing. She said she wanted to work next in a turnaround situation. That was where she had the most fun and felt she was contributing the most. Otherwise, she felt like she was limited in what she could achieve. She just put it out there. "This audience had heard me speak so often about my experiences at Southwest," she said. "It was part of my identity. Part of who I was." And she was giving it up.

Her audience's response was immediate. They gave her a standing ovation, as they broke into thunderous applause. They applauded her courage. They applauded her openness to exploring new possibilities. They applauded her for being so open to learning more about herself. And they applauded her for being so completely open with them. Libby soaked in the moment. And she felt emboldened.

"It was a great lesson," she said, "because so many opportunities opened up as a result of my sharing what was going on in my life."

After her speech someone came up to her, handed her a business card, and said that the head of human resources for Yahoo! had just left. Who knew? It might be worth looking into.

> **We've found that individuals who can keep growing share two distinct qualities: they are open to new experiences. And they are also open to learning more about themselves.**

To prepare for her upcoming job interviews, Libby was more thorough in her approach than she'd ever been before. Not that she had a lot of experience looking for jobs, but she knew, probably better than anyone else, what people who are running companies look for in top employees. "I hadn't been on a job interview for 13 years, and I had never been interviewed by the CEO before," she said. "So instead of just doing a bit of research on a company, then giving it my best shot during the interview, I found a coach to work with me. She helped me anticipate questions and articulate my answers in a way that would resonate with CEOs."

Libby also created her own mission statement, expressing the values and capabilities she would bring to an organization and what she was looking for in return. Essential to that was her answer to the question, "What are the things that you have to do no matter where you are?" For Libby, the first thing she had to do was align the goals of her department with the vision of the company, or create an internal brand, as she described it, which was a reflection of the company's brand in the marketplace.

She quickly received an offer from American Airlines, which seemed like a safe bet. She already had a stellar reputation in the airline industry and could have stayed in Dallas, so, in many ways, moving to another major airline would have been a natural transition.

Instead, however, Libby accepted the position at the helm of human resources for Yahoo!, at a time when the company's stock price had plummeted from an all-time high of $237 a share to a low in the single digits.

The dream of all dot-comers of becoming instant millionaires had become a nightmare that had played out just before Libby arrived; Yahoo! had just laid off 400 employees.

Why take such a risky career move?

"I was open to the challenge of turning around a situation, where I could make a real difference. When I signed on with Southwest in 1988, the company was small and struggling," she reflected. "There was something very exciting about being in on the ground floor of a venture you knew was going to succeed and where you knew that what you did mattered." After meeting with the executive team of Yahoo!, Libby became convinced that the company's troubles were really opportunities. "Everyone's stock options were underwater, so they knew they needed to reinvent rewards to keep an incredibly talented group of people motivated. They were focused on the culture.

There was new leadership at the helm, with a new vision. And they were looking to grow. How could I be anything but enthused about such a challenge?"

That's not to say it was smooth sailing. Hardly.

"We were in the middle of turning around a business and redefining what we were doing. So there wasn't a lot of clarity. In fact, there was much confusion, uncertainty, and frustration among the employees at that time," she confided.

One of her first goals was to pull her department together into a team. She wanted them to feel motivated about the changes they were going to be part of creating. One of their first challenges was to devise new incentive plans. Yahoo! still wanted employees to have a stake in the business, but becoming an overnight millionaire wasn't in the cards anymore. "One thing I learned at Southwest is that you manage the good times as if they were bad times, because the bad times are bound to come," Libby said. "The same thing applies to your career. We want people to think of options as a long-term investment in their company and their future. If they stay with us and build their careers here, we believe these options will become valuable."

As it turned out, there was another round of layoffs, which Libby oversaw, before the company made its turnaround.

Through all of this, what has Libby discovered that people really want from their jobs?

"The one constant," Libby has found, "is that most people really want to make a difference. And they want to feel they are part of a community that means something. Ultimately, they want to add value and they want to *feel* valued." She paused, then added, "We still have a lot of our dot-com millionaires active at work every day. How do we keep our most valuable people? We have to make sure that what they're doing is important and challenging, that they feel their jobs have real meaning, and that they're enjoying their work."

What advice does she share with young people about their careers?

"Most important of all is to find something to do that really drives you. I've come across so many people who pursue certain occupations because they think they'll make a lot of money, or it's what their parents expected, or some other wrong reason. You have to be open to yourself, to know who you truly are," she said. "Find something that you naturally gravitate to. Something that clicks with you. Something you feel really good about. Something you enjoy doing and look forward to. Then just pursue it with all your heart. You can certainly change along the way later. No doubt you will. But start off by going after something that you really want, with all you've got. That's how you'll stand out from the crowd. And make a real difference. Just be open to yourself, then go for it. And incredible opportunities will open up."

CHAPTER

21

Creativity

Michael Graves, *the renowned architect and designer, on how he stays inspired.*

Developing Your Curious Mind

IN PRACTICALLY ALL ANCIENT cultures the universe was thought of as chaos into which order was introduced by a creative, omnipotent hand. This is the essence of creation: a force stepping in. The nature of the force and type of order that people envisioned varied from culture to culture. But the similarities between these creation myths were more striking than the differences, as Joseph Campbell stated in his book *The Power of Myth.* It was important that light be separated from darkness. Day from night. That the sun, moon, and stars be assigned their proper place in determining the seasons. The cosmic egg from which proto-humans emerged is a feature of some Hindu, African, Greek, and Chinese myths. In other traditions the earth must be brought up from the primordial waters by a diver. Genesis, on the other hand, favors a rationally ordered process of creation. Whether the deity uses preexisting materials, whether he or she leaves once the creation is formed, how perfect the creation is, and whether the creator interacts with his or her creation varies among myths.

Creativity gets at the very heart of who we are and what we believe in. Creativity has a lot to do with understanding our environment and our relationship to it.

We have believed for a long time that there are two types of people in this world. Those who create and those who criticize. We recently heard a slight variation on this theme, which is that there are actually three types of people: those who make things happen, those who talk about what they think happened, and those who ask, "Did something just happen?"

Creative people make things happen.

"We are continually developing our curious minds, looking, analyzing, reflecting, then coming up with something different, something new. There is always an interest in continuing on to the next thing because there is always something new out there to learn," explained Michael Graves, who was hailed by *The New York Times* as "truly the most original voice American architecture has produced in some time."

Among his well-known projects are the Humana Building, which *TIME* magazine cited as one of "the ten best buildings of the decade (the 1980s)," Disney's corporate headquarters in Burbank, and the much-acclaimed, state-of-the-art headquarters and training center for the Philadelphia Eagles. In addition, he has teamed with Target Stores to bring his signature designs to the public at large in a wide variety of products.

When Michael looks around him, he sees "a crying need to improve the aesthetic design" of the buildings we surround ourselves with, along with many of the items inside them. He added, "In addition to wanting to make a good design generally available, I see the need to make it physically more accessible and usable. I see great possibilities in universal design, design for all of us."

To understand Michael's unique sense of creativity, first, we need to tell you that beyond seeing the world around him from a somewhat different perspective than most of us, Michael sometimes has a slightly different vocabulary for what he sees. His is a visual vocabulary. So you may need to shift your listening just a bit. It is well worth it.

One of the things that keep his creativity flowing is his sense of humor.

While his taste is exquisite, sophisticated, and cultured, Michael said, "I would love to democratize design, making good design accessible to everyone."

After receiving his architectural training at the University of Cincinnati and Harvard University, in 1960, Michael won the Rome

Prize, which enabled him to study for two years at the American Academy in Rome, of which he is now a trustee.

"Studying in Rome," Michael said, "provided an extraordinary opportunity that transformed how I looked at the world. Rome has such a rich architectural and cultural presence that I came to think of the city itself as a kind of artifact, a continuum of layers of history—from ancient Rome to the early Christian, Renaissance, and Baroque periods and thereafter. Because of that, I now view architecture as not just a style but as a language.

"It was in Rome that I learned the nouns, verbs, and adjectives of an architectural language and how that language fills architecture with meaning. In addition to my own work and travels, I enjoyed the company of the other fellows in residence at the academy—painters, writers, musicians, historians—whose insights allowed me to understand architecture within the broadest cultural context."

He added, "As a student, I would go out every day and walk the streets of Rome. I had my sketchbook and I would draw some of the world's greatest buildings." Michael's drawings helped him understand, from a scholarly perspective, how the ancient temples, amphitheaters, triumphal arches, bridges, villas, markets, and shops were composed. "Equally important to learning about these significant buildings," Michael said, "the so-called background buildings influenced me." He explained, "I learned to see things in a cultural sense. I do not just look at individual buildings by themselves, but how they relate to one another, their sense of purpose and belonging. That tells me much about the society and its beliefs—about what it values and what it doesn't."

Now when he is commissioned to design a building, he added, "I start by first analyzing the site and considering its context—what's there, what's likely to be there, and how this new building will contribute to that. I'm most interested in creating distinctive work that is fresh and contemporary, but that also draws on a knowledge of history and a respect for local context."

What were his initial thoughts when he was commissioned by Jeffrey Lurie, the owner of the Philadelphia Eagles, to create the headquarters and training center for the team?

"Jeffrey wanted a facility that expressed hope, optimism, and success. He had very clear ideas about making sure the public and the whole Eagles organization—from the players to the administration—

knew what the building stood for. So the first thing I wanted to do was symbolize the history of the team and create a place that would build camaraderie," Michael said. Then there were many practical considerations, such as where the athletes would eat, work out, relax, and meet with their coaches. Everything about it, from the rich cherry wood fittings in the locker rooms, to the spacious 200-seat auditorium, to the state-of-the-art fitness center, entailed creating an environment where a team could succeed. "Jeffrey especially wanted the entrance to make a statement," Michael added. "So we created a rather symbolic front door with stylized eagles over it that immediately lets you know you have arrived at a place that is significant." The goal was to create an entrance that would make anyone who walked in feel both impressed and comfortable at the same time. And most important, it had to be a facility that made the players feel they were part of something special.

Inside of Michael's creative decisions, as he explains them, are practical issues to consider.

"Ayn Rand's famous novel *The Fountainhead* was about an architect, Howard Roark, who was so single-minded that he insisted there was only one right way to make his buildings," Michael said. "But in today's world that just is not true. If you know your discipline well, you can approach any problem in a variety of ways. There are many ways of doing things, many alternatives. You must be smarter than the dilemma."

As a complete change of pace, on a much smaller scale, we asked Michael what his initial thoughts were when he was asked to design his famous teakettle.

"I was commissioned by Alberto Alessi to design the teakettle in the early 1980s. He had several very specific requirements. The teakettle had to hold a certain amount of water, the base had to be a certain size to fit on the stove, the water had to boil fast, and the handle had to stay cool to the touch. Then there were manufacturing considerations that took into account how the pieces were attached to each other, for example, the angle between the base and the side." Michael learned that water would boil most quickly if the kettle was shaped so that it was widest at the bottom and narrowest at the top. He also recommended a plastic that would not become too hot to hold when the water boiled. And the sleek figure was topped off humorously with a little red bird that whistles when the water reaches the boiling point.

Whether he's designing a building or a product, so much of Michael's creative process is constrained or at least influenced by practical considerations.

He said one of the things that keep his creativity flowing is his sense of humor. "Being able to laugh keeps me going, particularly when I'm under the stress of multiple deadlines, but it also actually infuses my work. I love to design objects with a little twist, sometimes a double meaning. I think my teakettle with the whistling bird spout captured the public's imagination because it was somewhat whimsical. The retail store Target, a major client of our product design practice, says I 'put the fun in *functional*.'"

Michael's interest in designing products for a broader audience initially met with some criticism from design and architectural circles. But then, he has never positioned himself as an elitist. Rather, he remains intrigued by the possibility of delivering creative designs at affordable prices—and firmly believes that design can enhance the world for all of us, not just cater to a select few. "The design of a single spoon gives me as much joy as designing the most complicated building," Michael added.

How does he know if an artistic work is successful in and of itself?

"In our popular culture, I suppose some people might think that the more you sell, the better you are," he said. "This is not necessarily so. We hear about composers, painters, writers and other artists who are highly regarded now but who were not popular in their day. They were not necessarily ahead of their time. Perhaps the critical debate at that time was simply not broad enough to encompass what they were doing."

When did Michael first know that he saw things differently from most people walking on this planet?

"I'm not sure," he said. "When I was younger, I would always draw. Drawing was what I did best. In fact, I was so preoccupied with drawing that my mother started worrying that I would choose to be an artist and would surely starve unless I was as good as Picasso, which I wasn't. She suggested that I choose a career path that used drawing as a way of working, perhaps architecture or engineering. I asked her what engineers did, and when she told me, I quickly said, 'Then I will be an architect.' She replied, 'But Michael, I haven't even told you what an architect does,' and I answered, 'It doesn't matter because I know I'm not going to be an engineer. I am going to be an architect.' From that day forward I drew with a new energy, documenting houses in our neighborhood in Indianapolis and taking as many drawing classes as possible in high school until they ran out of courses and had to invent new ones for me."

"He wouldn't teach how to do something but how to think about it."

Michael has built an organization with over 100 people around him who can carry on his distinctive style. How does he teach his style to other creative people?

"We have built an organization around ideas, not around one individual." The architectural practice, Michael Graves & Associates, has five studios which are headed by people who have worked very closely with Michael. "There's a real give and take of ideas," he explained. "It's not just me drawing everything. Architecture doesn't work that way. I might work on the initial ideas, then I may or may not continue to work with the studio on the building. And it is the same way with the Michael Graves Design Group, our product design practice. I meet with them every Wednesday morning and we have a session where they bring up all their questions and get feedback from each other as well as from me." It's a process that keeps Michael engaged in what is going on, able to offer alternative approaches to problems and compliment his creative team on solutions they've arrived at on their own. He is teaching a way to solve problems that can carry these projects and his company forward with or without him.

Karen Nichols, Managing Principal of Michael Graves & Associates, told us, "One of the things that Michael can't really say for himself—but those of us who have worked with him for a long, long time know—is that his passion for teaching is fundamental to the way he works. He was a professor at Princeton University for 39 years and during that time he taught thousands of students. What characterized the way he taught is that he wouldn't teach how to do something but how to think about it. He didn't say, 'Follow these steps.' Rather, he would engage his students in an intellectual dialogue where he would consider a variety of points of view. And as a result, many of his students have gone on to become deans of schools of architecture elsewhere, as well as practitioners. So they developed their own voices with his guidance. The way Michael taught is exactly how he works with his firm's designers. It translates into a very creative practice, where his voice is a major influence, but not the only one heard."

How would Michael himself describe the Michael Graves style?

"I want to emphasize that I do not have a single signature style. You can certainly drive down the highway or in town and see a building and say, 'I think that's a Michael Graves building.' But not knowing whether it is, you would have to find out. It might have a little more color than other people's work; it might reflect my interests in certain types of compositions. But I am not like Frank Lloyd Wright or Frank Gehry, who are known for their signature styles, where their last buildings look remarkably like their previous ones." He paused, then added, "What I like to think about is developing a building that has character, that conveys something about itself and its context."

These days, though he shows no signs of retiring, Michael has been thinking a lot about how his company could carry on without him. He has named six partners in the architecture practice and eight in the product design area, whose average tenure with the firm is more than two decades, so a succession plan is in place. And their voices had to become a little stronger in February of 2003, when a spinal cord infection left Michael's legs paralyzed.

Now, he said, he has good days and bad days, mostly good. "I still hurt, and I still take about a million pills. I used to have more stamina than I do now, but I'm building up my strength. I have a physical therapy session a couple of times a week, and that helps. One or two of the exercises I have to do keep the circulation going in my legs. So I do that religiously."

So that's helping?

"Well, it won't help me walk. No. It just helps with the circulation in my body. I stood up the other day, but that had nothing to do with walking. I have a plastic suit or armature that they put on me, then I stand between the parallel bars and try to take a step. And if I exert as much energy as I possibly can, I might move forward a few steps." He paused, then added, "But the only way I will walk is with the hope of regenerative stem cell research. What I need and a lot of people like me need in this paraplegic state is something that regenerates what is broken. And no amount of exercise will do that."

It came all at once?

"Yes. A cold turned into a sinus infection, which turned into lower body paralysis," he said.

Is there anything his disability has taught him that he would like to share?

"It has taught me to be more tolerant. More patient. And to keep being curious. Never stop being curious," he said. Then he switched gears. "Whenever I speak at commencement addresses, I like to tell the graduates to develop their curious minds. Continually look at things, analyze them, think about them, draw them, write about them, then create the next thing. And continue doing the next thing, because there is always something out there new to learn."

What else does he tell them?

"The only way you're going to achieve at the highest level is through serious dedication, diligence, and effort. Be sensitive to everything you see, the way people move and act. Read constantly—about your craft, about life. When you read a novel, don't just read the story line; think about the physical and metaphorical nature of the settings. And practice. Some practitioners of a discipline, once they become successful, go off golfing or something like that and leave the work behind for the worker bees. They leave behind all the joy of learning and creating, which for me is what it is all about."

22

Courage

Congressman John Lewis, *the legendary civil rights advo-cate, on pushing through fear and acting on your beliefs.*

Knowing What You Stand For

WHEN YOU COME ACROSS someone with courage, you know it. And it bowls you over. The strength of conviction is inspiring. Ernest Hemingway described courage as "grace under pressure." But Senator John McCain (R-AZ), a man certainly familiar with the subject, has argued that courage is more than just the style with which a situation is handled. He said, "There is only one thing that must always be present for courage to exist: fear. Because part of courage is overcoming fear."

We often think of courageous people as being totally fearless.

But courage really involves feeling fear, then moving beyond it.

Sometimes courage comes in a single, extraordinary act, when someone, in a moment of self-sacrifice, rises to the occasion and becomes a hero.

In Congressman John Lewis's (D-GA) case, courage is something he prepared for. To have a conversation with him is to talk with history.

Photographs show him kneeling and praying, with blood splattered on his shirt and tie, his head bandaged from the beatings he suffered at the lunch counter sit-ins in Nashville, Tennessee, in 1960, the Freedom Rides in Montgomery, Alabama, in 1961, and on that Bloody Sunday in 1965 when nonviolent protesters marching for voting rights were attacked at the crest of the Edmund Pettus Bridge in Selma, Alabama—a demonstration that caused President Lyndon Johnson to call on Congress to pass the Voting Rights Act of 1965.

Overall, John Lewis couldn't tell you how many times he was beaten by police officers as he led nonviolent protests in the early days of the civil rights movement. Official records show that he was arrested at least 40 times.

As he said, "I was caught up in the spirit of history." And he helped change the shape of America.

As a child, John Lewis grew up in segregated Alabama, near a town called Troy, just a few miles away from the place where George Wallace, a future governor of that state and the man who would become his nemesis, was raised. "But we might as well have lived on different planets," the congressman said. He recalled seeing only two white men when he was a child: the mailman and a traveling salesman.

His parents were sharecroppers, and John was expected to work alongside his siblings in the backbreaking toil of the cotton fields. "I hated the work," he said, "but even more than that, I resented what it represented: exploitation, hopelessness, a dead-end way of life." His family would pick 400 pounds of cotton a day and make $1.40.

But, through sacrifice and hard work, his parents eventually saved $300 so they could buy their own land. He recalled his mother saying, "It's good to have something you can call your own."

John's job was to tend to the chickens. "Each morning, as the sun was rising, I'd pull open the door to the henhouse, and the smell would hit me." It was too early for the chickens to stir, so instead of taking them to the yard to feed them, he would practice his preaching on them. "There was something magical, almost mystical, about that moment," he said. "It felt very spiritual. And I could swear those chickens felt it too."

But he watched his father toil in futility. "Even as a six-year-old," he said, "I could tell that this sharecropper's life was nothing but a bottomless pit. I saw my father sink deeper and deeper into debt, and it broke my heart. More than that, it made me angry."

You have to keep in mind that Troy, the town where John Lewis was raised, had a long history. As John explained, after President Lincoln was assassinated, a Troy businessman named Joseph Pinckney Parker wasted no time placing a white marble monument in his front yard on Madison Street. It read: "In Memory of John Wilkes Booth, Who Killed Ole Abraham Lincoln."

When John was in high school, he heard a voice on an old radio that mesmerized him. He described it as "a strong, deep voice, well versed in the rhythmic, singsong, old-style tradition of black Baptist preaching we call whooping. He really could make words sing." He heard that deep, resounding voice say, "No lie can live forever. Let us not despair. The universe is with us. Walk together, children. Do not get weary." He felt this man on the radio was speaking directly to him. The voice turned out to be that of the Reverend Martin Luther King, Jr.

John wrote to Dr. King, and they eventually met. As John described it, the first words Dr. King said to him were, "Are you the boy from Troy? Are you John Lewis?" That was the first moment of his involvement in the Civil Rights Movement.

Dr. King helped John get into the American Baptist Theological Seminary in Nashville to study for the ministry. There he learned about Mahatma Gandhi and the principle of nonviolent civil disobedience.

John soon became a leader in the student-led campaign to integrate the all-white public lunch counters.

What did it feel like to be involved in such a historic moment?

"We were ready," he said. "We had studied Thoreau, Gandhi, and King. We had accepted the philosophy and discipline of non-violence not simply as a technique, but as an entire way of life. And we had nothing to lose. We were young, free, and burning with belief. We felt a mixture of fear and excitement. There was a stirring inside. And a sense of power beyond yourself, a calling, a mission."

This is where courage kicks in.

"But doubt lingers," he said. "The feeling of not knowing what to expect. I don't care how many times you do something like this, how many times you sit in, or march, or in any way put yourself in the path of those who might do you harm. You can never know what's going to happen."

As his group entered a Woolworth's, they were confronted by young white men shouting, "Go home, nigger!" and "Get back to Africa!" They were called chicken for not fighting back. "We weren't playing by their rules," John said, "and that infuriated them further." Burning cigarettes were put out on their heads and on their backs.

They were spit on, and ketchup and mustard were poured all over them. But John and his group did not respond in kind. As he explained, "We didn't want to strike back. We didn't want to hate. We wanted to change things. We wanted to be reconciled. We wanted to win people over." But some of the onlookers were not ready to be won over. They started swinging. A television crew filmed one of the protesters being bloodied and bruised and silently pulling himself back onto his chair. It was one of the first instances of the way television made people aware of a reality they could no longer deny.

This was the first time John was arrested.

"I'd been told over and over again by my parents, 'Don't get in trouble.' And here I was getting in real trouble. But it was good trouble. It was necessary trouble," he said.

> **"I thought I saw death. I thought I was going to die. I looked death right in the face but was not afraid. My legs went out from under me, and I guess I lost consciousness. I just thought that this was part of the price I would have to pay to help make it possible for people in Selma, Alabama, and other parts of the south to be able to register to vote."**

When he was elected Chairman of the Student Nonviolent Coordinating Committee (SNCC), Bobby Kennedy, the president's brother and then the attorney general, called him and asked if they could meet. "I'll never forget what he said to me," John said. "Bobby looked me in the eye and said, 'John, the young people of SNCC have educated me. You have changed me. Now I understand.'

"That showed me something about Bobby Kennedy that I came to respect enormously. He was willing to listen, learn, and change. That same Bobby Kennedy who had resisted responding to so many of our pleas early on in the movement wound up out front, speaking against hunger, against poverty, going into Mississippi, into the Southwest, going to the Indian reservations, going into the coal-mining sections of West Virginia, standing up and speaking out for the dispossessed of all races—blacks, Hispanics, Native Americans, Appalachian whites. The man really grew. You could *see* him growing" (from *Walking with the Wind: A Memoir of the Movement* by John Lewis, page 215).

Still, John did not shy away from speaking truth to power. Shortly after meeting Bobby Kennedy, John gave a fiery speech, criticizing the Kennedy administration for moving too slowly in the struggle for civil rights. At the Lincoln Memorial, at what became known as the March on Washington, the young John Lewis walked up to the podium, looked hesitantly out at the sea of people, then saw a pocket of friends from SNCC cheering him on. "I said to myself, 'This is it.' I sort of had a quick executive session with myself," he said. Then he told himself, "All right. Let's go for it," and he called out to the crowd: "The revolution is at hand, and we must free ourselves from the chains of political and economic slavery. . . . Mr. Kennedy is trying to take the revolution out of the streets and put it into the courts . . . [but we are] on the march for jobs and freedom . . . and there won't be a 'cooling off' period. . . . Wake up, America. Wake up! For we *cannot* stop, and we will not be patient." His speech brought thunderous applause. Then came the next day's speaker, Dr. King, who gave his famous "I Have a Dream" speech, which he ended with the cadence we've all come to know: "Free at last! Free at last! Thank God Almighty, we are free at *last!*"

Herb, who was at that demonstration, asked Congressman Lewis if he knew at that moment that he was in the middle of a momentous point in history. John said he didn't think of it that way. "We knew it was big and important," he reflected. "But we were too much in the moment to have a sense of history."

John then returned to Selma, where, in his words, he "organized, mobilized, and tried to help people of color get out and register to vote." At one demonstration he was leading, Sheriff James Clark emerged from the courthouse, literally shaking with anger. John described him as having "a gun on one hip, a nightstick on the other, and an electric cattle prod in one hand. He looked like he was going over the edge. You could see it in his eyes."

"John," the sheriff said, "you're nothing but an outside agitator. You are the lowest form of humanity."

John looked him square in his eyes and said, "Sheriff, I may be an agitator, but I'm not an outsider. I grew up 90 miles from here. And we are going to stay here until these people are allowed to register to vote." Over the course of the next week more than 3,000 people were arrested, including John, and a young man named Jimmy Lee Jackson, who was shot by a state trooper and died a few days later.

In response, a march from Selma to Montgomery was planned.

Because Dr. King had been detained in Montgomery, John and Hosea Williams of the Southern Christian Leadership Conference led that march. The afternoon of March 7, 1965, will be remembered forever as Bloody Sunday.

To prepare for the march, John said, "I attended church with 600 others, where we organized a nonviolence workshop. Then we lined up two by two and started walking in an orderly, peaceful fashion. I was wearing a backpack. I assumed we were going to be arrested and taken to jail, so in this backpack I had two books, an apple, an orange, some toothpaste, and a toothbrush. I wanted to have something to eat, something to read, and, since I was going to be in close quarters with my friends, colleagues, and neighbors, I wanted to be able to brush my teeth."

But what happened next he could not have been prepared for.

He described the scene: "When we reached the crest of the bridge, I stopped dead in my tracks. There, facing us at the bottom of the other side, stood a sea of blue: blue-helmeted, blue-uniformed Alabama state troopers, line after line of them." Behind them was Sheriff Clark's posse. There were hundreds of troopers and sheriff's deputies, many on horseback, carrying clubs, prods, whips and wearing gas masks.

John recalled, "Hosea Williams, the young man walking beside me, asked, 'John, can you swim?' We both looked down at all of this water below us in the Alabama River. I said, 'No. Can you?' He said, 'No.' Then I told him, 'Well we're not going to jump, we're not going back. We're going forward.' And we continued to walk. Then a man identified himself as Major John Cloud of the Alabama state troopers. He said, 'This is an unlawful march. It will not be allowed to continue. I'm giving you three minutes to disperse and return to your church.' A minute later, he gave the command: 'Troopers advance.' I saw these men put on their gas masks and come toward us. They started beating us with nightsticks, cracking bullwhips, trampling us under their horses' hooves. I was hit in the head by a state trooper with a nightstick and had a concussion. I thought I saw death. I thought I was going to die. I looked death right in the face but was not afraid. My legs went out from under me, and I guess I lost consciousness. I just thought that this was part of the price I would have to pay to help make it possible for people in Selma, Alabama, and other parts of the south to be able to register to vote."

John was left bleeding badly. He said, "My head was exploding with pain. There was mayhem all around me. People were weeping, bleeding, vomiting from the tear gas. Men and horses were running right over fallen people."

That evening, ABC News interrupted its Sunday night movie and anchorman Frank Reynolds came on to show 15 minutes of footage of the attack in Selma. At one point in the film clip, Sheriff James Clark's voice could be heard clearly in the background, yelling, "Get those goddamned niggers." Viewers also saw John, lying on the ground, struggling to get back on his feet. Then they saw him collapse, unconscious, his skull fractured.

That touched a nerve deep in America's conscience.

Television, in this instance, verified reality and helped transform what would happen.

One week later, President Johnson addressed Congress, insisting on the passage of the Voting Rights Act. He said, "At times history and fate meet at a single time in a single place to shape a turning point in [our] unending search for freedom. So it was at Lexington and Concord. So it was a century ago at Appomattox. So it was last week in Selma, Alabama. . . . All of us must overcome the crippling legacy of bigotry and injustice. And we *shall* overcome."

John's life became a history of the Civil Rights Movement.

He was campaigning with Bobby Kennedy when he heard that Dr. Martin Luther King, Jr. had been assassinated. John recalled, "I was organizing a rally for Bobby. And there was some debate among his staffers about whether Kennedy himself should still attend. Despite the concern that there might be violence, Bobby made the decision to appear at the rally. He spoke from his soul and lifted us all up in spite of our sadness and shock and disbelief. And we hung on to his every word. And we hoped. I said to myself, 'Well, we still have Robert Kennedy.' I left for Atlanta the next day to prepare for the funeral of my hero, my friend, my big brother, my inspiration."

Just a short while later John was in California working with Bobby Kennedy's campaign when the announcement was made that Bobby had won the primary. Bobby told John, "Wait for me. I'll be back in 15 or 20 minutes." But just a few minutes later Bobby Kennedy was shot, and John would never see him again.

After serving in the Carter administration, then on Atlanta's city council, in 1986 John was elected to Congress from Georgia's Fifth District, where he continues to serve today. Even as a congressman, he said, "I still have to make a little noise and make people uncomfortable from time to time. You have to sort of get in the way if you really believe in something."

What does Congressman John Lewis feel has made the biggest difference in his life?

"I'd have to say it's courage. You must have courage. I describe it as raw courage. The courage to get in the way. The courage to disturb the order of things. When you see things that are wrong, you have to have the courage to stand up and agitate."

Did he ever think there might be another way to bring about social change besides nonviolence?

"I never ever did. And I never will. For me nonviolence is one of those immutable principles that you cannot and must not deviate from. I believe Gandhi said it best, 'It is nonviolence or nonexistence.'"

One of his fondest memories is of being asked to read from his book *Walking with the Wind: A Memoir of the Movement* at the public library in Troy on July 5, 1998. That opportunity was another milestone for him, another way to alter history, because, as he remembered so clearly, "As a child, I would go down to the public library in the little town of Troy, Alabama, trying to check some books out. And I was told by the librarian that the library was for whites only. Not for coloreds. So it was a thrill to return there and read from my book and sign copies for hundreds of people of every size, shape, and color. That was my destiny."

Congressman Rush Holt (D-NJ) said, "John Lewis personifies courage. I think of him as almost saintly. I just love that guy. He was handpicked by Dr. King to carry the movement forward. There's no question that Dr. King saw in John what he was to become: a man of strength, conviction, and courage."

And Senator John McCain echoed that thought: "I've seen courage in action on many occasions. I can't say I've ever seen anyone possess more of it, and use it for any better purpose and to any greater effect, than John Lewis."

Lessons in Success: What They Discovered About Themselves Along the Way

WE MET SO MANY INCREDIBLE people who shared personal stories and profound insights into the things they learned about themselves as they succeeded on their own terms.

If you are reading this book straight through, you may recognize a few of the people in this section. They were so introspective, reflective, and articulate that their voices became major themes throughout this book. Others in this section you'll be hearing from for the first time. All of them caused us to stop and reflect on our own experiences and what is yet to come.

As we listened to these stories, we found that they seemed to fall into two categories: "Knowing Yourself" and "Knowing the World around You." The individuals who succeeded by knowing themselves tended to focus on their inner strengths. Their stories are about how they succeeded by being keenly aware of who they were and knowing they could change things. The individuals who succeeded by knowing the world around them had a natural ability to sense the opportunities that came their way. Their stories are about how they used their radar to sense openings and make the most of them.

Whether focusing on their inner strengths or on sensing opportunities around them, all these people succeeded on their own terms.

As you read through the next two chapters, perhaps you'll learn more about your own strengths and your natural tendency to tune into yourself or into the world around you.

CHAPTER

Knowing Yourself

T*he individuals who succeeded by knowing themselves tended to focus on their inner strengths.*

I. Focus on What You Have Rather Than What You Don't

A CAR ACCIDENT LEFT 10-year-old Paul Schulte in a wheelchair, but it didn't alter his dreams of being an athlete.

Just slightly more than a decade after his accident, Paul made his Paralympic debut during the 2000 games in Sydney as the U.S. wheelchair basketball team's youngest player, helping the team secure a bronze medal. He's also earned an athletic scholarship for college, as well as traveled to Mexico City for the Pan American Games, to Kitakyushu, Japan, for the Gold Cup World Championship, and to Monaco as a nominee for the Laureus World Sports Awards.

After the accident, Paul realized that "the only thing I could change about my situation was my attitude." And his positive energy bowls you over. "I gained a much deeper understanding of what really matters," he said. "I truly believe that my disability is the best thing that ever happened to me, except, of course, meeting and marrying my wife, Meghan."

That's not to say it was all a breeze. It took a while for Paul to become so sanguine. Right after the accident, a few of his friends came by the hospital once or twice, but it was awkward for them and for him. Paul had to reinvent himself and get comfortable with who he was.

That's hard enough to do in the best of circumstances, let alone when you're just 10 years old.

"When I first got hurt, a close friend of the family came to the hospital and told me that eventually I would get to see this as a blessing, as something that was meant to be, rather than a tragedy. And I said to him, 'Look, I love you and everything, but I think you're missing the boat here. You don't seem to see the tubes I'm hooked up to or the cast that I'm in or recognize the fact that I'm *never* going to walk again.' But he was right. It just took me a while to get it."

Paul added, "My biggest challenge all along has been self-acceptance. It's important that I accept my disability. That I accept all aspects of it, all the challenges it brings to my life. And that is a continuing, ongoing process. For instance, right now, in terms of my relationship with my wife, Meghan, I've come to realize that any obstacles we've had in our relationship regarding my disability are the ones I've put in front of us. The ones I've been dealing with. And that I've sometimes pushed her away because I've been in my own head about accepting some aspect of my disability. That was a huge lesson for me. And there was nobody around to teach me how to deal with that. I had to sort of work on it on my own. It's not a quick process. It takes time."

> **"If you can look at adversity as**
> **an opportunity, it's completely different.**
> **Then you're ready to succeed."**

Paul and Meghan, whom he met in high school, volunteer once a month, visiting people who've just been in a disabling accident. He said, "We try to let them know that we understand what they're going through and that it is going to get better. I think more than anything we say, my being in a wheelchair and having a great relationship with my incredible wife helps in some way. Maybe not just then. Maybe they'll remember something we did or said later. That's the way it is. I know what they're going through. Wishing it was just a bad dream they would wake up from. The disbelief, the sadness, the anger, all of it. But Meghan and I try to assure them that they are the same people they were before. Their bodies have changed quite a bit. But they are the exact same people—maybe even better. And I let them know that I wouldn't want to change any aspect of my life right now, that I feel incredibly lucky, and that I'm definitely a better person because of the accident. It's helped me to live my life more fully."

If he can leave them with one message, Paul said, it is to "focus on what you have rather than what you don't have. In my life, there were 10,000 things I could have done before my disability. Now there are 9,000. You've got to focus on your opportunities and let the rest go."

He added, "For those of us who have been through a serious accident that alters our lives, there is much to gain. You can look at what happened and say, 'I'm a victim. This happened to me, and everybody should feel sorry for me.' Or you can look at it and say, 'This is an opportunity.' If you can look at adversity as an opportunity, it's completely different. Then you're ready to succeed."

2. Always Play Like You're Trying Out for the Team

The day Emilio Butragueño, Spain's legendary football player, was born, his father rushed out of the hospital and had his son inducted as a member of Real Madrid, the country's foremost football club. Shortly afterward Emilio was christened.

To say that Spaniards live and breathe their game of football would be an extreme understatement. The Real Madrid stadium is in the center of the city, and though it was built in 1947, it still helps define the city's character. The daily newspaper with the largest circulation in the city focuses entirely on sports. Football permeates the media as well as most polite, though impassioned, conversations.

Later, nicknamed "the Vulture," Emilio went on to become one of the most lethal strikers in the game during the 1980s.

> **"I have seen, time and time again, that the difference between a good player and a great one is the capacity to focus."**

"I was always competing against myself," he said. "Every game I would try to show that I belonged on the team. I was not big physically, but I didn't dwell on that. I just focused on all my advantages: speed, eagerness to play, and the drive to prove myself." Emilio, who is now the Vice President of Real Madrid, added, "I have seen, time and time again, that the difference between a good player and a great one is the capacity to focus."

His career had many high points, including becoming the first player since Eusébio da Silva Ferreira in 1966 to score four goals in a World Cup match.

We asked him to share with us the thrill of scoring his first professional goal.

"It was in my debut on the fifth of February, 1984. The day before, I was playing on the second division team. But the first division team hadn't won a title in three years. So people stopped filling the stadium. The coach knew he had to do something. And what he did was very unusual, very brave. He moved the second team up in the middle of the season. So all of us were very lucky. We were in the right place at the right time. And it turned out to be a great move. Four of those five players stayed with the club for a decade. And we formed one of the most famous groups in the club's history.

"So everything about that first game was like a dream come true. I started on the bench. Then, at halftime, we were losing 2–0 and I was called off the bench. We ended up winning 3–2, and I scored the first and third goals. And the third goal was in the last minute. My father was there to see it, which was one of the most special days of his life. There was no time left. There was a very long pass from our defender. It went in the air. Then our rebounder kicked it, but their goalkeeper saved it. But he didn't catch the ball. It was just lying there, a loose ball in the goal area. And I was there. So I tapped it in. I didn't have to do anything special. Only to be there. To be in the right place at the right moment."

What goes through your head when you're playing at that level?

"I thought. Then I didn't. When I didn't have the ball, I thought about what I needed to do to stop the opponent, to help the team, to score. But when I had the ball, I didn't think. I just turned on my pure instincts. In fact, if I did think when I had the ball, I would probably mess things up. So I learned to trust my instincts."

Those instincts would help him find the right place at the right time and keep him playing every game with the same intensity and desire to prove himself, as if he were trying out for the team for the first time.

3. Be Who You Are Right Now

José Luiz Tejon Megido's résumé makes him sound like several very accomplished people simultaneously. He is a professor, musician, author, motivational speaker, marketing expert, and head of a publishing house.

José Luiz grew up very poor in Santos, Brazil. One day, when he was just shy of four years old, his mother had just finished waxing the floor. She heated some wax at the bottom of a can to conserve it and pour the wax into another can. But the wax caught fire instead of just melting. As the can became too hot to hold, she threw it through her open doorway, just as José Luiz was walking in.

The flames engulfed his face.

He breathed in the fire. All he saw was a huge yellow light like a sun rushing toward him.

His mother stood paralyzed. A neighbor who saw what was happening grabbed a towel and covered his face, smothering the fire.

José Luiz didn't feel any pain, he said. Or, he doesn't remember the pain is probably a better way of putting it. But he does still remember the smell of the chloroform they used to knock him out.

"The doctors said it was a miracle that I did not lose my eyesight or my life," he said.

From that moment on he doesn't remember anything for about a year.

What José Luiz does remember is the hospital. From the age of 4 until he was 16 he spent most of his time in hospitals, undergoing countless skin grafts, some more successful than others. The technology at that time wasn't what it is today, and his family could not afford the top surgeons.

Once, late at night, he was crying because the result from one of the surgeries was worse than expected. José Luiz recalled, "An old man at the hospital called me over and said, 'Boy, why do you cry? Look around you. There are patients here who will only live a few days more. Don't just sit here and cry. Go and see them. And see what happens. Maybe you can help them by just being there.' It was a very simple message, but it changed my life and I carry it with me."

In the hospital he became an observer of people and a flier of paper airplanes. He would launch them over to someone then go to retrieve them and talk with whoever they landed close to.

During the times José Luiz was not in the hospital he just wanted to stay inside his parents' home because he didn't like the way he looked and, perhaps even more, didn't like the way other people looked at him.

But his mother said to him every Thursday that she needed his help selling their wares in the marketplace. And he would protest, "No, Mom. I don't want to. Please, no." Looking back, he realized that she didn't really need his help. "She was trying to help me. And eventually I lost my fear of the streets, of going out of the house. And the looks I would get didn't matter as much," he said.

> **"And I knew that I was more than how I looked. This gave me a new sense of confidence."**

The turning point came when José Luiz was 16 years old. "A great change for me was when I decided that I would not undergo any more surgeries. The doctors wanted to continue. They said there was more they could do. But I said, 'No. I am going to be who I am right now. Forget any more surgeries and recoveries and hoping for something else. This is who I am,'" he said. He paused, then added, "When I made the decision not to change anymore, to be fine with who I was, my life changed."

He had been playing rock 'n' roll guitar and writing music all along, and shortly after deciding to stop the surgeries, he joined a band and played in front of 5,000 people. "I could wear my hair long, so it fell over part of my face," he said. "That was the look. So it worked. And the music started to replace my face. And I knew that I was more than how I looked. This gave me a new sense of confidence. And when I heard the people applaud, I knew that everything had changed and that everything was going to be fine."

José Luiz does have a few photographs of himself before the accident. "People say I was a beautiful child," he said, as though describing someone else. "Assuming that's true, I could have grown to be a beautiful man. But I also would not know what I know now. So who can say what is best? If it hadn't been for the accident, I might have led a very normal, uneventful life. So I consider myself blessed, very blessed."

4. Pursue Something That Is Completely and Totally Interesting to You

When Angelo Sotira was still in high school, Michael Ovitz wanted to buy his online music-sharing business. The only catch was that his parents were firm about one thing: Angelo couldn't move out to Los Angeles until he graduated from high school.

That was in 1996, after he had developed a highly trafficked music site for downloading MP3s. "Fortunately, back then you didn't need a business model," Angelo explained. "You just put up a site, and word got out and people started coming and advertisers started paying you a lot of money. It was just something that worked very well at the time."

What Michael Ovitz recognized was that this high school kid knew how to make money on the Internet, a concept which eluded most businesses at that time.

This 15-year-old sophomore in high school (do we sound jealous?) was drawing up plans for what he wanted to do on his site during his chemistry and algebra classes at Our Lady of Lourdes High School in Poughkeepsie, New York. "Nobody understood the Internet quite yet," he said. "And I was completely and totally 100 percent dedicated to this idea. I couldn't allow anything else to get in the way. I was just focused on this; so it drove everything about me."

By his senior year he had it worked out. "I spoke with my principal about what I was doing, and he was very supportive. He embraced the idea and gave me total permission to pursue my business during school hours. He allowed me to have a cell phone in school, which no one else could have at that time. And if my cell went off in the middle of class, I was allowed to step out, no matter what my teacher said, because it was undoubtedly an advertiser. Some of the teachers did not take kindly to this, but I was talking about $50,000 deals, and I had permission from the top. So I just went about my business."

All the while, he added, "I was lying through my teeth because I couldn't tell the advertising execs that I was just a kid."

He added, "At this point, making money was an absolute toy. It was the most fun I could have. But there was an appeal that went far beyond that. I mean, I was the central figure in running a website. And there were hundreds of thousands of people visiting that site. I mean, it was a complete and total trip."

This was a time when the music industry was being turned on its ear. Artists and companies were up in arms because music was being downloaded for free. Then things started to get a little sticky for Angelo. Everyone was sending lawyers at him, every which way. He felt like he was dodging laser beams in a video game.

But Michael Ovitz realized the kid was onto something, and so a deal was struck in which as soon as Angelo graduated from high school, he would have an office in Los Angeles. The theory was that Michael wanted Angelo's perspective on potential investments, but Angelo found himself surrounded by a bunch of suits who were more interested in hearing the sound of their own voices. "I thought, maybe I should listen to them before sharing my thoughts," he said. "That was my mistake. If I had it to do all over again, I would have been more forthright from the beginning. That might have set a different tone. If I could have changed anything, it would have been that. I wish I had pushed forward a little more forcefully with my point of view and just gone for it a little bit more."

He left Ovitz in 2001, after two years, "because, in all fairness, Michael had a lot of other things grabbing his attention at the time, so he couldn't pay that much attention to what we were trying to do. It's completely understandable. But being with him was like an accelerated, advanced MBA program."

> **"At this point, making money was an absolute toy. It was the most fun I could have. But there was an appeal that went far beyond that."**

The most important thing Angelo learned from Michael Ovitz, "which calms me in the most insane circumstances, is the knowledge that life is full of conflicts," he said. "Michael got that. He greeted conflict head on. No problem. What's the solution? We'll figure it out and carry on. Conflict isn't to be avoided. It is one of the most valuable things that take place in a company. The best ideas and results can come out of conflict—if it is handled in a positive manner. Michael taught me how to embrace conflict, then enjoy what's going on around it," Angelo said, then added, "That's a very calming philosophy."

What advice would Angelo have for any teenager thinking about becoming an entrepreneur?

"Just choose something that is totally and completely interesting to you. Then give it your all. Behind every success story is someone who gave it every moment of his or her life. You've got to love it because it will consume your every waking hour and most of your sleeping ones too."

5. Embrace Your Roots

Knowing where you're from can help you appreciate where you are and feel more certain about where you're going.

Congressman Charles Rangel (D-NY) understands exactly where he comes from.

"I was born June 11, 1930, on Lenox Avenue and 132nd Street. Since I've become a big shot," he said, releasing his raspy laugh, "I've moved uptown to 135th Street and Lenox Avenue. All my life I've been in Harlem. I was basically raised by my mother, who was a seamstress, with the support of her father. I went to P.S. 89 and P.S. 139 and then DeWitt Clinton High School, but I dropped out to go into the army. So I went to Korea, where I got shot. And as I lay there bleeding, I told Jesus that if he got me out of that situation, he'd have no problem with Charlie Rangel anymore in life forever. The truth of the matter is, as a result of that experience, I can honestly say that I've never, never had a bad day since. How could I? Whenever anything is about to become a problem, my mind goes into automatic pilot and I think about how things could have been. How can I complain about the weather when I nearly died, freezing in combat, with temperatures of 30 degrees below?"

He was hit in the back, thrown in a ditch, surrounded by the enemy, high up in the mountains, near the Chinese border, in a place called Kuni-Re Pass, certain he was going to freeze to death before help arrived. With seemingly no way out, this 20-year-old sergeant led 40 men to safety from behind enemy lines over the course of three days and nights. Each night, he said, "we could feel our blood freeze and hear the bugles of the enemy. We couldn't sleep because they kept coming closer. It was a nightmare."

He won a Purple Heart and a Bronze Star after being treated for his wounds. "But I survived," he added, "so how the hell could I possibly find something to complain about? My life has been an incredible experience—from a high school dropout to a congressman," added the fourth most senior Democrat in the House, who won his seat in 1970 after defeating Representative Adam Clayton Powell, Jr., ending one of the most flamboyant congressional careers of modern times.

As one of the founders of the Black Congressional Caucus, he explained why they challenged both of President George W. Bush's declared victories: "The first election was stolen, no matter how you look at it. They hired a private firm to clean the voting records and eliminate anyone who had committed a felony, even though they had served their time. And they focused specifically on people with names like Jackson, Robinson, and Smith—any of the Anglo names that blacks have. The record makes clear that with all the intimidation in Florida, the election was just an absolute theft. And this is where the difference comes between whites and blacks when it comes to politics. First of all, whites just want to say, 'It's over, let's carry on.' But blacks have been on the losing end of these political things too long. And the vote was denied us for so long that we know how precious it is. And we just cannot accept these injustices the way someone else would. People died for our right to vote, and so we have to be outraged when an injustice occurs. So, as representatives of our people, we must stand up and let them know that we know what's going on and we don't approve. This last time, we had just one senator join us, Barbara Boxer, who has enormous courage, because, you can bet your life, Bush will never, never, never forgive her or forget her for what she did."

As far as his community is concerned, Charles knows it like he knows his own heartbeat. "There's no question I know my community better than anyone I can think of. I know its pulse, its feeling. Whenever there is an issue on the floor of the House of Representatives, I know that my feelings about that issue are those of the people I represent. We are one. I am from Harlem. It's in my blood. And it is such a good feeling to be validated when I come back home. I don't have to decide which way to vote and wonder what my constituents would think. I know what they think and feel. I grew up with the people in my neighborhood. We are all in this together."

> **"But blacks have been on the losing end
> of these political things too long.
> And the vote was denied us for so long
> that we know how precious it is.
> And we just cannot accept these injustices
> the way someone else would."**

Recognizing his roots, the Congressman has backed a commission to promote reparations for the descendants of former slaves and introduced legislation to reinstate the military draft, arguing that "a disproportionate number of the poor and members of minority groups make up the enlisted ranks of the military, while the most privileged Americans are underrepresented or absent."

Charles has what his friends characterize as an outsized personality, along with lawyerly powers of persuasion and a sense of humor that comes from enjoying life. He said, "Right now I spend a lot of time thinking about life and death. I guess I'm getting older. Whatever the reason, I tell all my friends who are ministers, 'If you see me talking with Saint Peter, don't you come trying to help me. You just stay where you are, because I feel better arguing my case on my own, rather than getting the church involved.'"

6. Customize Yourself

As one of the most legendary members of the Hell's Angels, Sonny Barger has lived a life of extremes, heading up what he calls one of the world's most misunderstood fraternities, habitually at odds with the law, often at the wrong end of a fist or a gun, spending serious time in Folsom prison where he says he got his *real* education, often found in his shop modifying a Harley, usually on the road searching for the ultimate ride, always seeking freedom.

Freedom is something Sonny has thought about a lot. Certainly more than most people. "America was born out of a revolution fostered by smart and tough renegades," he said. "Guys like Thomas Jefferson, Thomas Paine, Benjamin Franklin, Samuel Adams. They're all quintessential rebels, trouble makers and innovators who stayed loyal to one another and true to a single vision: freedom. When I say rebels, I mean it. Isn't it funny how the word *rebel* has taken on an entirely new meaning today?"

Sonny grew up in Oakland, California, where, when he was four months old his mother left him with a babysitter, ran off with a Trailways bus driver and never returned. "Leave it to my mother," he said, shaking his head. "She tried to get in touch with me when I was a teenager, but I didn't have any interest at that point." He described his father, Ralph, Sr., as "a hard working, hard-drinking, functioning alcoholic."

"If there's one thing—and it's the only thing—I can thank my mother for, it's the long-standing Italian tradition of calling their first-born Sonny. My real name was Ralph Hubert Barger, Jr., so Sonny sure beat being called Junior—not to mention Ralph or Hubert—all my life."

After serving in the Army, Sonny returned to the Bay area, where he decided he was either going to be a beatnik or a biker. "The beatniks were big in San Francisco in the 50's. But just before I went into the Army, I saw *The Wild One*. And Lee Marvin's character became my hero. He was cool, fun-loving and knew just the right thing to say. When some guy came up to him and said he'd been hit, he responded with the perfect answer: 'Well, hit him back.'"

So it was either a beatnik or a motorcycle rider. Both were unconventional. "They were the two major ways of life in the Bay area. Fortunately, I took up riding. Because most of the beatniks are now long gone. So that wouldn't have been a great career move," he said, smiling.

> **"Don't be so damned run-of-the-mill and buttoned down. There are already enough scared people out there occupying the middle of the road and afraid to show their colors or speak their minds."**

For Sonny, riding became more than just a pastime. "I built my life around motorcycles."

And riding has become a metaphor for many of his lessons in life. Like, *If you want to travel fast, travel light.* "Too many people complicate their lives by trying to have it all: the career, the money, the family, the respect, too many friends, too many cars and too many bedrooms in an empty house. For me, that's like the bike with so many gadgets on it that you forget why you're even riding it."

Another lesson: *There is no reverse gear on a motorcycle.* "I don't back down, nor do I retreat and retrace my steps. Instead of regret, I set my mind on forward-oriented goals. I'm a 'destination rider,' meaning I cover as many miles of road as quickly as possible. I'm covering maximum ground at maximum speed." He reflected, then added, "Have you been around people who dwell on the past, who are stuck in the good or bad times from another era? A real estate deal they should have made, a woman they should have married, the job they didn't take. They are going in reverse, big-time."

And he particularly likes to emphasize: *Customize yourself. Originals don't come off the assembly line.* "Don't be so damned run-of-the-mill and buttoned down. There are already enough scared people out there occupying the middle of the road and afraid to show their colors or speak their minds."

One of the lessons Sonny carries with him from prison is a clear sense of the importance of time. "For me, early is on time. On time is late. It's that simple," he said. "A lot of people like to be fashionably late. But if you deal with me (or anyone you respect), be on time. I'll go as far as to say, if you can't be early, don't even bother showing up. Keeping me waiting tells me all I need to know about you. You don't consider my time, or yours, valuable." He paused, then added, "I've 'done time' when time was an endless stretch in front of me."

When Sonny speaks, his voice sounds raspy and strained, as if it is hurting him to talk.

At book signings, when bikers bring their kids over to meet him, Sonny uses the opportunity to explain to them why his voice sounds so hoarse. "I think kids ought to understand what smoking does to you," he said. So he'll ask them, "Do you know why I talk this way?"

Staring at the gauze patch covering the hole in his throat, they shake their heads, nervously.

"Because I smoked cigarettes. And now I have a hole in my throat," he'll tell them. "Promise me you won't ever smoke cigarettes." He says the parents usually smile as their kid and Sonny shake hands on the deal. "Hopefully I've cost the big tobacco companies a few young customers."

As he was approaching his 44th birthday, he had a persistent, nagging sore throat that he suspected was serious. But he avoided getting treatment. By the time he was finally tricked into seeing a doctor, Sonny was told he was in the late stages of cancer of the larynx.

More than two decades ago, he was told he had less than two months to live. "Don't even bother to quit smoking, the doctors told me. I was a goner. So I smoked a Camel just before they wheeled me into the operating room to remove my larynx," he said.

After the operation, he was sent to a radiation treatment center. There he saw children who were laughing and running around the lobby, even though they were living on borrowed time. "That put things into perspective for me. I wanted to *live*," he said. "Fortunately, I defied the odds. So my advice to everyone is to not give up, just in case the doctors don't really know what they're talking about and you are that one-in-a-thousand cases that proves them all wrong."

A life without vocal cords meant relearning all the basics: eating, breathing and talking. "They cut a hole in the front of my neck, sewing my windpipe to my neck. When I recovered, they went back in and punched a hole in the back of my windpipe and inserted a plastic one-way valve through the front of my esophagus. When I put a finger over the hole in my throat, air gets trapped. I then vibrate a muscle in my throat, making the sound you hear when I talk. People tell me I now sound like Marlon Brando in *The Godfather*."

The Camel he smoked on the way to the operating room was his last cigarette. Since then, he's had his own personal campaign against smoking. While he is not a man who dwells on the past, he does admit to having one regret. "My biggest regret is that I smoked," he said. "Cigarettes are clearly one of the most deadly mass-marketed products. They are habit-forming, over-the-counter drugs that are legal only because tobacco has been such an important part of our economy."

Looking death in the face served as a turning point for Sonny. "I chose the option of reinventing my body and brain into a finely tuned machine, rather than letting it remain an abused receptacle for nicotine, booze and drugs," he said.

Beyond learning a new way to talk, Sonny said he has also learned a new way to listen. "Because speaking, for me, takes such effort, now, when somebody's talking to me, I not only hear their words, but I also study their faces and mannerisms. And since I intentionally hesitate a few moments before answering, I find that I'm able to think a little more about what's behind the words people say. My level of comprehension has increased. I've become a more succinct communicator. And I try to devote my full attention to whoever I'm talking to. And to make them feel special by looking them straight in the eye. If I regained my former voice tomorrow, I know that the qualities of being a better listener would stay with me."

What was it like being a leader of one of the most notorious biker groups?

"First of all, I have to emphasize that I am no longer a spokesperson for the Hell's Angels. So what I am sharing with you are just my own personal reflections. Essentially, I found that people would listen to me because I'd been around a long time. And because I would stand up and say what I thought."

But he was leading some really tough guys.

"We were all tough," he said, smiling enigmatically.

Sure. But some of those guys were six feet, six inches tall, weighing over 300 pounds, could bend metal with their bare hands and had tempers that would flare at a moment's notice. He couldn't just take them by the scruff of the neck and make them do whatever he wanted. How did he lead a group like that?

"First of all, I would never in my life ask somebody to do something that I wouldn't do right along side of them. Secondly, as a leader, I would listen to people. Leaders like to think they surround themselves with the brightest, the toughest and the best, but how many leaders have the balls to surround themselves with the most honest? There's bound to be lots of disagreement and dissent among dyed-in-the-wool individualists. That's the cost of surrounding yourself with real individuals," he paused, then added, "As a leader, my advice is: Don't confuse honest dissent with disloyalty. Take dissent as it is intended—provided it's honest. Listen hard. And don't take it personally. The voice of dissent may come from that lone, brave friend who will save you from making the biggest mistake of your life."

Was he a natural leader when he went to school? Was he popular?

"I don't think I went to school long enough to be popular," he said, laughing. "I was in tenth grade for three years before I finally quit. Then I went back to school when I was in Folsom prison. That's where I finished high school and got my associate's degree."

While Sonny's not shy about talking about why he landed in Folsom in 1973, what's most important, he said, is what he got out of it.

His criminal history, stretching from 1957 to 1987, includes 21 arrests on charges that include: possession of narcotics with intent to sell, assault with a deadly weapon, kidnapping, attempted murder, racketeering and conspiracy. As he said, you need a calculator to add it all up.

Ironically, Sonny talks about prison and the military with the same tone of respect. "Serving time in the barracks and behind bars teaches you discipline and survival," he said. "After doing the army and jail, you're ready for anything."

Ultimately, what Sonny is most ready for is working on and riding his bike.

"Messing around with motorcycles is what I do best. Modifying them, chopping them, customizing them to my own taste, then changing my mind, breaking them down and starting over again," he said.

That and the freedom he feels from being on the road.

"I've paid a terrible price for my freedom," he admitted. "I've learned the hard way that to understand my heart is to understand the evil that lurks inside. I can't hide behind religious traditions or superficial heroes. As a warrior, you've got to know pain and sadness alongside of joy and solitude."

Through it all, Sonny's underlying message is to *customize yourself, as you would your bike.* "You have to know who you are. Once you've figured that out, you're on your way," he said. "I'm me. I'm not you. I might be like you, without even knowing it. But I could never be like you by trying to be you. You've got to be yourself. Then customize yourself, so you're like no one else."

For now, just imagine Sonny on a long, open road, gripping the handlebars of his bike, with the wind in his face. Free as a bird.

7. Respond From the Heart When Disaster Strikes

Near the end of the movie *Starman*, Jeff Bridges, playing a visitor from another planet who takes on human qualities so he can somehow get the help he needs to return to his home, says to a scientist, "Would you like to know what I have learned that is most beautiful about your species?" Pausing for a moment, he then says, "You are at your very best when things are at their worst."

In difficult times, when we are challenged like we've never been before, we become more of ourselves. The shy become shier. The hiders go into serious hiding. The planners get out their paper and pencils. And the fighters start swinging for all they're worth.

David Oreck, Founder of Oreck Company, which makes one of the country's most recognized vacuum cleaners, the lightweight Oreck XL, found out what he and his company were made of when Hurricane Katrina struck the Gulf Coast, hitting the firm's corporate offices in New Orleans and its manufacturing facility in Long Beach, Mississippi.

Someone else might have taken this disaster as a sign that it was time to bow out gracefully, cave in to economic realities and take his manufacturing overseas.

But when David and his son, Tom, who is president of the company, got their executive team together the day after the hurricane turned their world upside down, relocating was not even mentioned.

"Inside that room, Tom directed the activities and he did a masterful job of creating teams," David recalled.

The world around them was falling apart.

"People have no idea of the devastation of that storm," David said. "Over a quarter of a million homes were destroyed. So many of those homes were under water. I mean right up to the rooftops. It was an extremely stressful, difficult time for so many people. More than a million lives were affected. We now know that one out of every three people lost everything they had. Living through that was like nothing I've ever experienced. I've served in the Second World War and I've been through countless hurricanes before, but I've never seen anything to compare to what happened with Katrina. The 120 mile sustained winds were gusting to 150 miles and you didn't know when your whole house was going to blow away."

> **"In difficult times, when we are challenged like we've never been before, we become more of ourselves."**

When the winds finally calmed down, Oreck's executive team hunkered down to determine what they would do without electricity or running water, with most roads undrivable, and with little hope of communicating with the outside world.

Keep in mind, also, that most of the executives had lost their homes, and their families were completely distraught. In that frame of mind, these executives took on projects they'd never before considered to get their employees a place to stay and to get their operations up and running again.

First off, they relocated about 150 people to Dallas, where they set up a crisis center and operated the administrative side of the business. Meanwhile, another team obtained state approval to have huge generators and fuel delivered. At the same time, a team was obtaining mobile homes to serve as temporary housing for Oreck's employees. The company's parking lot became a trailer park.

And the word got out.

Hundreds of employees who had lost their homes were put up in the temporary housing. The company also brought in food, medical care and crisis counselors.

Because the company's executive team knew what they stood for, they knew what they needed to do. So they could act on a dime. Oreck became the first factory along the hurricane-ravaged Gulf Coast to be up and operational.

"We were doing everything humanly possible to help our employees put their lives back together. We've all been there for each other. I'm glad we've been able to help make this difference for our employees—not just in terms of a paycheck, but to have meaningful work and a temporary place for them and their families. While this has been extremely stressful for all of us—all of our lives were turned upside-down and inside-out overnight—we've pulled through it together, with a stronger sense of loyalty and a clearer sense of what we are all about," David reflected.

He paused, then added, "You can't really prepare for the worst natural disaster in the history of our country. But it does test your essence. And gives you a chance to confirm what you believe in."

When you're in the midst of an ultimate emergency situation, how do you deal with the onslaught of questions, such as: How are you going to move a truck? How are you going to handle an order? How are you going to manufacture the merchandise? The answers to these questions becomes much easier when the tone of leadership is positive, clear and hopeful.

"When I look back, I wonder, 'How did we do all this?'" While incredulous, there is an underlying note of sureness in David's voice.

"All I know is that when our people are feeling good, it comes through to our customers. That's what we've always been about."

How many of Oreck's employees ended up returning to the manufacturing plant in Long Beach, Mississippi and its headquarters in New Orleans?

"Most are back," he said. "A few hundred are missing. They either haven't been located or just decided to move away entirely. But the majority are back. Of course, just moving them back is difficult because most of their homes have been destroyed. So we've been putting them up temporarily, while we help them find apartments or homes. But the important thing is that they have meaningful work, a community that supports them and a chance to start over. With that, we'll all get through this together."

8. Understand Your Past So You Can Create Your Future

Growing up in a village that was named for your family might seem like every kid's dream. Laura Kohler, who was born and raised in Kohler, Wisconsin, would tell you, however, that it was a mixed blessing, creating enormous possibilities along with daunting expectations.

The village bearing her family's name was incorporated in 1912 after her great grandfather started a small foundry and machine shop business. From that modest beginning, the company has grown into a world leader in resort hotels and golf courses, premier furniture, engines and power systems, and kitchen and bath products. The name Kohler has come to stand for integrity, understated elegance and the highest consistent standards. That's a lot for a young girl to grow up with, let alone live up to.

It was a circuitous route for Laura to become comfortable with her heritage and her potential. Now the Senior Vice President of Human Resources at Kohler, she is helping the company identify and develop talent that is transforming the company from an American-based multinational into a global organization.

> **Growing up in a village that was named for your family might seem like every kid's dream.**

While appreciating the privileges and opportunities that came with her family name, Laura was also driven to prove that she could succeed on her own terms. It was psychologically imperative to her that her personal achievements were seen as her own.

During the summers, she and her brother and sister worked in various capacities at Kohler, where they learned about the business from the bottom up. But, upon graduating from college, Laura headed for Washington, DC, where she earned a Master of Fine Arts Degree, managed a classical theater company, and then moved to Chicago where she earned an Equity and Screen Actors Guild Card, then founded and directed a theatre company called Address Unknown. The actors were homeless people and their performances aired on CBS's "Street Stories."

It wasn't until she was thirty that she interviewed for the position of Executive Director at the Kohler Foundation, an arts and education foundation, and found her way back to Kohler, the company and the village. For Laura, it was a matter of knowing she could come home again—on her own terms, knowing who she was and what she had to offer.

To be a leader in the company bearing her name is an enormous responsibility. "My father, brother, sister and I have to prove every day that we are not just figureheads, we are not just here because we carry the name. There is an incredible work ethic that comes with my family's name," she related. "In many ways, I find myself working much harder to cast aside any doubts that I am contributing in a very real way to this company." She paused, then added, "This company, which embodies so much history and achievement, is on the brink of such an incredible future."

The company now has more than 30,000 employees around the world, half in this country, half in Asia, Europe, the Middle East, and North Africa. It is a size and scope that her great-grandfather could never have imagined. As the company acquires other firms, enters new markets, introduces new products, opens new plants and is introduced to new customers around the world, Laura and her team are responsible for recruiting and developing the best talent from everywhere in the world. She and her team have to anticipate the competencies and skills required to lead what will be a global organization. She has to learn how to identify leaders who cannot just succeed today, but will help forge the company's future.

Laura focuses on identifying and developing leaders, because "the demand of leadership today, in my view, is much more complex than it has ever been historically. We are requiring more of our leaders today because of the complexity of the global marketplace. We need to identify someone who can lead in a world that is still being created. To do that, we look at psychological profiles as well the person's past accomplishments, how he or she works with others, analyzes situations, solves problems, shapes strategy, develops teams, builds trust, inspires others and continues to improve themselves."

She underscored, "As the world is changing, the very definition of leadership is also changing. The companies today that are thriving are those that are most flexible, most attuned to the market. It takes leaders who are constantly open, change-oriented, adaptable, looking for new challenges and can communicate very effectively—up, down and sideways."

The goal, Laura emphasized, "is to move our company from an American-based multi-national into a truly global company—with synergies and shared resources that help to fulfill an even larger vision." This, she emphasized, takes continual learning. "For example, when we first went into China with the Kohler brand, we realized that our U.S. print and TV ads needed to be modified beyond language to appeal to the Chinese sensibilities. We also discovered that the Chinese preferred European-designed products in some cases instead of our American designs, so we began utilizing designs from our European business as well. These are just two illustrations of how we are continually driving our business. We are in a constant process of learning, adapting and responding to the marketplace. And our leaders, in every market we enter, have to reflect that flexibility, have to be able to learn quickly, and know how to synthesize information to create vital, new synergies."

How does she help identify the right people for her company in markets that are completely new to her?

"Like much of my problem solving," she said, "I like to have my team with me. That's where I am my best. Some of the members of my team are more data-driven. Some have incredible experiences to draw upon. I am more intuitive and see the larger landscape. Once I have a clear understanding of the situation, I want to engage the best minds around me to challenge presumptions, question facts and work together to arrive at a solution that none of us could have reached on our own."

While she needed to prove her capabilities by first stepping outside the Kohler sphere, Laura has come to embrace both her role in driving Kohler's success and upholding the high standard the Kohler name symbolizes. And, from the shadows of the tower bearing her family's name, she has developed her own style of leadership that is very conducive to today's global marketplace, where information is shared freely, collaboration is vital and teamwork distinguishes the very best companies.

9. Be True to Your Convictions

Being a member of the minority party can be difficult when you're trying to accomplish certain goals. Do you compromise to get a little piece of what you're after or just make a statement, hoping that the strength of your convictions will cause others to reconsider their positions?

Congressman Rush Holt (D-NJ) said he sometimes feels he can be a little stubborn on issues that are dear to him. "Sometimes I think my sheer determination can get me in trouble with, say, the majority party. In other words, it might make it harder for me to compromise later because they have seen me in some situations where I have been uncompromising. There are some members of Congress who are just really good at working deals with the other side. And I certainly try to do that in various situations on a rational basis with personal contacts I've developed through the years. But I don't think I'm too good at it. I tend to believe so strongly in my convictions, that I will dig in my heels and the other side will see me as combatively liberal," he said, laughing in recognition. Then he added, "I'm not sure how I can do it differently, because it's just a natural reflex for me. Then afterward some of the key players on the Hill might dismiss me as someone who doesn't want to compromise, someone they can't work with."

Do you compromise to get a little piece of what you're after or just make a statement, hoping that the strength of your convictions will cause others to reconsider their positions?

Congressman Holt found himself in such a position over authorizing the current conflict in Iraq. "There were a lot of people around me saying, 'You've got to stick with the president.' The leader of the House at the time said there should not be an inch of daylight between us and the president on these issues of national security. But I just thought that was a wrong way to express it. But until the vote, I listened to everyone and tried to keep my mind open. In retrospect, however, I realize I couldn't have voted any other way than 'no' when it came to giving the president a blank check to go to war with Iraq. I told myself that I was really analyzing this and keeping an open mind, and I studied furiously everything I could get my hands on about the issue, but I had to follow my heart. Anything else wouldn't have been being true to myself."

The Congressman added, "The line between compromising and standing up for your beliefs is drawn a little more starkly in politics than anywhere else. In Congress, we vote one way or the other, and our votes are a matter of public record. But I think the principle of listening to your heart and standing up for what you believe in—that principle is the same for all of us in our daily struggles. In the end, all we can do is be true to ourselves."

10. Look in the Mirror and Be Able to Say, "I Did the Right Thing"

Francis Samuel's office is full of rugby memorabilia. He is particularly a fan of the All Blacks, the notorious rugby players from New Zealand, whose furious, resounding indigenous chanting before each match is enough to scare any opposing team into taking up some other sport.

Francis explained his decor this way: "Rugby is the sport that most resembles business."

But what if the other team is playing another game, say, basketball or football?

"Look, if you're playing rugby, it doesn't matter what game your opponent is trying to play; you're going to dominate," Francis said.

Francis is President of the Directory at CPR Billets, the leading wholesale exchange operator on the French market, which supplies financial institutions with foreign currency. In 2002 the company was turned on its ear when the euro arrived. Before that time CPR was transferring dollars into French francs into pounds sterling into

Deutsche Marks and back again. Then the Euro merged several of the currencies, so there were far fewer transactions. As a result, the company needed less than half its workforce. "It was a horrible, horrible situation," Francis said. "Suddenly we had more employees than we needed. But these were people who had worked for us for decades. Many of them had spent their entire professional careers giving everything they had to the company."

The European shift in currency became very personal for Francis.

What he did was devise an entirely new business model for his company. The game had changed, and he had to respond—like a rugby player. So, after a very quick analysis Francis led the way to converting CPR Billets into the cash hub for France. His company would still focus on transactions, its niche, but in a different way. It would make sure that all the banks and ATMs had euros. Because it was a major player but wasn't too big, it could adapt quickly. The company could adjust and still add value to the changing marketplace, thanks in part to Francis's new vision. He could imagine the future.

> **"I had to help everyone understand that the world had changed around us. It wasn't anyone's fault, and we didn't have time to get mad at anyone. All we could do was understand what was happening and respond to the best of our abilities."**

Do you remember the scene in *Butch Cassidy and the Sundance Kid* where they were trying to escape the federal marshals who were tracking them, and Butch and Sundance found themselves at the edge of an absurdly tall, jagged cliff? Bullets were whirring by them as Butch looked into the raging river below and said, "We'll jump," and Sundance responded, "Like hell we will." Then Butch tells him they have no choice. Finally, Sundance confesses, "I can't swim!" And Butch starts to laugh, saying, "The fall'll probably kill you." Then they look seriously at each other for just a moment, glance back at the posse firing at them, move closer to the edge, and step off.

That's about where Francis found himself. At the edge of the cliff, hoping he'd made the right choice, realizing the risk, and then diving into an entirely new situation, knowing he had no other options, all the while having to convince those with him that it was the right thing to do.

If he survived the leap, Francis knew he would have to let half of his people go. And that bothered the hell out of him. But if he didn't do something, the entire company would be wiped out.

He had to inspire the people around him and get them all enthused about a new vision while changing their jobs entirely.

He knew some people would make it and some wouldn't.

"I had to help everyone understand that the world had changed around us," Francis said. "It wasn't anyone's fault, and we didn't have time to get mad at anyone. All we could do was understand what was happening and respond to the best of our abilities. But there wasn't time to wallow. We had to move. For those who realized it wasn't terrible but saw it as an opportunity, everything would be fine. If they were going to keep saying, 'This isn't fair,' then they'd be stuck in the past and I couldn't help them. It wasn't going to be easy. It was going to take a lot of sweat. And it wasn't going to be as smooth as we might have liked. But, as a company, we had an objective, we knew our goal, and if you could help us get there, then you'd be valuable to the team. My role was to eliminate fear, help them understand the situation, then prepare them for the future."

Through the course of the most difficult professional transition in his life, Francis tried to be open, let everyone know what was happening, prepare them all for the future, and then, as a leader, make certain decisions to keep the company afloat.

The pain still coursed through him as he remembered having to let some people go who'd been with the company for more than 20 years but who weren't open to changing.

"But," he said, "what's important is that every day I had to look at myself in the mirror. I couldn't look away. I had to know I was doing everything I could to give everyone a chance. Then I had to deal with the reality of the situation that was surrounding us. And through it all, I was able to say to my reflection in the mirror, 'I did the right thing.'"

II. Know What You Stand For

Senator Debbie Stabenow (D-MI) knows a thing or two about facing difficult challenges. By the narrowest of margins, she unseated the

Republican incumbent, becoming the first woman elected to the U.S. Senate from the state of Michigan.

She inherited multiple constituencies that seem to be more in conflict with each other than ever before. But she holds them together through the strength of her convictions and by being very clear about what she stands for.

She stands firmly on issues such as reproductive choice, education, fair trade, and public funding for the arts, and she has strong support from labor and people of color.

How does she speak for groups that often can't speak with one another?

"The first thing I do is look for and emphasize the ways in which people are alike rather than different. I try to bring people together and focus on areas where we have common values. Politics is often the art of compromising in a positive way, but not compromising your values. For example, small and medium-sized manufacturers, and organized labor all now have a common interest, which is trying not to lose jobs to overseas companies. I spend a lot of time getting folks together who wouldn't normally agree to sit down with each other and help them arrive at the best possible solution," she said.

> **She holds them together through the strength of her convictions and by being very clear about what she stands for.**

Still, now more than ever, there seems to be so much money, time, focus, and energy spent on championing or defeating single issues, such as a woman's right to choose, gay rights, and stem cell research. Feelings run so hot and deep on these issues that conversations quickly turn into shouting matches. How does she stay above the fray, take strong positions on these issues, and still stay popular?

"I let people know who I am and what I believe in. I think people are most interested in somebody following their convictions, having integrity, and being able to stand up and fight for what they think is right," she explained. "Now, there are some people whose support I will never have. For instance, there are people who are opposed to abortion because they think it is a sin. They might never vote for me because I

am clearly pro-choice. So I just have to accept and respect their opinion—and know that there is nothing I can do about that. But most people have mixed feelings about this very sensitive issue, and so it helps
them and everyone else to know exactly where I stand and that I am
very clear about my position."

When Senator Stabenow voted against the war resolution for Iraq,
she knew she was taking an enormous career risk. "That was the most
important vote I've ever cast," she said. She weighed all the information available at that time about the possibility that Saddam Hussein
had developed weapons of mass destruction and the security risks that
could pose for our country. "Ultimately, I had to make my decision
based on the facts we were given and my own gut feeling. I'll never
forget how I agonized over that decision. So after making up my mind,
I spent a lot of time writing my position statement so that everyone
knew exactly why I was making a decision that was not popular at
the time."

Although the senator believes that compromise is possible, helpful
and necessary in much of politics, she added, "There are certain fundamental issues upon which you need to stand your ground—or you don't
stand for anything."

12. Sometimes You Just Have to Quit and Start Over

Howard J. Rubenstein, the nation's premier media advisor, has been at
the helm of the public relations firm bearing his name for over half a
century. His celebrity and media connections are legendary, with personal friends ranging from Larry King to virtually every president
since Jimmy Carter and clients ranging from BMW to the New York
Yankees.

Now in his mid-seventies, Howard maintains a gentlemanly manner. He runs in Central Park every day, which, no doubt, helps him
keep thinking so incredibly fast. He wears a New York Yankees World
Series ring, one of four he's been given by George Steinbrenner, with
whom he talks daily, on his left hand.

He still works 90 hours a week, but rarely uses a computer and
doesn't send e-mail. "You lose caution, and when you press a button, it's
gone forever," he explained in his measured manner. "When you write
or dictate, you are more thoughtful."

"'So what do you want to do for a living?' And I didn't know how to answer his question. I didn't have a clue."

Howard has developed a reputation as a man of his word in a field where that is a rarity. He has a succession plan, which recognizes his two sons, for his firm that employs nearly 200 professionals, though he has no plans to retire soon.

Just how did it all start?

"My turning point," Howard explained, "was after I graduated from the University of Pennsylvania. I entered Harvard Law School. And two months into the first semester, to my parents' consternation, I quit."

Why walk away from such a coveted opportunity?

"I just knew it wasn't for me. I liked the rigor of law, and I didn't have trouble learning the material. But I didn't like the combative nature of the legal profession. And I just knew in my heart that I didn't want to do that for a living."

So he left Harvard's ivy-covered walls without the faintest idea of what he was going to do. "I might have to be a shoe salesman or just do anything to make ends meet. I had no idea what my next move would be. But I just couldn't become a practicing lawyer. I knew that. My parents were terrific, though they were heartbroken. They just said, 'You've got to find your way and do what you like.' This was when reality knocked—real hard.

"My father, a crime reporter for the *New York Herald Tribune*, said, 'So what do you want to do for a living?' And I didn't know how to answer his question. I didn't have a clue. I was really lost. The only thing I knew for sure was that I did not want to be a lawyer."

Howard's father, whose statue greets clients in Rubenstein Associates' waiting room, leaning over an old typewriter, pounding away on the keyboard, with his green visor forever protecting his eyes, said, "Well, son. Why don't you try public relations?"

Howard started his fledgling business at his parents' kitchen table, searching for possible clients. "The first day I was typing away, when the phone rang, and I said, 'Mom, do me a favor, would you pick it up and say, "Rubenstein Associates. May I help you?"' She made it amply clear that she was not about to do that," he said, laughing. "So I had to find a new location for my business."

His father taught him how to write a press release, how to develop a media list, how to start pitching prospects, and that he would succeed by always telling the truth. Apparently those lessons took.

How has Howard seen his profession change?

"When I first started, they called us hacks. They'd bring us in after a decision was made and ask us what to do," he explained. "Now we are an integral part of the decision-making process because major corporations and governments know that perception needs to conform to the truth and reality. So you now see public relations elevated to the corporate boardroom, which is very gratifying for me."

Is there any advice he gives across the board to his clients?

"I advise all the corporations I work with to seek out good causes to back economically and with their time. The cause could be the environment, health, welfare, or anything focused on improving the human condition. I urge them to select a cause that excites them, then adopt that cause, move in heavily, back it financially, and give it time and talent—so you can leave your mark on society. There's more to success than making money," he said. "And all the individuals and corporations that do this find it personally very gratifying. It connects us all in a very real, meaningful way."

13. Don't Let Others Define You

Representative Bill Shuster (R-PA) won a special election in May 2001 to succeed his father, Bud, who cited health concerns for stepping down.

Bill was running in a district in south-central Pennsylvania where his family name is very well known. Interstate 99, which runs through the district, is named the Bud Shuster Highway after his father, who was known as the legendary "Congressman Concrete" because of the enormous amount of funds he'd acquired to improve roads and other public works projects in Pennsylvania and the rest of the country.

Bill acknowledged that his father was a tough act to follow.

Growing up with a father who was, as Bill described, "an icon" was not a breeze. His dad was bigger than life in many ways. Before becoming a congressman, Bud was a successful business executive in Washington, DC, who also owned a 500-acre cattle farm in central Pennsylvania.

Bill grew up in Washington until he was 11, when his family moved back to Bedford County in central Pennsylvania. Though only two hours away, the two locations were separated by worlds. As Bill said, "James Carville, who is not one of my favorite political people, once described Pennsylvania as Philadelphia in the east, Pittsburgh in the west, and Alabama in the middle. It is very rural." The largest town he represents is Altoona, with about 50,000 people. The next biggest town is Chambersburg, with about 17,000, and the next largest town has about 5,000. As he described it, "It's a lot of rural areas and small towns."

His father set quite a standard, and every day growing up Bill dealt with that. "It was always a challenge for me. As a kid, I thought that if he can succeed, I've got to. I didn't have to do it exactly as he did. But the bar was set high. Right or wrong, that's just the way it was. Every day I had to deal with that. And I had to come to terms with the fact that I have much of my father in me, but I am more than that. I also have a lot of my mother. And I've got other strong influences. The simple truth is that I always felt I was very much my own person. I think people recognize that."

Still, when he was playing high school sports, there were people who would say, "The only reason he's starting is because of his father." As Bill explained, "I knew that wasn't true. If there was anything I knew for sure, it was that I was an above-average athlete. And I knew I worked harder than anyone else around me. That's just part of who I was."

> **Growing up with a father who was,
> as Bill described,
> "an icon" was not a breeze.**

When the playing field changed, he found the same kind of people saying the same kinds of things. "When I first walked onto the floor of Congress as an elected official, it was daunting because I was Bud Shuster's son. And everyone knew him there. So they expected me to be either a complete asshole or a hard-driving, brilliant, hard-nosed guy. And they were just waiting to see what would come out," he said, laughing at the memory. "The truth is, I'm somewhere in the middle but hopefully have none of the worst of either of those qualities."

Bill explained, "Most of the representatives in Congress knew my father at the end of his career, when he kept his emotions in check and became harder. Then one day, one of these gentlemen who had been on the losing end of a clash with my father came up to me and complimented me on my style and approach without any reference to my father. Just talking about how I had handled a particular situation. And afterward I thought, that validates it. I'm my own person."

14. Reinvent Yourself

When Susan Magrino graduated from college, she was poised to do exactly what she wanted to do, which has absolutely nothing to do with what she's succeeding at today.

In her early twenties Susan was working at the Biltmore Hotel in Los Angeles as a florist. There was no question she had a talent for it. She was setting the stage for major Hollywood parties and helped coordinate the look for the Emmy Awards and the fiftieth anniversary of the Academy Awards.

Then she broke out. In a rash. A rash that wouldn't go away. Somehow the pollen built up in her system, and she became allergic to flowers. Her work was making her sick. Once she had to be rushed to the hospital, swelling up, unable to breathe. She sometimes had to slam a needle into her hip to try to stop the reaction. It was getting serious, and the more times she had allergic reactions at that level, the less time she had to get medical treatment. The last job she did was the Grammy Awards. "I had to wear gloves up to my elbows. And a gas mask. It was ridiculous. What was I going to do?" she asked, as if we might know.

"I was sick of my job," she said, laughing at the way it sounded. "And the crazy thing was that I loved what I was doing. But I just couldn't do it anymore. It was literally dangerous to my health."

She got a job as a marketing administrator for AT&T. And as she worked her way through various promotions, she realized she could sell. When they first came out, she sold fax machines to people who didn't have the faintest idea why they might want one.

If you just step back and think about it for a minute, the person who sold the very first fax machine was the ultimate salesperson. Who were they going to fax anything to? Selling is easier when something catches on. You want to be in early. But not too early.

At any rate, Susan was doing incredibly well. In fact, she eventually became their number one salesperson in the country. But then something happened. The branch manager adjusted the quota, retroactively changing the game, and that diminished the commissions of her last huge sale. Susan went in to talk with her boss about how unfair that was. He just shrugged his shoulders, saying things like, "What are you going to do?" Without thinking that long about what she was going to do, she hauled off and gave him an uppercut to the chin, knocking him down into his chair. It was the last thing either of them expected. "And it derailed my career there for about four years," she said, laughing at the memory.

It became a strange time for her at the company. "The workers were on my side. They were like, 'Yeah, Susan. This guy lied, and you nailed him.' And management and I weren't exactly on speaking terms," she said. "So it was strange. Until that point my career was all about climbing. I wanted to be on the side of management. But I became the dividing line between these two worlds."

> **The person who sold the very first fax machine was the ultimate salesperson. Who were they going to fax anything to?**

Years later all was forgiven, and she went on to manage Northern California and Hawaii for AT&T. There she learned to identify people's potential and give them a second chance. But as the company grew and changed, she didn't find herself connected to its changing values. So, when the company came up with a voluntary retirement package for 30,000 people, she signed up.

During her exit interview her boss wanted to know why she was leaving. She had developed a loyal team of individuals who had grown personally and professionally and would do anything for her. So why?

At first she gave him the corporate spiel. You know, I think it's time to move on, it's me, not you. Then she said, "I can't lead anymore for AT&T." And he said, "I don't buy that. What do you mean, you can't lead anymore? You've been leading here for years. You're an incredible leader." And she said, "I can't lead anymore because I can't follow where the company is going."

So she reinvented herself again.

She left AT&T, not sure what she was going to do next. She had not been unemployed since she was 12 years old, working part-time as the fish girl at Howard Johnson's.

A headhunter gave her the best advice: "You need some time to sort things out. Don't just jump at the next promising opportunity."

That's the hard part, Susan realized: "I had to figure it out for myself."

After much careful consideration she discovered that what she found most rewarding was helping other people to first recognize their potential, and then realize it.

She took her pension from AT&T and invested it in a company she founded, WorkForce OS, which helps individuals and companies identify each other's skills and talents and match them for the future. Through advanced technology, she's looking to help managers, employees, and potential employers recognize what they're looking for in each other, determine if there is a match, and find the best way to move forward.

15. Accept Your Own Challenges

"I had a tremendous fear, a real fear, of underachieving and being unable to fulfill the expectations of other people." This voice belongs to the New York State Senate Minority Leader and Lieutenant Gubernatorial candidate, David Patterson. "I just didn't want to hear the comparisons," he said. Those comparisons invariably were with his father, who was the first person of color to serve as New York's Secretary of State and to run for Lieutenant Governor on a major party ticket. When a father and son have so much in common, establishing your own identity can be difficult. The comparisons started as a child. "I could speak well in front of an audience. I had a certain rhythm, and audiences could feel it, and I could hear them say, 'He's really going to do something. He's really going to be something.'" At that time he loved to hear the enthusiasm behind those accolades. But as he got older, those pressures created an anxiety that stemmed from David's not believing he was living up to what was expected of a strong leader's son.

He wanted to avoid the scrutiny and disappear.

"My dad's always been there for me. And I'm very proud of him. It just took me until now to escape being compared to him. First by others, then by myself."

While David was in law school, a teacher asked him to come and share his experiences with nine sight-disabled students in the high school where she taught. She had heard David, who has been blind since birth, speak in public before and couldn't help being impressed. But he put her off, saying he was cramming for exams and couldn't find the time. That went on for three years, until she said to him, "You once sold me a ticket to the Black Law Students Dinner, where you admonished your colleagues to always remember where they came from. But aren't you forgetting where you came from? Why won't you come speak to these students? Wouldn't it have been meaningful to you if some successful older blind individuals had come in and talked with you about their experiences?"

David said her cutting remarks upset him greatly. "I was very angry toward her. How dare she?" he said. "Then, over the course of several restless nights, I realized she was right. So I called her up and apologized for taking so long and accepted, and said that she had hit the nail on the head: I had insecurities about being represented as a blind person. But I was glad she had pushed me. I told her she could count on me to be there."

David said he actually spent hours studying the latest technology, research, and potential cures for blindness. Then, after his prepared remarks, he opened it up to questions. That was when he realized that he had lost touch with his audience. "They wanted to know how I got dates when I was their age. And how did I get rid of my escort so I could have some time alone with my date? And how could you tell if someone wanted you to kiss them?" And David just laughed to himself and opened up, speaking to the kids from his heart about his experiences. Reaching inside himself, he remembered those awkward moments, and sharing them became very freeing.

After graduating from law school, he was tapped to run for state senator. It was a tough campaign. He gave it all he had. And the night of the election, he remembers his father asking if he was prepared for the possibility of losing.

David said, "I feel I'm going to win," which he did. Then he added, "I've given it everything I have, Dad, so whatever happens, I'm fine with it, because I have no regrets."

As David recalled the story, he still had mixed feelings about his father's question. "I'm not sure if he was trying to protect his son from the possibility that I might get hurt. Or if he didn't really think I would win. Or if he thought that if I did lose, I might be so caught up in the moment that I wouldn't be graceful. I'm not sure where his question came from, because he was an astute student of politics. He could read the tea leaves. And he knew me. So I'm not sure why he asked me that the night I had my first victory. Maybe it was just a reality check. Maybe he feared losing every time he ran, though nobody would ever know it from the confident way he carried himself."

At any rate, that comment still troubles David, even though he's been a formidable political force in New York City politics for many years, having gone on to become the minority leader of the state senate, and often is spoken of for higher office in New York City and the state.

Is his father protective? Or a force to be reckoned with?

The answer is probably a bit of both. His father is a highly accomplished individual who declined to be the keynote speaker at his son's high school graduation because, as he said, "This is David's day. It is his event. I don't want to upstage him in any way. I want to celebrate my son."

"My dad's always been there for me," David said. "And I'm very proud of him. It just took me until now to escape being compared to him. First by others, then by myself." He thought about what he had just said, shrugged, and added, "In Dante's *Inferno*, he writes about going through a transformation in the middle years of his life. That's probably all I'm going through."

16. When You Get Sick of What You're Doing, Stop Doing It

In studies we have conducted in virtually every industry, we have discovered that approximately three out of every four employees are what we term "misemployed." By that we mean they are performing in jobs that do not play to their core strengths. As a direct result, they are missing out—for their employers and for themselves—since they do not feel fulfilled by what they are doing and do not perform as well as expected. They may be getting by adequately, but that's about it. They are hardly succeeding. And the unfortunate truth is that more often than not these misemployed employees have other talents, which they are wasting because they are in the wrong job. Misemployment creates ill-fated results for employers and individuals alike, not the least of which are poor productivity, low morale, and, in the case of Jane Sanders, literally getting sick of her job.

Jane had been succeeding very nicely on the corporate track. Carnation, now known as Nestlé, had paid for her master's degree in business administration while moving her through the ranks of the marketing department. Then, as she approached the next position of group product manager, a feeling she couldn't deny started seeping in. She came to realize she didn't fit into the corporate environment. She felt like she was faking it. And she didn't recognize who she was becoming. Ironically, the executives at Carnation recognized her as having sales, marketing, and management potential—a great combination in the corporate world. Yet, Jane was experiencing a growing discontent, a disconnect between her job and herself, and between what she was doing and who she was becoming. So she left and worked for companies that sold their graphic design capabilities to Fortune 500 firms. Then, when a recession hit, Jane was really struggling. She was working harder than she ever had before. Then, the day she pulled in a million-dollar account that virtually saved the company, instead of celebrating, she told her boss that she had to go on disability.

As it turned out, Jane had chronic fatigue syndrome and Epstein-Barr syndrome, which was depleting all her energy. Before that she had gotten up early and headed out to scuba dive or run or ride horses. But then she started noticing that two or three days a week she'd just turn the alarm off and go back to sleep for a while. "I knew it was unusual for me," she said. "But I didn't think much of it. I was working extremely hard, so I just attributed it to all the pressure and concerns at work." Then she started getting migraines, which she never had before. Then her fatigue level took over.

> ## "I realized that working so hard at something that was not really fulfilling had contributed to my getting ill."

At that point all she knew was the pain of the headaches and the constant fatigue. She moved back home with her parents for a couple of months, where, as she described it, "I would just sit in a chair. I couldn't even watch television. It was just too much stimulation." As she collapsed into herself, Jane ran out of money, lost her home, and, as she said, "went into all kinds of financial problems."

Everything she was used to feeling was gone. "I was just this thing in a chair," she said. It was completely debilitating.

Then, as she slowly got some of her energy back, Jane started thinking she had to get back to work. The only thing she knew for certain was that she absolutely didn't want to go back to what she had been doing. She knew her boss would have her back in a heartbeat, but that was no longer what her life was going to be about. "I realized," she said, "that working so hard at something that was not really fulfilling had contributed to my getting ill."

Now Jane is able to look back on those times and smile a bit, saying, "It brings a whole new meaning to being sick of your job."

"The truth is," she explained, "I knew I wasn't doing what I was supposed to be doing. And I wasn't doing anything about it. So, I believe that God stepped in and said, 'Okay, if you're not going to do anything about changing your life, I will.' And the rug was pulled out from under me. Because I kept ignoring the signs that I was spending my life doing something that I was not supposed to be doing."

Although Jane had time to reflect on it, she still had no idea what she should be doing with her life. As she began to recover, she embarked on a very intense personal growth mission. She read all kinds of things, attended seminars, talked with people. She focused on the favorite parts of her past careers—speaking and teaching. And she started to realize that wherever she landed, it would have to do with the journey she'd just been on. "I've got a story to tell about not being true to myself and how it affected me," she realized. She joined Toastmasters and the National Speakers Association and honed her presentation skills. Then groups such as the Society for Human Resources Management asked to hear her story, and she gathered the confidence to go out on her own as a speaker. "It was terrifying," Jane recalled. "Absolutely terrifying. The only thing I knew for certain was that I did not want to go back on the corporate track. So I faced the fear and branched out on my own."

The first year, she said, "I made only $7,000."

Now, as a speaker, trainer, facilitator, and consultant, Jane has an extensive client list, including Prudential, MassMutual, Ford, and Toyota. Her passion, as she explained, is helping people, especially women, reach their personal and professional potential, whatever that means for them. She is able to inspire individuals and audiences when she starts out one of her programs by asking if they feel overwhelmed, stuck, or unable to pursue their true dreams. They know they are listening to someone authentic, someone who is genuinely searching and can point out some road signs, detours and alternate routes on the way to true self-awareness.

24

Knowing the World Around You

T*he individuals who succeeded by knowing the world around them had a natural ability to sense the opportunities that came their way.*

17. Challenge the Status Quo

WHEN REPRESENTATIVE Jan Schakowsky (D-IL) was elected to Congress, she began hearing horror stories about the long lines and poor service at the Immigration and Naturalization Service's downtown Chicago office. "People who simply needed an update on their immigration status were telling me they'd wait all day only to be told to come back the next day. They'd wait in the rain, they'd wait through unbearable heat advisories, they'd wait through freezing cold, they'd wait with snow falling on them. They'd just wait and get nowhere. Frustrated and powerless, they didn't know where to turn for help. They were afraid that if they took more time off from work, they would lose their jobs. Then, if they were lucky enough to finally get to see an official, they'd be told the INS didn't have their fingerprints or had misplaced something else, so they'd have to start all over. They felt like they were trapped in a game with no official rules except one: they couldn't win."

"Power is to share and transfer and understand so it can empower other people."

Congresswoman Schakowsky decided to do something about it. One afternoon she showed up at the INS office without identifying herself. She stood in a discouragingly long line that barely moved for more than three hours, only to be told she had to go home and try again some other day. It was as if the Great and Powerful Oz had spoken, but she wasn't going to play the part of Dorothy. When she didn't leave fast enough, a worker told her to get moving or she'd be hauled off to jail. The Congresswoman replied that she didn't appreciate being spoken to that way, and that didn't go over well. The worker, in an all-too-official tone, demanded to know who she was. The Congresswomen replied, "First of all, I'm a human being. And you shouldn't be speaking to anybody that way. Second, I'm a United States Representative."

The worker replied, "That's not fair."

Congresswoman Schakowsky replied, "Actually, it's very fair. I got more votes than anyone else. That's how these things work."

The flustered worker disappeared and then came back, saying that the district director would very much like to meet the congresswoman upstairs.

"I said that if he wanted to see me, he could come downstairs and explain to me and all these other people why they had waited all day and couldn't be served and why they were being treated so rudely," she said.

In a matter of a few weeks the lines had disappeared.

That story defined how Congresswoman Schakowsky wants to use power. "Power is to share and transfer and understand so it can empower other people," she said. "Ultimately, the goal is to make a difference. To challenge, shake up, and change the status quo."

18. Admit When You've Made a Mistake, Then Turn the Situation Around

When leaders talk about their defining moments, their successes are not what come to their minds first. Instead, the leaders we've assessed and interviewed view their defining moments as the times when they weathered unexpected storms that tested their very essence.

They've shared, with enormous candor, failures and mistakes they made that could have derailed their careers. And they've reflected on what they've learned through adversity, how those times hurt, and how they carried on with more determination and focus—and a clearer understanding of their own strengths.

Sara Mathew, the Chief Financial Officer of Dun and Bradstreet, recalled one of her defining moments when she was with another Fortune 500 company. She had decided to completely revamp the firm's investor relations program and make it one of the most enviable in the country. To pull that off, she knew she had to move very rapidly. As part of the introduction for that program, she coordinated the firm's first live webcast, with hundreds of investors tuned in. But the webcast fell apart at the seams. "I did a terrible job, as nearly every major financial publication in the country cited," she recalled. Overnight, everyone in the industry knew who she was, but not as she wanted to be known. "I could go on and on, citing what went wrong," she said. "It was years ago, and I can still remember every detail like it was yesterday. That should say a lot, right?"

> ## "I let him know that the problem was not the direction. It was the poor execution. And I owned that. And my team and I could fix it."

As it turned out, several months later Sara did create for the company one of the best investor relations programs available.

But we're getting ahead of ourselves.

How did she turn the situation around? As she recalled, "My CEO was immediately firm about one thing: that we would never do this ever again." How did she convince him that the company needed that program? That the company's stock would rebound? That the company needed to do it right? And that she deserved a second chance?

Sara says it took her a few days to pick herself back up, shake off the dust, and figure out what she needed to do differently. She knew her window of opportunity had closed, and she had to get it open again. Time was finite and not on her side.

"I think the most important time is immediately after something goes wrong," she said. "It's recognizing the situation and admitting that yes, I made a colossal mistake." Then she went back and figured out exactly where, when, and how things went wrong, how she could have handled the situation differently, what resources she had within the organization, and, most important, how to convince the CEO—who, as she said, "had already decided never to try that approach again and had written a letter to that effect"—to ignore the media and the stockholders. How could she persuade him to give her a second chance?

"The first part was helping him understand how the world was changing around us," she explained, "and that we couldn't continue down our current path regardless of how safe it felt. Meanwhile, I let him know that I completely understood his position and why he had closed the door." But she emphasized that there was a limited period of time to connect their innovative new program with an innovative technology. If they didn't come back and do it right, a competitor would. And the competitor would own that new territory while her firm would be remembered as only a failed footnote in their innovation. "Then I let him know that the problem was not the direction. It was the poor execution. And I owned that. And my team and I could fix it," she assured him.

At that point she expressed, as only she could, her unwavering belief in the project and how it could differentiate the company from its competitors. "I do believe," Sara said, "that passion goes a long way in persuading people to try certain things. When you are passionate about doing something, people sense it and want you to succeed. In this situation it helped to open a door that had been closed and locked. If you are passionate about something, it impacts you as a person because it won't allow you to give up. If you don't have passion for doing something, it's better not to do it at all. I genuinely believe that."

Sara's belief in herself and her cause, her disappointment in its failure, her feeling the sting of rejection very personally, her ability to learn quickly from her mistakes, her persuasiveness, her open style of problem solving, and her carrying on with a newfound confidence embody the key qualities that distinguish top leaders.

19. Realize When You're Lucky and Grab Your Opportunity

After Danny Goldberg dropped out of college, he got a job with Lee Solters, a Broadway public relations maven with clients who included Barbra Streisand, Frank Sinatra, and Ringling Brothers.

Back in 1973 Danny was, as he described it, "a long-haired rock guy," and so he was the natural choice to represent Led Zeppelin when Lee Solters signed the band as a client.

What did he do as the publicist for Led Zeppelin besides say, "They did what? I can't believe it. That's terrible. I am so sorry. Don't worry, we'll pay for everything."?

Danny was busy arranging interviews with mainstream media, including radio and television stations and front-line magazines. First and foremost, he explained, he connected with the group's stars, singer Robert Plant and guitarist Jimmy Page, who were fascinated by the American hippie era. They were breaking the Beatles' records for attendance at live performances and they liked the fact that Danny was a little younger than they were and had long hair but could still communicate with people in suits.

Working with Led Zeppelin would be the turning point in Danny's career. His job was to help move them from a major cult band to having the rest of the world know about them.

"Nobody exactly knows what anyone does in the entertainment business," he said, laughing, "so you're judged solely on who you work with and the fact that they think you're okay. There is nothing better than being associated with someone who is admired. It puts you in a different category. What you have to realize is that once you're there, that's your entrée to the next people you're going to meet. So you've got to get lucky. But then you've got to recognize when you're getting lucky and grab the opportunities that are around you."

He paused, then added, "You also can't forget that success has a short shelf life. You have to keep refreshing it and repositioning it because the present becomes the past every minute."

Now, there's a guy who's listened to a lot of Dylan.

Danny went on to manage Nirvana, Bonnie Raitt, and the Beastie Boys, then was at the helm of Mercury Records, then Warner Brothers Records, then Atlantic Records before forming his own record label, Artemis, where he released albums by many notables, including Warren Zevon and Steve Earle.

Nirvana and Led Zeppelin seemed in many ways to live in parallel universes. "But it was an entirely different time. I was older when I was with Nirvana, so it was a very different relationship. The similarity was that both bands had geniuses and both were very, very important to the story line of rock and roll. And both bands lived the life. Dave Grohl, the drummer in Nirvana, was always asking me about Zeppelin's drummer, John Bonham. But there were important differences also. Zeppelin was much more flamboyant and much more about money. They were the epitome of rock excess, whereas Nirvana was a product of the punk rock tradition, which was really a reaction against rock excess."

For a while Danny was also the nemesis of Tipper Gore, who wanted to label certain lyrics as offensive so that parents could prevent their children from listening to them. "She represented the sensibility of people who were offended by what was then considered dirty rock music," he explained. The two of them wound up on many television talk shows, debating the issue. "I thought she was dead wrong, but I liked her personally," Danny said. "I don't think you can legislate morality or impose an aesthetic on an entire country. I know there's a whole argument now that Democrats don't get moral values, but I don't think it's moral to impose your views on others. I'm more of a free-market, change-the-channel-if-you-don't-like-it kind of guy."

He added, "The problem with censorship right now is that, for instance, the Federal Communications Commission regulates certain types of media but not others. So the ones they regulate will lose younger audiences, who will just migrate to other forms of media. Then, when the lines of censorship become blurry, you get the worst situation, which is self-censorship. That becomes the most onerous form of censorship, because it stops free thinking dead in its tracks."

> **"You also can't forget that success has a short shelf life. The present becomes the past every minute."**

Censorship certainly gets at the heart and soul of rock 'n' roll. At the request of the largest retail chain in America, the title of the Matthew Good Band's album had to be changed from *A Boy and a Machine Gun* to *A Boy and* followed by three dots. "In Canada we could say what we wanted on the album cover," Danny said, "but you can't buy guns in the same store as the album. At the largest retail chain in America, you can't have the word *gun* on the album cover, but they sell real guns!"

Danny wrote a book *Dispatches from the Culture Wars*, which he subtitled *How the Left Lost Teen Spirit* to clarify his "liberal, political, activist thinking" without having Tipper Gore interrupt him.

Most recently, in keeping true to his philosophy of grasping the opportunities that present themselves when you're lucky, Danny has taken a new leadership position at the helm of Air America, the unapologetically liberal radio network.

20. Find Something That No One Else Is Doing and Make It Yours

The first thing we have to tell you about Fergal Murray, the Guinness Brewmaster, is that he's not on this planet to conform to anyone's Irish stereotype—even on Saint Patrick's Day. He's not here to keep people laughing with humorous anecdotes and winding tales. Fergal is a scientist and an ambassador, who is serious about upholding Guinness's reputation as a brand that is Irish, yet transcends its roots. "First of all, we're talking about tradition," Fergal explained with more than a hint of reverence in his unmistakable brogue. "The four principal ingredients in Guinness Stout are the same today as they were in 1759: a roasted and Irish-grown malted barley, our unique Guinness yeast, water from the Dublin mountains, and hops, from around the world."

To a beer lover, Fergal seems to have a dream job. He is recognized as the expert and spokesperson for his favorite product. This scientist has an MBA as well as a Master Brewer degree. (Hey, what do you have to do to get one of those degrees?) Fergal's advanced degrees and unmatched understanding of the Guinness brand have enabled him to work for the company in Nigeria, the United States, and at the birthplace of this cultural icon, the Guinness Brewery at St. James's Gate.

Although Guinness is known as an Irish brew, it is made in 51 countries around the world, including places like Jamaica, Ghana, and Indonesia. And Fergal told us there are over ten million pints of Guinness sold every day around the world.

Does he have to taste every batch?

"No. Part of my role includes tasting—which certainly makes this an unusual (and some would say perfect) job. But I spend a lot of my time as an ambassador for the brand. What I deliver is an incredible knowledge and a personal passion for the brand and its brewing legacy and heritage with Ireland."

It's not just a beer to Fergal. The dark black nectar under the creamy head is the same one that was served to Padraic Pearse before Easter Sunday, the same one that William Butler Yeats sipped before writing "A Terrible Beauty Is Born," and the same one that any respectable rugby player will demand after winning or losing an important match.

"The more I practiced, the more positive feedback I got, which pushed forward the idea that there was something here. An opening for me. So I went for it."

So how did Fergal get to be an ambassador for Guinness?

"It evolved," he said. "The brand's rich tradition has a lot to do with mystical, magical, mythical misconceptions. People love to talk about where you can get the best pint. How should it be poured? Does it travel well? These types of conversations are unique to Guinness. They don't occur over any other beers. Our brand brings out something different. And it's my job to clarify these conversations."

But how did the job evolve?

"You never know when you identify these things clearly. But I think what happened to me was that I started to hear from people that journalists and customers were interested in having these questions answered. I enjoyed it and felt comfortable doing it. So I thought, 'Maybe I should work on that.' And the more I practiced, the more positive feedback I got, which pushed forward the idea that there was something here. An opening for me. That I had something else to offer. So I went for it."

He started something, got positive feedback, understood there was an opportunity, built on it, tested it out, learned his trade, and went for the opening with everything he had.

"As I was doing this," Fergal said, "some of the key executives in the business seemed to recognize that I had a talent for being a Guinness ambassador and there was a need for it. So the stage was set. I started traveling around the world, speaking on behalf of the brand, doing something I liked enormously and filling a need for the company, something that wasn't being done before. And it seems to be working out for all of us. So I've become a player on the team with a unique position, like a central striker on a football team. You always need someone on your team with a unique talent, you know? I was just able to recognize that, realize I had a talent for it, and create the opportunity."

An important lesson. Look around for something that needs to be done that nobody else is doing. Then request to do it and give it your all. Then ask your supervisor what he or she thought of your performance. If you hear back that you're doing well, ask about how you could do more of it. It can get you and the people you work for thinking on an entirely new level. It also could open up new possibilities for your career, maybe even create a new position that plays to your strengths and that you may have never imagined before.

21. Develop the Strength of Your Own Voice

Susan Rice was an undergraduate student at Wellesley College when she met a graduate exchange student from Scotland who was on a year's fellowship, studying history at Harvard. "We met at a party, just by pure chance," she said. "And one thing led to another, and here we are now, ever so many years later, married and living in Scotland." The "here" she's referring to is Lloyds TSB Scotland, where she is the Chief Executive.

A large part of being a leader, she said, is getting listened to. "It's not a matter of having the loudest voice but of having something to say," she told us. "It's being worth listening to. Early in my career I can remember contributing an idea in a meeting; then, a few minutes later, a male colleague across the table said, 'I really liked Sean's idea. We should pick up on that.' And fortunately, Sean, who was sitting on my right, had the wherewithal and fortitude to say, 'That wasn't my idea at all. It was Susan's.' Afterward I thanked Sean. But I've shared that experience with other women leaders, and they all seem to have been in that same room. Afterward, whenever anything like that would happen, I would simply speak up for myself and say, 'The reason I thought that was. . . .' And inside of that speaking up for myself, my voice strengthened. Now I just find that people listen. Maybe it's because I've got something better to say or it's because of my title. But I think it's because I feel more comfortable speaking, so it comes across in my voice."

The thing about speaking, as Susan knows better than most, is that it starts with listening. A child cannot imitate words if the words can't be heard. But many adults seem to forget that.

Susan's style of leadership starts with listening. "I don't come in with a plan. Instead I surround myself with really bright people. And I learn a lot by listening to them. I often say to people, 'I don't have all the clever ideas. I just have the occasional one. But I can recognize a good idea when I hear it.' And if I hear all the ideas, I can see the space where we should go, where no one else is. That's how I lead. It's by listening before I speak. But that listening, I've found, has helped develop the strength of my ideas and my voice."

The best answers, she's found, come from the best questions.

Susan is also able to listen to a group of bright, impassioned people talking over one another and sift through the noise and identify a synergy in the ideas that proves stronger than any of the original ideas. "I simplify things," she said. "Very often people in business, particularly in large companies like this one, get into very convoluted conversations and processes. I try not to get caught up in that. I just think, 'If I were the customer, what would I want?' And that usually tips the scales."

An incredibly candid and unusually modest leader, she confided, "I really knew very little when I came into this position, and I was utterly aware of my ignorance. But what I found was that by taking a simpler view of things, always keeping in the forefront the customer's point of view, I've been able to ask the right questions and get us to a place where we wouldn't have been otherwise."

Susan added, "To learn, you have to keep asking. What's most important is that the people I work with know that my questions are not about questioning their abilities. The process takes a lot of trust. My questions may sometimes only be for me. But they help us clarify our thinking and come out a little sharper."

Susan's leadership style started when her voice got just a little stronger, a little more sure. Then people started listening more. And it became more comfortable for her. And she became more confident. And her questions got better.

The best answers, she's found, come from the best questions.

22. Don't Leave Your Past Behind

Whenever Annette Verschuren finds herself in a particularly difficult situation, a quiet, self-assured voice calmly whispers to her that she can do anything she wants. That voice takes her back to the dairy farm on Cape Breton Island, Nova Scotia, where her Dutch family emigrated in 1951. Sometimes in the wind on that island, she can still discern the unmistakable cadence of her father, who, when she was just ten years old, had a massive heart attack, which left him incapable of working on the farm with his previous vigor. But his presence was always felt by Annette, as she and her brothers, sisters and mother took on the round-the-clock work of keeping the farm running.

"I had about 40 cows to milk before I went off to school," she recalled. "I remember one time in particular when my brother and I pulled a calf from a cow that would have died if we hadn't helped. That early responsibility proved to be a great advantage for all of us later on in life. I have no fear of hard work or long hours. Because that's what my family did. I've seen some people cower when problems or challenges seem to be too big to handle. But I just take it in stride, as part of what needs to be done. After that beginning on the farm, nothing seems hard."

Annette is now the Division President of Home Depot's Canadian operations and EXPO Design Center. While her professional responsibilities have her constantly shuttling between Toronto and Atlanta, part of her is always on the causeway connecting the mainland to Cape Breton. It is the home she carries with her and returns to often. When she describes the island, she makes you want to book a flight to see its rugged landforms, scenic roads and spectacular views. As the rest of the world rushes by, somehow Cape Breton has managed to keep its Celtic essence. It is from a different era, a simpler time.

Annette went on to graduate from St. Francis Xavier University in Nova Scotia. After ignoring the advice of a professor who recommended she polish her typing skills because she would never make it as an executive, she evaluated several job options. "I think it is very important to make sure that your first job is the right job," she said. "Don't take the first offer that comes along. Always look at a few alternatives. Then write down your strengths and limitations, then look at the job and do the same thing. And see if there is a match. I believe it is also vital to assess the boss. Will you be able to work well with that individual? Will he or she encourage you to grow?"

> **"A lot of the innovation we brought about occurred because I didn't have the baggage that can weigh people down when they have too much experience in a particular industry."**

The first job Annette took was very unusual for a young woman at the time. But it gave her enormous responsibilities, significant experiences and the opportunity to be recognized for her successes. She became a development officer with the Cape Breton Development Corporation, helping displaced coal miners and others without jobs on the island find new jobs. It was a difficult assignment, because the miners, most originally from Scotland, had been working in mines for generations. It was central to their identity. In Nova Scotia, these men had been extracting coal from underneath the sea. It was a harsh existence and dangerous beyond belief. There were cave-ins and floods and everyone knew someone who had died in the mines. But that's what these men did. And there didn't seem to be a need for them any longer. Most of the men figured they would just find mines in other parts of the country, and come back home when they could. But for those who were open to changing, Annette helped them tap into a new potential. Many found new positions as mill workers, teachers and entrepreneurs.

Then, the '70s energy crisis hit with full force, and the mines were reactivated. As the miners were called back, Annette was promoted to a management position, where she found herself the only woman in a decision-making capacity.

One of the first things she learned was that whenever she would go into the mines, some of the miners would stay home because they were superstitious about women going underground. So she would often disguise herself as a man in order to take government officials down into the ground or under the sea to show them how awful the conditions were.

What was it like?

"Completely dark. The only source of light was the flashlight on your helmet. There was a constant dripping from the ceiling. The face of the mine was supported only by wood. And you felt that something could collapse at a moment's notice."

And it often did.

After that, Annette was offered a six-week contract with the federal government to privatize companies. That assignment stretched for three years, during which time she learned an enormous amount about how successful companies operate and how they adapt to change.

From there, she felt confident enough to go off on her own.

She convinced the CEO of Michael's, The Arts and Crafts Store that his venture could succeed in Canada—and that she was the person to make it happen. "It was one of those situations where we were building a business from the ground floor up, and we had to move fast. I glued my first desk together myself. I personally guaranteed payment for the telephone system to be set up. We didn't have time to do anything but succeed," she said.

"I think my biggest advantage was that I didn't have a lot of retail experience. Instead, I thought like a customer. And I believe that drove me to take a different position in the retail business. A lot of the innovation we brought about occurred because I didn't have the baggage that can weigh people down when they have too much experience in a particular industry," she reflected.

She developed a very energetic team around her, opening 17 stores in just 26 months.

That's when Home Depot came knocking.

At first, she was reluctant to talk with Home Depot because she had invested so much of herself in Michael's.

But Home Depot was persistent.

232 SUCCEED ON YOUR OWN TERMS

And, eventually, she saw it as a bigger opportunity, needing strategy and organization, with the distinct possibility of growing at an incredible clip.

It was a chance to make her own mark and turn around a major company.

And she has.

Since 1996, Annette has taken Home Depot in Canada from just over 4,000 associates to more than 25,000 today, with nearly 140 stores.

Then in 2003, she was asked to also take over the company's Atlanta-based EXPO Design Center, which features a premiere approach to home improvement.

Where does her motivation come from?

She paused, considering the question. "I'm sure it has to do with my past. I do look to the past to stay in touch with where I'm from. While I've left the island, I'm never really gone. I go back at least once a month to be with my brothers and sisters and their families. And to breathe the fresh air. I'm building a home there now. I know where I'm from. And I carry it with me wherever I go."

Those ties are strong.

To get a sense of the open, expansive views Annette saw growing up on her family's farm, all you have to do is see her office. It offers a stunning perspective of Toronto's skyline, stretching for miles. And the rest of her office is all windows. There are no walls. Everyone can see in. It is completely open. It's not just that her door is open. Her entire office is open. As is everything about her. "I have nothing to hide," she said, matter-of-factly. "I'm very transparent. I don't need walls. Or some private area. I want my team to know that we're all in this together. Because that's honestly the way I feel. The openness of this office reflects my leadership style."

And the connection to Cape Breton is also clear. And strong.

"I didn't leave until I was 30 years old. The place is hypnotic. It holds you. There's Celtic music everywhere. Gaelic is still spoken on the island. My family is still there. The island is part of me. With its trails, rugged coastline, rolling farmlands and stunning views. From the moment you arrive there, you breathe the air—and it's so clean. You know it's different from whatever you're used to. And wherever I go, I know I can always go back."

You *can* go home again.

23. Know How to Retire

A little more than 12 years ago Pierre Ralet retired from the advertising agency he founded in Belgium. It was there that he learned the art of catching the public's attention. As an advertising executive Pierre knew how to point the public lens in a certain direction. Through advertising, he learned how to make things happen for his clients.

Then, at the end of his professional career, he started working longer hours than he ever had before. With the financial security he'd acquired, Pierre was perfectly positioned to do whatever he wanted. Some people might have bought a couple of cases of sunscreen and headed for the nearest beach. Others might have looked for a top professional to teach them the secrets of hitting a golf ball.

Pierre had other ideas.

"The end of my professional career was when my real life started," he said. "I was able to take all I had learned about advertising and apply it to social and cultural causes I truly believed in."

His list of associations he now does work for pro bono is twice as long as the number of clients he had when he was being paid.

"Being retired is very freeing," he said. "I have more energy than I ever had before. And working on my own schedule, not worrying about money, allows me to do whatever I want. And what I want to do is contribute in some meaningful way to the world that is swirling around me."

Among his favorite associations now is the Special Olympics in Belgium. "I've been offering my services to this cause for over a dozen years. And nothing brings me more fulfillment than seeing the look on the faces of these kids when they are interviewed by a television crew. They are on top of the world. And I am touched to know that I had a little something to do with making their day incredible. What I do is put myself in the skin of the parents of these children, knowing the love they have for their children. And I take everything I've learned from my professional craft and try to help those parents share the feeling they have for their children. When I see the children striving and their parents cheering and the crowds roaring, I am thrilled beyond belief. And if I can do anything to spread that message, then that's what I was put here for."

> ## "What I want to do is contribute in some meaningful way to the world that is swirling around me."

He paused, then added, "If you ever think there is no reason for hope, do yourself a favor and watch children compete in the Special Olympics. You'll see that anything is possible. In each of their faces, whether they win, come in second, or whatever, you'll see a winner's mentality."

24. Assert Yourself

When Governor Jon Corzine (D-NJ) was a U.S. Senator, he wrote an article in *The Nation* called "A Time to Be Bold." That time seems to be constant with him.

Being clear about his position and asserting himself has gained him respect and wealth while also getting him in hot water more than once.

On January 11, 1999, he was ousted as the Chief Executive Officer of Goldman Sachs, Wall Street's most prestigious investment bank, after he orchestrated the firm's initial public offering. "For 25 years executives at Goldman Sachs debated whether they would go public," he explained. "But nothing happened. In the meantime, we were on our way to a trillion-dollar balance sheet, and we were still operating like a candy store organization as far as the structure. But nobody was willing to take the political risks, to change the status quo. And I basically said, 'This is my whole purpose for being here,' and I set the agenda. For me, it was about protecting the existence of the organization so it could be vital and strong for at least another half century. And it ultimately cost me my job because I fractured my relationships with some of the people on the executive committee. But I just feel that people in positions of authority should set important agendas. If not, why are we there?"

As one of Goldman's biggest owners, Jon had hundreds of millions of dollars tied up in the firm, according to *Business Week*. He went on to become a U.S. Senator initially known for spending more than $60 million of his own money to win his seat, a self-financing record. Like the Roosevelts and the Kennedys, he convinced the party faithful that, in spite of his enormous wealth, he had the interests of the working class at heart.

"I have a very simple philosophy on this stuff," he told us, "which is 'when much is given, much is expected.'" Truth is, he grew up on a small farm in central Illinois, where he took his first job at age 13 to help his parents make ends meet.

When he left Goldman Sachs, what made him decide to run for the Senate rather than continue to succeed in business, which he had just proved he could do exceptionally well?

"The simple answer is that if I made another dollar, another hundred million dollars, or whatever, it would not change any aspect of my life. I wouldn't feel better about myself," he said.

> ## "I just feel that people in positions of authority should set important agendas. If not, why are we there?"

Although most new senators take their time to learn the lay of the land and are known as the "junior senator," Senator Corzine came out swinging against President Bush's proposals for the deepest tax cuts in two decades. The Senator insisted the money would do more good if it were spent on Social Security, Medicare, universal health care, the environment, and education.

He then asserted his point of view by opposing the law authorizing the war against Iraq even though that was a very unpopular position at the time, possibly even life-threatening to a politician's career. "While it was a tough vote to cast, I had to assert my point of view," he said. "The classified information I was reviewing did not support the assertions the President was making."

"We have to fight for our convictions," he explained. "If we begin to negotiate from the middle, the end result inevitably takes us to the right of where I believe our nation should be."

His need for a challenge and to be the key voice in asserting his point of view, is ultimately what motivated him to run for governor, where now having won, as he's used to, he is poised to set a new agenda.

25. Surround Yourself with the Right People

We recently surveyed the presidents and chief executive officers of over 300 companies and asked them, "What is the best part and what is the worst part of being a leader?"

"Surrounding yourself with the right people" was at the top of both categories. How can it be the best part *and* the worst part of being a leader?

At first this might sound contradictory, but what they were telling us is that surrounding yourself with the right people is an either-or proposition.

When it doesn't work, it's the worst part of being a leader. It keeps you up at nights, worrying. It makes you fill in for others. It forces you to make very tough decisions about letting people go, or spending a lot of time trying to develop people who aren't really cut out for their jobs. Worst of all, it keeps you from doing what you're best at.

Surrounding yourself with the right people.

When it works, it's the best thing. It frees you up to do what you're best at: to plan for the future, to set a new course, to feel a real sense of confidence in the people who surround you, and to play to *your* strengths.

> **"I've seen leaders who couldn't succeed
> or grow because they were not comfortable
> with the idea that most of the people
> on their team were smarter than
> they were in many ways."**

As H. Edward Hanway, Chairman and Chief Executive Officer of CIGNA Corporation, will tell you, it all starts or stops with who you surround yourself with. When there was an opening to run CIGNA International in 1989, as Ed described the situation, "I didn't have any previous corporate leadership experience. I had done some time in the purgatory of corporate staff positions. Still, I went to the CEO and said, 'You may think this is a crazy idea. I've never run anything in this organization. But I think I know what our international business needs, and I'd like the opportunity to run it.' And he said, 'Okay.' And

I said, 'I beg your pardon.' And he said, 'I've been thinking about you for this position, and I'm glad you approached me. I'm going to put you in charge of international.'

"This turned out to be the most meaningful growth experience for me," Ed said. "I quickly realized leadership is not having all of the right answers to all the questions. My success depended on getting the right people around a table and getting them to work together effectively, focusing on the right questions. It was at that point in my career that I realized I needed to have people working for me who knew a hell of a lot more about certain things than I did. And my job was to be fine with that and to just let that go. Because they needed me to convey confidence and to build a coalition and to make them realize they were part of something very important and to create energy and to foster an environment where the incredibly talented people I chose to surround myself with were able to accomplish more together than they would have otherwise."

Ed added, "The truth is, I've seen leaders who couldn't succeed or grow because they were not comfortable with the idea that most of the people on their team were smarter than they were in many ways. Some leaders limit their own growth because they can't get beyond that. Their identity just won't allow them to get comfortable with the idea that there are people who know more than they do about certain things. A true leader is able to get beyond that. It took me a while to fully understand that. My job as a leader is not to be the smartest kid in the class. My job as a leader is to set a direction, then populate the organization with people who are talented enough and enthused enough about that direction to help get us there. It is one of the most difficult lessons for a leader. But when you get to the point where you're comfortable surrounding yourself with people who know more than you do, ironically you become even more confident. And that confidence allows you to deal more effectively with the complexities of an organization like this one. But if you don't get to that point, I don't think you'll ever be a true leader."

26. Set Your Watch for Now

Some people have a need to get things done immediately. Then there are those who can't wait that long.

238 SUCCEED ON YOUR OWN TERMS

Liz Elting brings a whole new meaning to the term *urgency*.

She founded TransPerfect Translations in her dorm room in 1992, immediately after obtaining a master's in business administration from New York University. Her partner was still in school, so the dorm room gave them a roof over their heads.

Some people just can't wait.

"The great thing was, I had nothing to lose," Liz explained. "I had just graduated and didn't have a job, so I could throw myself into it 16 hours a day 7 days a week—and if it didn't work, I could always start over."

At that time the officials at NYU were not aware that one of their dorm rooms was being used as an incubator for a new business. Liz said she and her partner didn't want to cause a stir, so they kept a very low profile. Now she frequently lectures at the school, and her story has become iconic.

Starting the new company brought together Liz's entrepreneurial spirit and her love of languages and cultures. She had already lived in Portugal, Canada, Spain, and Venezuela. Equally important, it enabled her to fulfill her need to get things done immediately. This way she wouldn't have to wait to get her first job, then wait to get promoted, then wait to oversee a staff, then wait to get the experience and confidence to branch out on her own.

Since she was planning on eventually running her own company, why not start there?

That's urgency.

They had six months to get out of the dorm and be in their own office, which they did. Their next goal was to grow into the world's largest premier translation company.

> ## "Even for entry-level positions, we look for people who could one day run a department."

"We wanted to make something happen," she said. "We wanted to transform the translation industry. We wanted to set a new standard in coming through for our clients." The translation industry, the way Liz described it, was very fragmented at the time, and customers' expectations were rarely met.

As the world becomes smaller, the need for immediate, accurate translations is more and more in demand. Just before Liz started her company, Pepsi had a major snafu with the translation of its slogan "Come alive with Pepsi." It had been mistranslated in Mandarin to "We will bring your ancestors back from the dead." Hardly what you'd expect to hear in an upbeat jingle for a carbonated soft drink.

Liz has built her company into one of the world's largest foreign language service companies, working with most of the Fortune 500 companies. TransPerfect has offices in 30 cities in 11 different countries, working in over 100 languages, with more than 300 full-time employees. The languages most frequently translated from and to are Chinese, English, French, German, Italian, Japanese, Korean, Portuguese, and Spanish.

What does she look for when hiring a new employee?

"Even for entry-level positions, we look for people who could one day run a department," Liz said. "We tend to hire with a career path in mind. I'm most impressed with people who are bright, conscientious, flexible, diligent, have a lot of energy, and, of course, a strong sense of urgency."

Of course.

What's the most difficult part of leading her company?

"Not being able to hire enough talented people quickly enough."

There you go.

The waiting is the worst part, particularly for someone with a strong sense of urgency. It's that need to get things done immediately, and keep moving on to the next venture, that helps make Liz successful.

27. Don't Take It Personally

Mara Swan, Senior Vice President of Global Human Resources for Manpower, candidly shared some personal insights about rebounding and learning from professional setbacks.

Certainly part of what has helped Mara succeed in various business environments is her ability to step back when she makes a crucial mistake and realize how it can become a major learning opportunity.

The first time Mara was promoted and found herself sitting at the executive table, she realized that the rules were different. "There was a debate going on about a subject I cared about," she said. "So I chimed in with a point of view based on my experience, and sparks started to fly. Different beliefs and viewpoints were shooting back and forth like arrows. And you had to duck to make sure you weren't hit with one of the tips, which were getting quite poisonous. I thought, 'Geez, this is some introduction to the big leagues.' And I went home and talked with my husband about it and had a very restless night. Then I went in the next morning to talk with one of the guys who was really in the heat of this debate about what was going on, and he said, 'Mara, that was nothing. Everyone's fine. You're taking this way too personally.' I left his office shaking my head. But the more it sank in, the more I realized: that's what's going on. These guys don't take it personally. Two of the guys in particular who were going at each other played golf together the next day. So what was I worried about? It wasn't natural to me; I had to think consciously about changing my approach toward such conflict. But the one thing I've learned from men in the workplace is not to take it personally. I share this story with young women all the time. Because it took me by surprise. I didn't understand it at first. I prefer to connect with people on a real level. But in business it's not personal. It's just about the goal and delivering results. It's that simple."

Another piece of advice she likes to share with young women also has to do with not taking things too personally. "I think the biggest mistake a lot of us make is that we look at things from our own perspective. If you really want to succeed in corporate America, you need to be able to put yourself in the other person's shoes. A lot of times I'll hear women complain, 'They don't understand.' And I'll say, 'Well, guess what? It doesn't matter that they don't understand us. The burden is on us to help them understand and change,'" she said.

Mara added, "So you have to figure out how to change things. If your presentation didn't go over, you have to find a different way to get through to your audience rather than just ranting and raving about your audience. If you want to change things, you have to understand who you're trying to change."

"But the one thing I've learned from men in the workplace is not to take it personally. I share this with young women all the time. Because it took me by surprise."

She also points out that women need to know and be very clear about what they want and need. Then they have to be able to ask for it and not be afraid of rejection. "There are so many things I've asked for from my boss, and I think he really likes me, but he's said 'no.' Now, generally, at that point, women cave in. We don't like to hear, 'No.' So we won't ask unless we're 100 percent sure that we'll get a 'yes.' Well, again, in business you can't take that stuff personally. It might have to do with budgets or priorities or moods. You've got to accept it, shrug it off, and work around it. As women, we read way too much into all this stuff. We need to get a little bit better at asking for what we need. What we really have to understand is that business is about making money. It's business. Nothing personal. As women, we have to understand that we need to take some of the feeling stuff out of it. It's nothing but a business proposition. What I've learned to do is to ask for what I need. 'Here's what I need. Here's why I need it. Here's how it is going to help us both achieve our goals. Here's how that is going to help the company become more profitable.' Simple. Straightforward. Nothing personal."

Mara concluded, "Of course, for me, if I don't get what I want from my boss, I don't quit there. I'll keep pushing. But that's just me. I'm not sure I'm ready to share that with young women as a piece of sound advice because sometimes it works and sometimes it backfires."

The point is, you've got to be who you are—and not take things personally.

28. Don't Be Afraid to Be First

The truth of the matter is that nobody, except a few studious pilots, knows who the second woman to fly across the Atlantic was. Amelia Earhart was the first. We all know that. None of us know who the third one was. If we were asked on Jeopardy, we would definitely lose some money.

Being first means you will be remembered.

Melinda Large, who is currently Regional People Director–Americas for Wal-Mart, has made a career of being first.

That doesn't necessarily make for the smoothest career moves, but it does make for an interesting career.

As a young woman of color, she grew up on the south side of Chicago, a Sox fan. But then she went to college at Western Illinois University. "I'd come out of my classes, and there were cows there. You know what I mean? I was the first in my family to go to college, and the only guidance my father gave me was, 'I want you to learn how to work with different people, I don't want to send you to a traditional black college.' He said, 'Real life is learning how to work with all kinds of people.'"

She wound up getting a fine education, majoring in geology, because she liked rocks.

Then, when she was off her parents' payroll, as she called it, she got a job overseeing some major construction sites in Chicago.

Now, the time frame here is important. This was during the early part of the women's movement, when women were coming to terms with finding fulfillment in the domestic and business worlds. "So here I am, a woman of color, out here on these jobs telling Bubbas that I could yank out everything if it wasn't inspected and approved. Do you understand the authority I had? Because if it was wrong, people could get killed, and it would be on my shoulders."

She figured out how to lead authoritatively while managing the crew and having fun at the same time. There was nobody teaching her this at the time. Melinda was all on her own. She described one scene she remembered fondly. "We were all sitting on the construction site at break time, and everybody knows what construction workers look like on the job. We're covered in grime, with our hard hats on, all looking very much the same, drinking our coffee. Ugly, dirty. And some attractive women come past, and all the men—keep in mind the time frame—are hooting and whistling. So this attractive man comes past, and I start whistling at him. Well, he just about died. So I took my hat off, and he saw that I was a woman, and he said, 'Whew!' Can you imagine? Those are the days you remember. The guys with me were all laughing, busting a gut. They were like, 'Oh, my *God*, I can't *believe* she just did that,'" Melinda said, laughing at the memory. Then she added, "What I realized I knew at that point was how to lead a project, how to manage people, and, most important, how to make sure that a building was firmly planted in the ground."

As a leader, how does she make difficult decisions?

"I think what has played to my advantage is that I have a keen sense of discernment."

What exactly does she mean by that?

"It's a matter of listening to yourself and to what's happening around you. I think all of us have it. I just trust my inner voice implicitly. When I hear that voice inside of me that tugs at me and points in a certain direction, I'm pretty much hearing it and doing it. Because it has never led me wrong," she said.

"So here I am, a woman of color, out here on these jobs telling Bubbas that I could yank out everything if it wasn't inspected and approved."

Fast forward to the 1990s. Melinda was accepted at the University of Chicago's master's program in business administration. The company she was working for at that time wouldn't pay for it, but she knew it would take her someplace she hadn't been before. So she took a deep breath and went for it on her own.

For two years it was an incredible, almost unbearable grind. But she made it, learning more about how to connect with and depend on people who could help her realize aspects of herself that she had never been aware of before. By the time she graduated, she knew she could lead a team and a project that would break new ground.

For one of her next job interviews, she flew into Bentonville, Arkansas. "I don't know if anything can prepare you for that. Once I left the airport in my rented car, there were no street lights. I was driving on completely dark roads, afraid I was going to drive off them," she recalled, laughing. "Then a cow walked in front of the road, and I slammed on my brakes. I thought, 'Oh, my God, I'm going to hit a cow. How will I explain this?' I finally made it to my hotel and barely slept through the night. The next morning, for my interview with Wal-Mart, I was beyond the point of exhaustion."

That day she went through a dozen interviews. In one there were six people.

Why the grueling interviews?

"I was an outsider," she explained. "Back then there weren't a lot of people who looked like me applying for senior jobs at a company like this. So it was new ground for all of us. I've never been one to tone down my image or hide my opinions. So they had to figure out if I made sense for who they were and where they wanted to go."

Apparently she did, because Wal-Mart took Melinda on seven years ago. Since then she has contributed in leadership roles in the firm's domestic and international units, with the hope of bringing a true sense of diversity to the world's largest retail store.

29. Defy the Odds

Dr. Eric Braverman believes that death is a concept worth defying.

His battle with mortality traces back to November fifteenth of 1980. That was the day he got a telephone call from his mother saying that his stepfather, who had adopted him, just had a stroke. As he was on his way to Virginia to be with his parents, he got a call from his brother saying that his natural father had just died of a heart attack.

Then, when he got to Virginia, Eric discovered that his adoptive father's condition was very bad. "Here was the man who was really my mentor, asking for a piece of paper. Then he scrawled, barely legibly, the words 'I love you.' That's the last thing he was able to communicate," Eric said. "After that he went into a coma and was essentially brain-dead."

He paused, then added, "In the same day I lost two fathers. I'm sure Freud could tell you that's why I keep fighting the establishment, searching for a larger truth."

Eric and his natural father had just reconnected after his dad had disappeared from his life for about 15 years. "I got to know him a bit and understand, at least from his perspective, why he felt he couldn't be around," Eric said. "At least we had that last year to try to resolve things and link up with each other."

What meaning could he find in such overwhelming loss?

In his stepfather's last message, Eric realized what was missing from the medical profession. "Love and caring," he said. "That's what's been lost in medicine."

> **"We have perfected the ability to kill one another down through the years. Now we have to figure out what we're really here for."**

That was when Eric first started to be at odds with his chosen profession.

At that time he was still a student at New York University Medical School, studying to be a doctor. Since then, his conflicts with traditional medicine have occasionally found him in a courtroom, arguing on behalf of his alternative approach to medicine, which emphasizes brain chemistry and electricity. At the same time, his views have also garnered a strong following of loyal patients who believe in his methods for defying the aging process.

Eric is now a leading figure in the practice of brain-mind body health care. He believes that the key to longevity and well-being is balancing the brain's four neurotransmitters, modifying our diets and taking supplements to live healthier, longer lives with more energy, less weight, clearer thinking, and sharper memories.

"As a physician," he said, "I went into this profession to be a healer. I am most interested in seeking a deeper meaning for our purpose in this world. So I am going after the number one enemy of humankind, which is death."

He views death as the number one enemy of humankind?

"Absolutely," he said. "We have perfected the ability to kill one another down through the years. Now we have to figure out what we're really here for, which is to live longer, healthier, more abundant lives."

He added, "Age is just a barrier that needs to be broken. There was a time when the four-minute mile was considered unachievable. Now high school kids are doing it. Once a milestone is attained, new possibilities unfold. Right now most people aren't doing very well when they get to be 80 years old. But that is changing. That 80 could become 800 years. Who knows? We are not just talking about getting older but along the way living every stage of our lives more fully."

Does Eric feel confident that he will live forever?

"My backup plan, if I die," he said, "is to put on my tombstone, 'I'll be right back.'"

Is he on to something?

We'll check back in 800 years.

**PART
IV**

Defining Moments, Lessons, and Qualities and What They All Mean

CHAPTER

25

Recognizing Your Defining Moment (Before It's in the Rearview Mirror)

*W*ith insights and reflections from Paul Schulte on competing in the Olympics; Rocky Bleier, who recovered from being shot in Vietnam and went on to help win a Super Bowl game; Gaston Caperton on needing to leave his home state in order to keep growing; Marc Koska on inventing a device to save people from getting AIDS; and Dave Power on starting his own business because he could not bear to have his work misrepresented.

THERE ARE CERTAIN TIMES when opportunities or tragedies occur and everything in our lives changes as a result. When we look back on those times, we know they were defining moments. Our lives can be divided into before and after.

While interviewing and assessing people who've succeeded beyond their wildest dreams, we've found that there was often a defining moment that they could call their own.

Those turning points fall into two categories.

The first category consists of those defining moments that happen to us, which we can't do anything about. They can range from winning the lottery to being in a terrible accident. What matters most is how we respond. Often, during trying times, you'll hear people excuse their behavior, saying they just weren't themselves. In our interviews we found the case to be quite the opposite. During difficult times, as you'll see in some of the stories we're about to introduce, we usually become more of ourselves. We find out what we're really made of. What comes through the loudest is the way in which we react.

The second category of defining moments consists of those we create for ourselves. In some ways these defining moments may be harder to identify as they're happening. We'll share with you stories of people who grabbed their defining moment because it spoke to them so loudly that they couldn't ignore it. However, some of those opportunities just whisper to us. And all of them can be easily missed because we're so caught up in our day-to-day activities. The common thread running through the stories of the people who created their own defining moments is that they were ready for them. They wanted to make something happen.

Regardless of whether their defining moments were thrust upon them or they created them, what mattered most was their incredible attitude.

For **Paul Schulte**, his defining moment came crashing down on him.

For the first decade of his life, all Paul wanted to do was become a professional athlete. When he wasn't dreaming about sports, he was playing. He'd take time out for lunch and dinner, but even then he'd be talking about sports.

That was the case until March 6, 1989, the day after his birthday, when the 10-year-old Paul was riding in the backseat of the car his mother was driving. His older brother was in the front seat. Their car had only a lap belt in the backseat, and Paul had it on. He didn't hear the sound of the head-on crash. He just felt his body being whipped around—really fast. He fractured his vertebrae and bruised his spinal cord. "So, as they say, I'm a spinal cord injury, incomplete," Paul said, as if describing a scientific phenomenon. *Incomplete*, as he explained, means he has a blur of a feeling. All in all, he "pretty much lost more than half of my leg function," as he said, which occurred immediately after the accident.

What was it like?

"They say I was awake the entire time, from when they took me out of the car, to when I was in the hospital, to just before I went into surgery. The whole time. But I have zero recollection. Absolutely zero," he said.

"Then my father got a phone call. Can you imagine? 'Mr. Schulte, you need to come to the hospital.' He knew my brother and I were out with Mom. So he knew something was bad. My mother's face hit the steering wheel, and her entire face got turned to really little pieces of bone. Her entire face. So it was very scary. I can't comprehend how my father dealt with it. He got to the hospital and they said, 'Okay, this is what happened,' and they told him everything. The next day they said, 'We're going to need pictures of your wife, a lot of pictures, because we're going to put your wife's face back together. Just bring us as many pictures as you possibly can.' So I can't imagine how traumatic it was for my dad. He went from Mom—fortunately my brother Peter was really not that bad off—to me. And I said, 'Dad, I can't feel my legs. What's wrong?' I don't have any recollection of it, but he described what happened, and it's become part of my reality. But it's not like I can honestly remember."

His first memory was at least a month later, while he was still in a body cast, listening to the physical therapist and trying to respond, though he didn't know how. Those memories were very fuzzy, almost dreamlike, like those just before you wake up.

What was it like when he saw his mother?

"She carries a great deal of guilt about it. It's difficult for her. Because the accident, it seems, was her fault. So she has a hard time with me. But I've hugged her and told her time and time again, 'Mom, it was supposed to happen. It was a blessing. I'm telling you, I'm a much better person. I'm stronger. I appreciate life more. I am a better person because this happened to me.' Many times I've told her that. I'm not mad. I don't wish my life was any different. I know my mom still carries the accident with her. That's Mom. That's all right."

How did the reconstructive surgery on his mother's face turn out?

"It's just amazing. Bones have been replaced with titanium. It was quite an ordeal. But my dad will tease her that they actually made her prettier. The doctors who worked on her were just fantastic. She sustained a closed head injury, so she has difficulty remembering things. But her heart has never changed. That was the constant. She was the same person before. You know, relatively speaking, the same person after."

Immediately after the accident, Paul withdrew into himself. It was a very lonely time. He started playing sports on a video game system. Some of the parents in the neighborhood chipped in and bought it for him. "And that became my focus as I got better," he said. He would spend his allowance on more games. "That was where I was able to be competitive again," he said. He'd spend countless hours practicing.

"My crazy determination or competitiveness wouldn't quit," he added. "And I had plenty of time on my hands to practice, so I just kept getting better and better at beating the video games. I worked on my coordination and my speed, and I knew that persistence was my trump card."

Four years later he started playing wheelchair basketball. "At first I wasn't really interested because I had the stereotype of 'Oh, the guys in the wheelchairs aren't going to move very fast.' Then I remember the first time I got invited to come out to a practice for wheelchair basketball. I came to the gym, and the first guy I met, well, his arm was bigger than my head. And I thought, 'These guys are for real.' And that's what I like about it too. It was a lofty goal. I came in, and it was not kids my own age. The youngest guy in the gym was 23 years old, and I was 14. I was like, there's a challenge. I saw all these men going back and forth, with huge arms, and they were really fast. Great shooters. And I was like, all right, this is cool; I'm going to lose for a while. But then, you watch. I knew there was plenty of opportunity to learn to get better and to push myself."

Paul Schulte took his defining moment and reinvented it—and made it his own.

Seven years later he made his debut in the Paralympic Games. In Sydney, in the year 2000, as the U.S. wheelchair basketball team's youngest player, Paul helped his team secure a bronze medal.

When a defining moment, like a terrible car accident, happens in the wink of an eye and changes everything, the only thing you can change is your attitude.

Paul Schulte's attitude bowls you over. We've rarely come across someone with more positive energy.

"For lack of a better phrase, the accident was 'a reality check,'" he said. "You start saying, 'Whoooow. Okay.' And you shift gears a bit. And you appreciate everything. You certainly don't take things for granted as much as you did before because you know how quickly things can change. So I feel it realigned my values and better enabled me to live my life because I've gone through such a hard thing. So now I figure, 'All right. Bring it on! What's the worst thing that can happen?' So if you're aiming for a dream, keep aiming. It's exciting to be in it. Don't worry about failing or succeeding. Just go for what you know is important."

"When a defining moment, like a terrible car accident, happens in the wink of an eye and changes everything, the only thing you can change is your attitude."

Rocky Bleier was drafted by the Pittsburgh Steelers right after graduating from Notre Dame, where he was captain of the Fighting Irish's football team.

A few months later he was drafted again, this time by the U.S. Army.

In May of 1969, at the height of the conflict, Rocky was sent to Vietnam.

On August twentieth he had his defining moment, after which he was awarded a Bronze Star and a Purple Heart. One sure way you can tell you're having a defining moment is if you find yourself talking with God. We'll tell you more about Rocky's conversation shortly.

The night before, Rocky's platoon was helicoptered in to help rescue another platoon that had been hit in Heip Duc. "We took only our weapons, our ammunition, and poncho liners to carry the dead. It was an eerie night, black and cold," he recalled. They walked about a mile through tall elephant grass, scraggly bushes, and dense underbrush. The farther they went, the darker and smokier it got. He heard firing from a distance, then closer. Finally, in the middle of the night, they arrived. There were 10 dead men and 20 wounded. They were deep in enemy territory. Then he heard it: the repeating sound of an automatic weapon. They dove for cover into a rice paddy. Rocky grabbed his rocket launcher and grenades and crawled on his stomach for about 20 yards to the front of the paddy. As he rose to sight his weapon, he felt a dull thud in his left leg. Looking down, he saw blood gushing through two neat holes in his pants. He fired a few rounds and then saw four or five machine-gun rounds rip through his pack. Rocky was down when he heard his lieutenant on the radio saying, "They're all around us. There's no place to hide. There's no cover. They're everywhere."

That was when Rocky had his conversation with God.

He said, "Dear Lord, get me out of here if you can. I'm not going to bullshit you. I'd like to say that if you get me out of here alive and okay, I'll dedicate my life to you and become a priest or build a church or something. But I can't do that because I know that's not what I'll do."

He paused. Here he was making a deal with God, but he didn't want to be two-faced about it. He didn't want to promise something just to get out of the situation, then forget about it or conveniently alter his promise when things got better. This was big, and he didn't want to be playing some kind of shell game with God. Rocky wanted to be honest, but he didn't know what he could offer that would matter.

Finally he said, "Okay. Honest to God. What I'll do is this: I'll give you my life to do with whatever you will. Here it is. I'm not going to complain if things go wrong. If things go well, I'll share my success with everybody around me. That's it. Whatever you want to do, wherever you want to direct, that's fine. This is the best I can come up with."

That was all he said at the time. It was somewhere between a deal and a prayer. "All we really have is our life and what we do with it," Rocky said later.

Reflecting on his deal with God, he added, "Why do we turn to God at moments like that and say, 'Please take care of me'? Why? Maybe that's the kind of animal God created. I'm not sure, but for me those conversations are the most conclusive proof I've come up with for the existence of a supreme being. Perhaps if I hadn't spoken to God in that rice paddy, things might have worked out exactly the same. But one thing's for sure: when my self-preservation instinct was on the line, I said the most fervent prayer of my life."

After he prayed, a grenade landed at his feet and exploded. He saw his right leg quivering uncontrollably. He could see places on both legs where shrapnel had shredded his fatigues. The pain in his right foot was piercing.

Of the 32 men in his platoon, nine were now dead, two were missing, and the rest were seriously injured.

Then, for some inexplicable reason, the enemy stopped firing and fell back in the jungle. The lieutenant speculated that they had killed or wounded their commanding officer. Whatever the reason, another platoon arrived to carry Rocky and his platoon to a medevac helicopter that was waiting about two miles away.

A guy slung Rocky over his shoulder and carried him most of the way fireman-style. "I never knew his name, and I don't think he knew mine," Rocky said. "But he helped save my life. That's a special kind of love that you find in life-and-death situations."

When he saw the helicopter's whirling blades, Rocky said, "Thank you, Lord."

When he woke up the next day, he learned that the blast had gashed his foot in three places and shattered the bone. The damage to his legs and knees would leave scars but would heal. With therapy, he was told, he could learn to walk normally again. He started to read an article in *Stars and Stripes*, the army newspaper, about "Rocky Bleier, ex-football player, now serving with the 196th LIB in Hiep Duc." But he stopped at the phrase "ex-football player" because he didn't want to consider the implications.

Fast forward to Rocky returning to the Pittsburgh Steelers.

Art Rooney, Sr., the team's owner, absorbed the cost of a third operation for Rocky, paid him his full year's salary, and suggested he become a scout for the team. Rocky was grateful and okay as a scout, but he kept up with his rehabilitation. His motivation? "I'd rather be a third-string special-teams player than the greatest scout in the world," he explained.

He worked out, with a vengeance, running cockeyed on the heel and side of his damaged foot several miles every day. He didn't have strength or flexibility, but he had sheer drive, determination, and self-discipline. He ripped a hamstring muscle in the leg that had been shot in Vietnam. He was advised countless times to give up football. But he'd tape up his leg and return to the field, again and again.

Why?

His explanation: "I have an amazing ability to persuade myself that reality is not what it seems."

By 1972 he was timed faster than he had been before suffering his wounds. He was playing every game with the Steelers on their specialty teams. Then, in 1974, he moved into the starting backfield and, with Franco Harris and Terry Bradshaw, became a key element in Pittsburgh's emergence as the dominant NFL team of the 1970s.

Steelers fans still talk about how high he jumped to catch a pass in the end zone to nail Pittsburgh's third Super Bowl victory.

For Rocky and Paul, their defining moments were thrust upon them. What mattered was what they did afterward. What mattered most was their attitude.

There are other kinds of defining moments: the ones we create for ourselves. And some of them aren't as obvious as you might think.

"During difficult times, we usually become more of ourselves. We find out what we're really made of."

In 1987 *Gaston Caperton* was at the helm of a highly successful insurance business in West Virginia. It was actually the country's tenth largest privately owned insurance brokerage firm, which he had taken from 15 people to over 600.

When Gaston told his family and friends that he was considering a run for Governor of West Virginia, they said, "You've got it made. Why would you want to run for Governor?"

He had an incredibly successful business life, thoroughly enjoying the people he was working with, and everything he was doing. But something inside him said, "It's time to do something more purposeful." Around that time, there was an article in the newspaper that mentioned about two dozen people who should run for governor and help West Virginia get back on track. And Gaston's name was among them.

At first he was just flattered. Then he started to consider the possibility, and something about it made sense.

Before deciding to run, he hired a pollster who put him at three percent in the polls. When he asked the pollster what that meant, he said, "Everybody gets three percent. So you're starting at zero."

The polls didn't tell him to take a chance. But something inside him said that he could be a real leader of the state if given the chance.

So, for the next 15 months he campaigned tirelessly. "The harder I worked, the luckier I got," he said. "I had enormously talented people join the campaign. My campaign manager was a state senator who was very young, driven and insightful. I had great consultants and advisors. And West Virginia was ready for a change. And we were able to articulate a vision that made sense. It was a lot of luck, great strategy, great people supporting me, great execution, and a lot of very, very hard work."

"I ran against a person who was running for his fourth term as governor, as a Republican, and he was a tough opponent, and I was really lucky to win the election," Gaston reflected.

His inaugural address was short and to the point. It contained clarity, vision, a love of words, a sense of history, a promise for the future, and a passion for what he was about to do. That came from two things. "One was someone who once told me, 'Gaston, nobody will ever say, "I wish you spoke longer."'" And the other was the simple fact that I'm dyslexic, so I have to know my speeches by heart."

He said, "I don't suffer any illusions. I know how tough it was to become your governor, and I know how tough it's going to be to make West Virginia turn around." Then he told his audience, "The truth is, West Virginia does have serious problems, and it is time to attack those problems. . . . Our education system has not kept pace, our economy has not created the needed jobs, our environment has not been protected, and our government has not functioned responsibly. However, it is not my purpose today to mourn West Virginia. On the contrary, it is my purpose to call us to action." He went on to outline a three-part plan for improving the state's economy. Then he stated, "My vision of West Virginia is one where these mountains are alive with better schools, challenging jobs, responsive and efficient government, and a protective environment."

There's a terrific photograph on his office wall, taken the night he was elected, of Gaston with his two sons. The expressions are of exuberance. Underneath is one of Gaston's favorite quotes, from Theodore Roosevelt. In part it says, "The credit belongs to the man who . . . knows in the end the high achievement of triumph and who, at worst, if he fails while doing greatly, knows his place shall never be with those timid and cold souls, who know neither victory nor defeat."

Not surprisingly, Gaston went on to be re-elected.

Throughout those eight years, Gaston became comfortable with the idea that he was a very good team leader. "I was a quarterback in school, and some of those skills translate. As a leader I had great respect and appreciation for the people who worked for me. I never thought it was just about me. It was about everyone working together for a common purpose and belief, with a clear mission and a common set of goals."

After eight years he was ready for his next challenge.

He taught courses on leadership at Harvard and Columbia before moving on to his current position as President of the College Board, where he has made such pronouncements as: "The single most un-American aspect of our great society is the lack of truly equal educational opportunity." His goal is to change the disparities in college enrollment between affluent white students and low-income minority students.

Pardon the obvious question, but deciding to run for governor was certainly his defining moment, right?

Hardly.

"No," Gaston replied. "Running for governor was a big thing. No question. It was certainly a wonderful opportunity. But I wouldn't describe it as a crossroads. Intuitively, I knew that running for governor was the right thing for me to do. And I am very, very happy I did it. It opened my life up to a whole new world of possibilities, and I'm glad I had that chance to serve. But it was just an evolution. I think life sort of flows through." He paused, then added, "The most difficult choice I have had to make was the decision to take a job outside of West Virginia. West Virginia was my life, where I grew up, where I have my friends and family. When I looked around for what I should do after serving as Governor, I realized that it would have been easy for me to stay at home and live my life in the past rather than in the present and the future. But I had to take advantage of an opportunity to make a contribution to education, something I have a great passion for. I was fortunate enough to be given the offer to teach at Harvard and Columbia and later to work for the College Board in New York.

"Ultimately," he explained, "I think life is about moving forward and doing today what you can and dreaming about tomorrow. So in many ways, leaving West Virginia was the hardest thing for me. I love that place, it's my soul. To leave was really more than an evolution. It was a real crossroads for me. I had to change where I lived. But not where I came from. I still have my home in West Virginia and I get home as often as I can. Nothing can take the place of old friends. Moving to New York was difficult. But it was also a critical turning point for me. I'm sure I made the right choice." He paused, as if looking in the distance. Leaving where he came from. That was his real defining moment.

Note to self: Make sure you ask what might seem like an obvious question. The answer can knock you over.

"Our defining moments can come to us from every possible direction: from accidents, from crazy twists of fate, from newspaper articles, from knowing we could be doing something more important."

Marc Koska's defining moment came while he was reading an article in a British tabloid.

Before that he was enjoying a life of leisure.

He'd been living in Saint Croix, where, as he describes it, "the native people were working for Martin Marietta and Hess Oil, and there were about 2,000 white lawyers living off of personal accidents on the island." And there were lots of accidents, Marc says, including chains breaking, cranes crashing down on a dozen people eating their lunch, all sorts of things like that. For the lawyers, Marc used to create scale models of accident scenes to be used in court.

On Monday through Thursday he'd create models of crime scenes out of Styrofoam, plastic, cardboard—whatever was at hand. Then on Friday through Sunday he'd professionally race sailing yachts.

"It was nice," he said, smiling as he remembered. "I was in my early twenties, with long hair and a British accent, on an American island. Now that's a recipe for either disaster or success," he added, laughing.

Then, in the early 1980s, HIV became a serious issue and there was a lot of confusion and panic. "The upshot of that was that I had to get educated," Marc said. "It was affecting everyone's life, and certainly would affect mine."

All he knew was that he had the ability to create models that were accurate enough to simulate reality in a courtroom and that he was scared out of his wits about this new virus that was changing everything around the world.

One day Marc was reading a newspaper and came across a line, buried deep in a story, that said this new virus was being transmitted by people who were sharing and re-using disposable syringes.

Time froze for Marc.

He described the moment as well as he could. "It was like a lightbulb went on. I decided that was it. There was no choice at all from that moment on. I was going to do it. And I was very calm. It was an ethereal moment. That was it. It was decided in a split second, and I was there. But I don't know how much I had to do with it. I just knew what I was going to do. Simple as that."

At that point everything became crystal clear. He was going to develop a disposable syringe that could be used only once—even though he didn't know the first thing about it. Could it really be that hard?

He started by researching the problem. He knew he needed to understand the problem completely before he could find the right solution. Once he was clear about that, he decided, the solution would arrive.

He spent time with junkies in Liverpool, trying to understand their habits: how they shot up, where they shot up, the extent to which they would go to get high. He discovered that junkies have the most varied uses of syringes. The end users, he discovered, had far more creative uses of syringes than did the doctors.

Then he knew the only way to change the situation was to come up with a new way of looking at the syringe. But how? Manufacturers weren't going to spend more money on their manufacturing process. He studied how they made syringes and using the same process, with one minor difference which would not cost more to produce, he came up with a way to make syringes that were guaranteed single use. They were referred to as Auto-Disable syringes.

It was an enormous breakthrough, and he thought he had the answer.

He had designed an Auto-Disable syringe that the same manufacturers could produce at no extra cost. But there was no demand. And it was driving him crazy. He knew he had the answer. If there was absolutely no way for a syringe to be reused, it could not spread disease.

Marc believed he had the idea and the methodology. But he didn't have the market. He needed money to help create the demand for his invention.

That was when he met an investor who believed in him. "And it was unbelievable," Marc said. "We liked each other straight away. And there was no doubt in my mind that this guy was genuine. And he saved the day. Our conversation went along the lines of: 'Well, we'll give you the money you need and share the company with you.' Then there were questions like, 'How much of a salary do you need?' and 'Do you need a car?' Then it was, 'Fine. How are we gong to do this program?' So it was like, 'Let's get the horrible bits out of the way. And let's get on with it and make this thing successful.'"

Marc is now producing disposable syringes in Brazil, Nigeria, India, Saudi Arabia, Iran, China, Korea, Vietnam, Indonesia, and Malaysia. And he employs just five people, including himself. It is all done through simple arrangements with manufacturing companies that pay royalties to license his patent.

To date, Marc has been credited with saving more than two-million lives. And this number is growing exponentially each year.

For Marc, the moment of lucidity, his defining moment, was reading the article in the newspaper about the need for something he knew he could create. "It was very personal. I know it sounds crazy," he said. "It was just an article in a newspaper. I know it wasn't written for me. I could have skipped over it or not read the newspaper that day. But I did. And there was a personal connection that I could not deny. It was so strong that I knew that if I walked away from it, it would be committing treason to myself. At that point, I didn't have a choice. There was no backing away. There were no half measures. If I was going to do something about it, now was the time. It was my future. I had to decide. And there was no question from where I stood. It was a total knowingness. A total commitment. It was me."

That's a defining moment. No question.

So what are you going to do about it? The answer is up to you.

"At that point, I didn't have a choice. There was no backing away. There were no half measures. If I was going to do something about it, now was the time."

There are other defining moments that don't knock us over the head. They just gnaw at us and take away a little piece of our hearts.

That's the way it was for *Dave Power*, the founder of J.D. Power and Associates, whose award has come to mean excellence in customer satisfaction.

Dave was working in Detroit for a company that was doing consumer research for one of the major domestic automobile manufacturers.

But he was very frustrated.

"By the time we got finished conducting a study and it went through the organization and finally got to top management, what we had written in our analysis was totally changed to give management what their subordinates thought the executives wanted," Dave explained.

That convoluted process and distortion of his work was driving Dave crazy.

That wasn't why he'd gone to Wharton and earned a master's in business administration. Dave was intrigued by understanding what drives customer satisfaction, and the last thing he wanted to do was pretend.

Unfortunately, he found himself in the middle of a game he had no interest in playing. "Often our research was done to justify the decisions management had already made," Dave said. "I saw it as torturing the data until it confessed," he said, adding, "We worked hard to have data that we thought was very informative, and then everything we had done was virtually destroyed in the process."

Dave realized he was part of a system that was designed to check upon itself, but then hide any real information, and continue on undaunted.

"The powers that be wanted to hear the good things," Dave said. "And some of them also knew that something was going on that didn't measure up. So they hired me to tell them the truth. But they weren't ready to handle it because the truth might reflect negatively on the person who hired me."

So Dave found himself stuck in a situation he wanted no part of. But what could he do?

Dave cashed in his chips and said he didn't want to play the game anymore. Then he started his own game.

At his kitchen table, with his pregnant wife helping, Dave started his own company, conducting independent research. One of the first studies he conducted was on Mazda's rotary engine, which was a revolutionary concept in the industry. They were interviewing customers and tabulating responses, when his wife said to him, "What's an O-ring?" Dave said, "I haven't the faintest idea." And his wife replied, "Well, I don't know either, but Mazda better figure it out, because that's a real problem for them." It turned out to be just that, with Dave's research serving as an early indication of things to come.

From there, Dave had to figure out how to create a business model.

Who was he for? The manufacturers or the customers?

Certainly there were mistakes along the way.

"One year we had a ranking of the top three automakers in each category. Seemed simple enough. But in 1983, we cited that Mercedes was the number one automaker and Subaru was in the second slot. Truth be told, Subaru had only one model at that time. And we were dealing with the difference between customer expectations and experiences. So you might expect some differences between expectations for a Mercedes and a Subaru in 1983. At any rate, it came back to haunt us. Here I was, relaxing, watching the Super Bowl of 1984, and during the halftime break there was a commercial for, you guessed it, Subaru, saying that according to J.D. Power and Associates, they were second only to Mercedes in customer satisfaction."

Monday morning, Dave got a call from a furious executive of Mercedes, asking how dare he authorize Subaru to use its name.

"The truth was," Dave said, "we did not authorize anything."

That was when he changed his business model.

"Advertising agencies can drive us absolutely crazy," Dave said. "There can be a built-in conflict. Just think about it. We're trying to uncover the truth, and they're trying to promote a product. So if we said that a certain manufacturer had 'the best door handle,' the next thing we knew, there was an advertisement saying that J.D. Power and Associates says we have 'the best car.'"

"If I didn't change that, I'd have no reason for existing," Dave said.

At that point, he decided that he would announce only one award for each category. There would be no runners-up. "In this way," Dave said, "everybody knows who is on top that year. Because of what they did. Period. Nobody is changing our information or making it anything other than what the customers honestly said."

To convey what the customers were honestly saying, Dave had to employ a roomful of advisors and lawyers who could agree on how the information he was gathering could be used.

"It's a crazy game," David admitted.

Of course, throughout the years, J.D. Power and Associates has moved beyond automobiles to numerous other products and services, including newly-built homes, telecom services, hotels, and airlines.

But how do we judge the difference between expectations, experiences, and reality?

"It becomes increasingly difficult," Dave admitted.

Consider what has become known as the FedEx paradox. "When FedEx started," the marketing guru Seth Godin said, "it was a miracle. You put something in an envelope, and it showed up anywhere in the United States the next day. It was breathtaking—for about a week. And then, if the letter was five minutes late, you heard, 'I want my money back.' Companies keep raising the bar on expectations."

How do you keep all those expectations and realities in check?

That's where Dave Power steps in.

He was just invited to Germany "because one of the German automobile manufacturers was upset with some of the results of one of our latest surveys," Dave said. "The people at the top of the best companies want to have all the right information, the good, the bad, and the ugly. Then they can make the best decisions. They're not interested in having some of their underlings gloss things over. If they are misled by someone in their company who is trying to justify his or her existence, it could doom the company. The people at the top of these excellent companies want to know the truth so that they can do something about it. In fact, there are now several auto manufacturers who are basing some of their executive compensation on the results of our customer satisfaction or quality surveys. The companies that used to balk at our surveys and question who we were to speak on behalf of the public now see the value of the unvarnished truth. This is incredibly gratifying to me."

Think about it: He's created his own little world with his own standards for reporting on reality.

So, why did he name his company J.D. Power and Associates? What does the J.D. stand for? Why not call the company Dave Power and Associates?

"For anyone who's counting," Dave pointed out, "I'm actually the third person in my family to be called James David Power. That is what the the the "J.D." stands for.

"The name implied that we had a staff of people at the time," he said, laughing to himself. "It sounded more prominent than just my wife and me conducting surveys at our kitchen table, which is what we were when we started. Actually, the name helps us even today," he explained ever so simply. "When people call and say, 'I'd like to talk with J.D.,' we know they don't really know me, since everyone knows me as Dave."

The difference between fact and fiction can be a thin line. You have to know what you know.

"We can pay attention and take a shot at it. Or we can look the other way and pretend we are too busy with whatever it is that is filling our days."

We'll leave you with these thoughts about defining moments:

Our defining moments can come to us from every possible direction: from accidents, from crazy twists of fate, from newspaper articles, from knowing we could be doing something more important.

Some of us have our defining moments thrust upon us, and we can either see them for what they are or miss them entirely.

Some of us can sense our opportunities. Some of us create them.

Ultimately, what matters is our attitude.

We can pay attention and take a shot at it. Or we can look the other way and pretend we are too busy with whatever it is that is filling our days.

The choice, ultimately, is ours. What do we want to do?

Sure, some people can regale you with sad stories about all the opportunities they missed. There are plenty of sad songs about that. Skip them. Or just dance to them.

For real inspiration, think about the people who recognized their defining moments before they were in the rearview mirror.

The trick is knowing when your defining moment is here, tapping you on the shoulder, knocking you over, or just staring you in the face.

Having a Lesson for Your Children

What would you like a child to learn from your life?

SOMETIMES OUR CHILDREN do things that remind us of ourselves and we can't help smiling. There's something about them carrying on our quirky little habits. Maybe it's just the realization that we actually do have an influence on our children, even if it has nothing to do with what we may have intended.

One of Patrick's children was in a very long line at a supermarket that had come to a grinding halt. Nobody was moving, and she was thirsty. Colleen unscrewed the cap on a bottle of Yoo-Hoo, the chocolate drink, and started sipping from it. By the time she reached the cashier, the bottle was empty. When her mother saw this, she said, *"Where* did you learn that?" Colleen just smiled and said, "From Dad. He does it all the time. Then, as he pays for it, he jokes with the cashier that the bottle seems to have a leak in it." Colleen's mom just shook her head and sighed.

Well, maybe those aren't exactly the kinds of things we want to pass on to our children.

One of the questions we asked the successful people we've featured in this book was, "What one lesson would you like a child to learn from your life?"

Some of them answered the question with profoundly universal lessons. Others had extremely personal ones.

It's an interesting question to ponder as you plan your own success. Here are some of our favorite answers.

"What lesson would I want a child to learn from me? Never give up," Muggsy Bogues, the shortest National Basketball Association player of all time, said. "If you believe in something, go all-out and see it through. Don't be afraid to reach for your dreams. If you fail, so what? As long as you gave it everything. You'll get there. Believe in yourself and go for it."

"When I'm talking with young people, I tell them the story of the Movement," said Congressman John Lewis, the renowned civil rights advocate. "And sometimes I tell them that if someone had told me when I was a kid growing up on a sharecropper's farm that I would one day work with Dr. Martin Luther King, Jr., and with President Kennedy and with Robert Kennedy and that I would be a member of Congress, I'd say, 'You're crazy.' But it happened. So I say to young people, 'Don't give up. Don't give in. Don't become bitter. Don't become hostile. Don't get lost in the sea of despair. Keep the faith. Hold on to your dreams. Do everything you can to make those dreams real.' And I tell them to love. It is better to love than to hate. Always."

Rebecca Stephens, the first British woman to climb Mount Everest, said, "I hope my daughter Anna will know that each of us is born with a different spirit and she should follow whatever path she wants. I think my parents gave me that message, and I have every intention of giving the same message to her."

> **"If you fail, so what? As long as you gave it everything. You'll get there. Believe in yourself and go for it."**

Senator Barbara Boxer, who knows how to stand for what she believes in, even when she stands alone, would say, "The most important thing is: Don't say what you want to be. Say what you want to do. I never said, 'I want to be a senator.' What chance would I have of that? Instead, I said, 'I want to help children and promote justice and protect the environment. Those are things I want to do.' And, when I put it like that, I have a lot more options open to me, a lot more ways in which I can succeed."

Janet Lasley, an inspiring cancer survivor, said, "I want my children to know that cancer taught me to be compassionate. And I want them to have compassion for others without having to get cancer to find that out. And I want them to know that the joy I get from them keeps me alive. That insecurity is a waste of time. That they should stand up for what they believe in. And I want them to know that I believe they can do anything."

João Carlos Martins, one of the world's foremost interpreters of Bach, who lost the use of his right hand, said, "I would advise my children to control their emotions in a way that I did not. I let my emotions run away with me. It was good for my music, but not for some of the personal decisions I made. I would advise them to be a little bit cooler than I was. But one thing I would like them to have from me is to love life the way I do. Because this is the way we can have a hope for tomorrow. To love life. I love life every minute of the day."

"To prepare yourself," said Congressman Rush Holt, a former physicist with a patent for a solar energy device. "The trick is to be prepared for a lot of different eventualities. Now, I also believe that you have to keep your options open. I don't have, and have never had, a clear career goal. Of course, I understand that this is not the usual thing you read in self-help books or management manuals. But if life favors the prepared mind, it means life is going to throw you curveballs and you've got to be ready for anything. You never know when you will learn something that will become very meaningful in your life. I heard an incredible story about a 10-year old girl who was studying tsunamis. And when she and her family were vacationing in Thailand, she saw the water recede very suddenly, and she said, 'This is exactly what happens before a tsunami.' And she and her family and everyone around them got back to their hotel before the tsunami hit. She was a hero because she was prepared. But she had no idea what she was preparing for. That's life. The truth is, we often don't know exactly what we're preparing for."

Representative Jan Schakowsky, an unapologetic progressive voice in Congress, said her advice to young women in particular is as follows: "This might sound like an odd message, but we have to be a little easier on ourselves. As women we tend to focus on the one inadequate thing we said or did, instead of the dozen really articulate and smart things we've said and accomplished. Everybody makes mistakes. And we have to be a little lighter on ourselves. I think men have an easier time dusting themselves off and focusing on what they achieved. It's something we women have to learn. To be easier on ourselves and celebrate when we do achieve our goals. Then to just keep going for it. That's my advice."

Angelo Sotira, whose online company was purchased by Michael Ovitz while he was still in high school, said, "School is busy trying to make people well-rounded. And if you have an edge, you might not fit in. Though I'm a great admirer of education, people without edges are often less interesting. And well-rounded people can be quite boring. So learn what you can from school, but realize it's only one place to learn. There are plenty of other places. When I was in high school, there wasn't a textbook or a course on online societies. We invented it. Perhaps they'll eventually be in case studies for some college course. But that will be so far after the fact. My advice is: if you're interested in being on the cutting edge, if you have it in you to go out there and tear things up, do it. Granted, that's not great advice for everybody. But if you're built that way, you know what I mean."

You know what he means?

"People without edges are often less interesting. And well-rounded people can be quite boring."

Advice either rings true or it doesn't.

All we can tell you for certain is that the last piece of advice children generally want to hear is the one that comes from their parents.

Still we all pass things on. Even when we don't mean to.

Maybe that's why we asked this question of these successful people.

Okay. We accept that it is presumptuous to think that our children will learn from us what we believe they should know. No, it's ridiculous. They are here to sample what we've said and done, then take the best, and leave the rest.

The only messages that will endure are those which resonate with them.

That is why we'll continue to open bottles of Yoo-Hoo and gulp from them—as long as we're already in line and have enough change in our pockets to pay for our little quirks.

CHAPTER

What Does It All Mean?

*I*t's all about focusing on your strengths, being self-aware, taking chances, and loving what you are doing.

THE INDIVIDUALS IN THIS BOOK epitomize the capacity to succeed on your own terms. As we've shared with you, each of them had his or her own definition for success, as well as distinguishing qualities and a defining moment that helped him or her succeed.

In addition, we found that each of these individuals have succeeded because of four other overarching factors. They all focus on their strengths, have a keen sense of self-awareness, are willing to take risks, and love what they are doing.

Focus on Your Strengths

First of all, although we have been concentrating on the strengths of these successful individuals, we should also note that they all acknowledge having equally significant limitations. What matters is their perspective. Do they focus on their strengths or on their limitations? It makes all the difference in the world.

Muggsy Bogues, the shortest professional basketball player of all time, knew he was talented. But he also knew that his real strength was his incredible resilience. He refused to be discouraged by all the people who said he should give up and try something else. When he was selected as a first-round draft pick, he said, "That was it. All the naysayers telling me I would never make it. All the folks saying, 'He's too small.' And here it is. I'm walking up there to accept my hat and shake

Mr. Stern's hand. You know, five feet, three inches. I tell you. That was just amazing. The whole universe was just lifted off my shoulders."

**What is really motivating you?
How do you affect others? Do you like what
you are doing now? Is there something
you could be doing that would be
more fulfilling and a lot more fun?**

Every one of us has core strengths that can put us in the top ten percent of the population in some attributes. However, we are all also in the bottom ten percent for other qualities. That is the human condition. No one, not even the incredible individuals presented in this book, has all the positive attributes and none of the limitations. What we need is to understand our inherent strengths and develop them. Of course, anything we can do to tone down our weaknesses will do us no harm. But we don't want to be in a position where we are futilely attempting to succeed at something that we are not cut out for, that we don't enjoy, and that we haven't a snowball's chance in hell of being anything except mediocre at. Real success starts with getting ourselves out of such situations. Real success comes from recognizing, understanding, developing, and concentrating on our strengths. That's the underlying message of all of the individuals featured in this book. That's the road to success. The real winners in this world are those individuals who are in positions that play to their strengths.

Have a Keen Sense of Self-Awareness

Individuals who are self-aware know what drives them, and they do not let the outside world define them. This takes a combination of reflection and action. To succeed on your own terms, you first have to know how to check your own temperature. This means asking yourself some tough questions, such as: What is really motivating you? How do you affect others? Do you like what you are doing now? Is there something you could be doing that would be more fulfilling and a lot more fun?

Being self-aware means asking yourself these questions and not allowing yourself to get away with any easy answers.

People who are self-aware are not just reacting to the whims of the world around them. Instead, because they are in tune with themselves, they are making things happen around them.

It was his keen sense of self-awareness that enabled Jon Corzine to shift careers after he left Goldman Sachs. Could he have taken over the helm of another company? Of course. Were there offers? Many. But that was not what was driving Jon anymore, and he knew it. As he explained, "The simple answer is that if I made another dollar, or another hundred million dollars, or whatever, it would not change any aspect of my life. I wouldn't feel better about myself. I felt what I needed to do was to give back." So he went on to become a U.S. Senator initially known for spending more than $60 million of his own money to win his seat, a self-financing record. Yet, like the Roosevelts and the Kennedys, in spite of his enormous wealth, he has fought tirelessly for the interests of the working class.

Likewise, Liz Elting was keenly aware that she loved languages, wanted to be an entrepreneur, and wasn't very good at waiting. So she started a translation company in her dorm room immediately after receiving a master's in business administration from New York University. Some people just can't wait. "The great thing was, I had nothing to lose," Liz explained. "I didn't have a job, had just graduated, could throw myself into it 16 hours a day for 7 days a week—and if it didn't work, I could always start over." TransPerfect Translations is now one of the world's largest foreign language service companies. That's because Liz knew herself, knew what she wanted, and wasn't about to listen to the dozens of reasons from the outside world about why she should take her time, learn her craft, and find out about the intricacies of running a business before she took the plunge.

Knowing yourself and not letting the outside world define you is a thread that winds its way through the stories of everyone we met who was succeeding on his or her own terms.

Be Willing to Take a Risk

Without taking a risk, very little happens. Even for those who prefer to be cautious, there is no way to be insulated from risks. We run a risk by just going about our business: driving to work, getting on an airplane, swimming in the ocean. There's no way to avoid risk.

If you do not act, life can be very boring. So you might as well take your risks on purpose.

Of course, if you take a risk, you might fail. Then what?

Does someone who fails in the first start-up he or she undertook accept that defeat as a verdict, or does that person say, "Oh, well, I made some mistakes, but at least I've learned from them. So let me at it again. And the mistakes I make next time will be new ones."

We were recently speaking at an MBA class at the University of Michigan. There were about 30 students taking a class in entrepreneurialism, all brilliantly successful in their academic careers, on the verge of graduating. Then, in the middle of the presentation, Herb started telling them about some of his business failures. As a successful entrepreneur, he shared, with enormous candor, times he was fired, colossal mistakes he'd made, and ventures that went belly-up. The room became electric. The students couldn't get enough. Keep in mind that these students would not have been considered for this program unless they had arrived with the highest academic ratings. None of them had ever failed at something significant before. Most of them had never gotten a grade as low as a B-plus. But in the room, as Herb spoke, you could almost hear a huge collective sigh of relief. It was like an enormous weight being lifted off their shoulders as Herb conveyed his underlying message that it is okay to make a mistake—it is okay even to fail—if you possess the resiliency to learn from your mistakes and failures and then come back even stronger.

Being willing to take a risk means being all right with the possible consequences. What's the worst thing that can happen? Are you fine with that? Could you handle it? If so, then go for it, because the worst probably won't happen. What are the odds? If you're an optimist, you know they're on your side.

If you don't take a risk, you'll never know. Remember the line from the poem by John Greenleaf Whittier: "For all sad words of tongue or pen, the saddest are these, 'It might have been.'"

Love Your Work

The successful people in this book all love what they are doing. You can sense it when you are in their presence. When João Carlos Martins sits at the keyboard and plays Bach with his left hand, his passion fills the room. When Senator Barbara Boxer stands up for a noble cause, even if she knows she is not going to win the day, her enthusiasm is palpable. When Rebecca Stephens talks about reaching the top of Mount Everest, her audience is transfixed by her intensity. While all these individuals have different core strengths, such as passion, a willingness to take a risk, and being goal-oriented, they are also able to amplify their strengths because they love what they are doing.

And everyone around them knows it.

To paraphrase Freud, life adds up to two things: love and work. Since most of us spend a great deal more time at work than at love, true happiness comes when we combine love and work by loving what we are doing.

What Does This All Mean For You?

The lessons for succeeding on our own terms are the same for employers as they are for individuals. The fundamental message is to look for potential—in yourself and in those around you.

Don't get trapped by the past. The simple truth of the matter is that we tend to rely on past experience entirely too much.

Employers do it with help-wanted ads. What's the first thing they write? "Need a manager, salesperson, or whatever the job is with at least one year of experience." No. Wait a minute. This is a much more important job than that. Let's say instead, "Need five years of experience." But when you think about it, how often have you come across people who have 12 years of experience, which adds up to just one year's bad experience repeated a dozen times?

For employers looking for people to help move the company forward and for individuals looking to move their careers to a new level, our message is the same: look for potential.

If we've learned anything through interviewing and assessing incredible individuals who have succeeded on their own terms, it is that their achievements have less to do with their experience than with their potential.

We're not saying to forget about experience completely. Just keep in mind, to paraphrase Aldous Huxley, "Experience is not what happens to you; it's what you do with what happens to you."

For employers, our advice is as follows: Don't concentrate on what promising job candidates have done. Look for what they've learned from what they've done. How have their experiences altered their lives, formed their philosophies, defined who they are? What have they learned from their growth experiences?

Most important, look for potential.

For individuals who want to succeed on their own terms, our advice is to look at your own experiences the exact same way. Whatever your next career move—whether it is seeking a new position or starting your own company—consider what you've learned from what you've done, what you can carry with you from the past. Perhaps more important, have a clear sense of your potential and think about how you can express it in the most compelling way possible.

Our hope is that the insights derived from the successful people in this book will provide you with a new perspective for thinking about how you are going to succeed, whether you are an individual looking to change your direction or an employer seeking to hire people who can help take your company to a whole new level.

We have found that people who succeed on their own terms in business, sports, the entertainment world—whatever their pursuit—are those individuals who know who they are and know how to play to their strengths.

They are willing to take risks on their own potential—and maybe on someone else's as well.

Find those qualities in yourself, surround yourself with like-minded people who see infinite possibilities in themselves and others, and new doors will open.

How to Discover
Your Own
Defining Qualities

*A*sk yourself some serious questions and take a free personality assessment to help you discover and develop your own defining qualities.

WE WANT TO HELP YOU discover and understand your own
defining qualities by providing you with two approaches to assessing
your potential. The first is a list of open-ended questions; the second is
an online personality profile.

Your First Step

The first part is subjective. It has to do with asking yourself some
very serious questions about who you are, what you believe in, and
where you'd like to go.

The key is not to let yourself off too easy. These are difficult questions that get at the heart of who you are, what drives you, and what you
believe in. We asked these questions of the people featured in this book.
Some of the questions required a great deal of thought. And some of
their responses bowled us over.

There is no time limit on these questions. Take as long as you need.
If you'd like, write down your answers. Then come back to them later
to see if there's anything you'd like to change.

Each of us approaches this journey from our own starting point.

"It has to do with asking yourself some very serious questions about who you are, what you believe in, and where you'd like to go."

If you've been reading this book in a linear fashion, you've no doubt come across a few incredible responses to these questions. Those answers wove their way into the stories about the qualities and moments that define Roger Staubach, Senator Barbara Boxer, Ben Vereen, and many others.

The point is that it is important to be honest and yet subjective at the same time. That's not an easy thing to do, particularly when we're focusing on ourselves.

So here's another suggestion: After you've written down your answers to these questions, ask some friends, who you know can be honest with you, how they would answer the same questions about you. That can get a little tricky, as your friends will want to keep you as a friend. So they are likely to be kind. That is good. If you are serious about exploring your next move, you will want to surround yourself with friends you can trust, who are also kind. But if you listen closely, you will hear some of their subtle hints. Pay close attention because they may well be pointing you in a particular direction. Possibly the direction you intuitively knew was best for you all along.

With that in mind, here are some of the questions we asked of the individuals in this book—and dozens of other incredible individuals with equally compelling stories and growth paths whose voices we weren't able to include because our editors wouldn't let the book expand into a set of encyclopedias.

These questions were designed to help you get in touch with what drives you. There is only one right answer: Yours.

Thirty-Five Questions to Ask Yourself and Then Ask Your Friends

1. What do you enjoy most about your current job?

2. If you could change one thing about your current job, what would it be?

3. A year from now, how will you know if you are succeeding in your current job?

4. If you have a difficult decision to make, how many people do you discuss it with?

5. How do you go about getting things done?

6. Are you hard on yourself when things go wrong?

7. What is the first thing you do when you want to convince somebody to go in a direction you want to take?

8. How often do you find yourself going against the tide?

9. How hard is it for you to assert yourself in a difficult situation?

10. How do you solve problems?

11. How do you start thinking about a new project?

12. When you were a child, did you have a hero? If so, who was it?

13. What has been your biggest mistake? What did you learn from it?

14. What is the worst thing that ever happened to you? What did you learn from it?

15. What's the biggest risk you've ever taken in your career? What's the biggest risk you've ever taken in your personal life? Do you think differently about the two situations?

16. In your first job, did you have a mentor? If so, what was the most important thing you learned from your mentor?

17. Did you always know what you wanted to do?

18. Do you consider yourself lucky?

19. What is the biggest difference between your parents' generation and yours?

20. What is the biggest difference between your generation and the one coming up behind you?

21. What challenges have you had to overcome to get where you are?

22. What drives you in the face of defeat?

23. What helps you overcome a failure?

24. How do you define success?

25. Do you consider yourself successful?

26. If you had to name the one thing that drives you to succeed, what would it be?

27. Have you had a defining moment (an event that changed the direction of your life)? If so, did you recognize your defining moment when it was occurring?

28. What makes you happy?

29. Where do you get inspiration?

30. What is your next big challenge?

31. Do you remember anything you learned from your first job that you carry with you today?

32. When your back is against the wall, the odds are against you, and there seems to be no way out, what quality in you comes out?

33. When you were a child, what did you want to be when you grew up?

34. What lesson would you like a child to learn from your life?

35. What would you most like to do with the rest of your life?

Your Next Step

All right. After answering those questions, we'd recommend taking a breather. Let it all sink in gradually. Hopefully you've discovered something about yourself that you weren't aware of before—or confirmed something you knew but never said out loud.

Consider your next step to be our contribution to your journey.

This is a way to get some objective insights into the qualities that drive you and distinguish you from others.

We are offering you the opportunity to take an online, in-depth personality profile, which can provide you with an introductory assessment of your defining qualities. This personality profile is the same assessment used by FedEx and Johnson & Johnson to assess the potential of employees, and was also the same assessment completed by most of the participants in this book.

You are welcome to take this free profile and receive a report pinpointing the qualities that distinguish you.

This *developmental guide* will provide you with some interesting and valuable insights into the qualities that drive you, along with suggestions for developing your potential. It is not a complete road map to your next career move. Rather, it is a starting place that outlines some of your key strengths and motivations. The results can help clarify whether your motivations are aligned with your aspirations. It may solidify your current thinking or trigger some new ideas as you explore your future possibilities.

Consider this to be our contribution to your personal and professional growth. If the insights from this assessment help you identify and understand just a little more about your defining qualities, we will feel more than gratified.

To access your free online assessment, go to SucceedOnYourOwn Terms.com. Click on the button that says, "Take Caliper's Free Assessment." Enter your 6-digit access code, which is located on the inside bottom back flap of the book's jacket. Then follow the directions.

Of course, if you are interested in further assessments, coaching, or counseling, we are always available to you. And, if you are a manager or employer, you can get guidance in hiring, developing, coaching, team building, succession planning, and organizational development.

The next steps are all yours. Consider the results of your online assessment. Reflect on the stories in this book that resonate with you most strongly. Keep asking yourself those tough questions. Talk with friends about what you are considering. Look around you for inspiration. Keep looking inside yourself. Your road map will come into focus. It's just a matter of getting from here to there. You've known the direction all along. The destination is to *succeed on your own terms.*

Acknowledgments

This is where we run into one of the biggest risks of writing this book, which is leaving out so many of the people who helped us to make this dream a reality.

FIRST AND FOREMOST, as in our first book, *How to Hire & Develop Your Next Top Performer*, we want to thank Mary Glenn, our editor, who showed enormous confidence and enthusiasm in our initial concept, then helped us frame our vague notion into a truly unique book. And thanks also to Peter McCurdy from McGraw-Hill for his patience, understanding, and professionalism, particularly through all of our last minute revisions.

In addition, this book would not exist without the nearly 300 employees in Caliper's 14 offices around the world, who all teach us so much every day. Their voices, and those of the executives from the more than 25,000 companies we consult with, resonate throughout this book.

We also want to thank our colleagues at Caliper who so capably assumed the burdens created by our absence as we disappeared for large amounts of time throughout the past two years to research, interview and write this book.

And we want to express special thanks to: Melanie Quiambao, who arranged interviews, stayed on top of details that we would have certainly missed and, along with Debbie Dlabik, made sure that we always had flights and places to stay as we traveled to over a dozen countries; Ricardo Roman who was always there, providing insights and constant support; Amy Yates-Wuelfing who was invaluable in helping to identify and piece together some of the themes that run through this book; and Jim Marmon, Meg Tuttle, and Claudio Salvucci who saved us countless times from grammatically embarrassing ourselves.

And if we wore hats, we'd take them off to Debbie Dreessen, our editor-in-chief, who did an extraordinary job of coordinating and refining the sundry revisions between the initial manuscript, which was turned in by two authors who never met a deadline they didn't try to stretch, and the final version of the book that you are holding in your hands. We are exceedingly grateful to her.

In addition, our dear friend Gerhard Gschwandtner shared with us many inspiring conversations about success, convinced us that *succeed* was a better first word than *succeeding* for the title of our book, and also introduced the image of the torch on the cover, which our designer John Mulvaney then refined.

We also want to thank each of the incredible people who so generously donated their time, personal stories and profound insights to this project. They shared with us so much about succeeding on their own terms. Never accepting failure, defeat or any other setback as anything but a temporary condition, they always had the courage to carry on and prevail. From Holocaust survivors to Hell's Angels, from star athletes to entrepreneurs, from climbers of Mount Everest to individuals who overcame seemingly insurmountable odds, the stories they shared keep inspiring us.

Bibliography

Bennis, Warren G. and Robert J. Thomas, Geeks & Geezers *(Harvard Business School Press, 2002).*

Bleier, Rocky, Fighting Back *(Stein and Day, 1975).*

Bogues, Tyrone, "Muggsy," In the Land of Giants *(Little, Brown and Company, 1994).*

Boxer, Barbara, Strangers in the Senate *(National Press Books, 1994).*

Braverman, Eric, The Edge Effect *(Sterling Publishing, 2004).*

Bronson, Po, What Should I Do With My Life? *(Random House, 2002).*

Deford, Frank, The Heart of a Champion *(Tehabi, 2002).*

Dubal, David, Conversations with João Carlos Martins *(Labor Records, 1998).*

Erikson, Eric H., Identity and the Life Cycle *(International Universities Press, Inc., 1959).*

Frankl, Victor, Man's Search for Meaning *(Beacon Press, 1959).*

Goldberg, Danny, Dispatches from the Culture Wars *(Miramax Books, 2003).*

Gladwell, Malcolm, The Tipping Point: How Little Things Can Make a Big Difference *(Little, Brown and Company, 2000).*

Greenberg, Herb, Harold Weinstein, and Patrick Sweeney, How to Hire & Develop Your Next Top Performer *(McGraw-Hill, 2001).*

Grunitzky, Claude, Transculturalism: How the World is Coming Together *(True Agency, 2004).*

Ibarra, Herminia, Working Identity *(Harvard Business School Press, 2003).*

Kanter, Rosabeth Moss, Confidence *(Crown Business, 2004).*

Lewis, John, Walking with the Wind *(Simon & Schuster, 1998).*

McCain, John, Why Courage Matters *(Random House, 2004).*

Mikulski, Barbara (et al.), Nine and Counting *(William Morrow, 2000).*

Morgan, Howard, Phil Harkins, and Marshall Goldsmith (eds.), The Art and Practice of Leadership *(John Wiley & Sons, Inc., 2005).*

Myers, Daisy, Sticks 'n Stones *(York County Heritage Trust, 2005).*

Pisar, Samuel, Of Blood and Hope *(Little, Brown and Company, 1979).*

Rogers, Carl R., On Becoming a Person *(Houghton Mifflin, 1961).*

St. John, Bob, Landry, The Legend and the Legacy *(W Publishing Group, 2000).*

Sartain, Libby, HR from the Heart *(American Management Association, 2003).*

Seligman, Martin, Learned Optimism *(Pocket Books, 1990).*

Staubach, Roger, Time Enough to Win *(Word Books, 1980)*

Index

Disaster response, 196–199
Discernment, sense of, 243
Disloyalty, dissent vs., 195
Disney corporate headquarters, 162
Dispatches from the Culture Wars
(Danny Goldberg), 225
Disposable syringes, 260–261
Dissent, disloyalty vs., 195
Dogwood Hollow Social Club, 115
Dunbar High School, 74

E
Earhart, Amelia, 241
Earnhardt, Dale, Sr., 105, 106
Education, segregation in, 8
Ego-drive, 117
Elston, Dave, 148
Elting, Liz, 237–239, 272
Embracing your roots, 189–191
Empathy, 31, 99–104
Employers, lessons for, 274–275
"Energy of despair," 42
Erikson, Erik, 135
Euros, 203–204

F
Family time, 95–96, 98
Fear, 169
Fear of being first, 241–244
Federal Communications Committee,
224
FedEx paradox, 264
Feedback, 227
Feinstein, Diane, 82
Financial Times, 56–57
First, fear of being, 241–244
First impressions, 9–10
Focus:
capacity to, 183–184
on opportunities, 20–21, 181–183
on strengths, 270–271
Football, 85–89
Football (soccer), 183–184
For the Left Hand Only (CD), 34,
133
Fosse, Bob, 19, 65–67
Foundation Fighting Blindness, 147
The Fountainhead (Ayn Rand), 164
Freedom, 191–192
Freud, Sigmund, 274
Freudian therapy, 10
Friends, 277
Friendships, 35, 144

Frustration, 153
Fun, 15, 35, 149–153

G
Gandhi, Mahatma, 171
General Motors, 9
George Washington University, 138
Ghadar, Fariborz, 22–23
Goal-oriented quality, 28, 56–62
Godin, Seth, 264
Gold Cup World Championship, 181
Goldberg, Danny, 222–225
Goldman, Lionel, 6
Goldman Sachs, 234–235
Gore, Al, 21
Gore, Tipper, 224
Gould, Glenn, 130
Graves, Michael, xiv–xv, 98, 161–168
on alternatives, 164
on architectural language, 163
architecture projects of, 162
on context of architecture, 163
creativity of, 36
on decision to be architect,
165–166
on drawing, 165
health of, 167–168
on humor, 165
on learning from disability, 168
in Rome, 163
stadium designed by, 126, 162–164
on his style, 167
teaching style of, 166–167
on teakettle design, 164, 165
training of, 162
visual vocabulary of, 162
The Great Escape (film), 127
Greenberg, Herb, xv, 3–15
and Boy Scouts, 6
Caliper started by, 9
and color, 7
on ego-drive, 117
on empathy, 99
on establishing trust, 14, 15
on fun, 15
and learning from mistakes, 273
limitations of, 7
management style of, 12
mastoid infection causing blindness
in, 4–5
and prejudice in job market, 8
and rejection, 8
at Rutgers, 8–9

Jackson, Jimmy Lee, 174
J.D. Power and Associates, 261–264
Jesus Christ Superstar (play), 66
Job market, prejudice in, 8
Johnson, Lyndon, 37, 169, 175
Johnson, Magic, 75
Jones, Stephanie Tubbs, 21
Journals, 95

K
"Kaddish" (Leonard Bernstein), 55
Kanter, Rosabeth Moss, 124
Kennedy, Bobby, 172–173, 175–176
Kennedy, Edward, 54
Kennedy, John F., 52, 53
Kennedy administration, 173
King, Martin Luther, Jr., 37, 171, 173, 175
Knowing the world around you, 180, 219–246
  and admitting mistakes, 220–222
  and asserting yourself, 234–235
  and challenging status quo, 219–220
  and defying odds, 244–246
  and fear of being first, 241–244
  and finding unique opportunities, 225–227
  and luck, 222–225
  and retirement, 233–234
  and sense of home, 229–232
  and sense of urgency, 237–239
  and speaking up for yourself, 227–229
  and surrounding yourself with right people, 236–237
  and taking things personally, 239–241
Knowing yourself, 179–218
  and accepting challenges, 213–215
  and being true to your convictions, 202–203
  and being yourself, 191–196
  and capacity to focus, 183–184
  and defining yourself, 209–211
  and embracing your roots, 189–191
  and focusing on opportunities, 181–183
  and integrity, 203–205
  and misemployment, 216–218
  and pursuing interests, 187–189
  and reinventing yourself, 211–213

Knowing yourself *(Cont.)*:
  and respecting your heritage, 199–202
  and responding to disaster, 196–199
  and self-acceptance, 185–186
  and starting over, 207–209
  and your values, 205–207
Kohler, Laura, 199–202
Kohler (company), 199–202
Korea, 189
Koska, Marc, xiv, 259–261
Ku Klux Klan, 32, 110, 115

L
Landry, Tom, 87, 88
Large, Melinda, 242–244
Lasley, Janet, 91–98
  construction company of, 97–98
  fatal cancer prognosis of, 92
  journal keeping by, 95
  on learning from cancer, 98
  lesson for children from, 267–268
  on living in present, 94–95
  optimism of, 31
  in remission, 93
  return of cancer in, 93
  on taking trips, 95
  on time with family, 95–96, 98
  transition in, 96–97
  video made by, 93–94
Lasley Brahaney Architecture and Construction, 97–98
Lasley Construction, 97
Laureus World Sports Awards, 181
Leaders, identifying, 200–201
Leadership:
  Sonny Barger on, 195
  and inner voice, 141
  and respect of employees, 257
  and sense of discernment, 243
  style of women's, 81
  and support advisors, 236–237
Learned Optimism (Martin E. P. Seligman), 92
Led Zeppelin, 223, 224
Leiomyosarcoma, 93
Lessons for children, 266–269
Levitt, William, 112
Levitt & Sons, 112
Levittown, Pennsylvania, 32, 110–116
Levittown Betterment Committee, 115